FileMaker® Web Publishing

A Complete Guide to Using the API for PHP

Allyson Olm, Stephen Knight, and Michael Petrov

Wordware Publishing, Inc.

Library of Congress Cataloging-in-Publication Data

Olm, Allyson.
   FileMaker Web publishing : a complete guide to using the API for PHP / by Allyson Olm,
   Stephen Knight, and Michael Petrov.
   p. cm.
   Includes index.
   ISBN-13: 978-1-59822-041-4
   ISBN-10: 1-59822-041-1
   1. FileMaker (Computer file).   2. Web publishing.   3. PHP (Computer program language).
   I. Knight, Stephen, 1968-   II. Petrov, Michael.   III. Title.
   TK5105.888.O465 2007
   005.75'65--dc22   2007026436

© 2008, Wordware Publishing, Inc.

All Rights Reserved

1100 Summit Avenue, Suite 102
Plano, Texas 75074

No part of this book may be reproduced in any form or by any means
without permission in writing from Wordware Publishing, Inc.

Printed in the United States of America

ISBN-13: 978-1-59822-041-4
ISBN-10: 1-59822-041-1
10 9 8 7 6 5 4 3 2 1
0707

All inquiries for volume purchases of this book should be addressed to Wordware Publishing,
Inc., at the above address. Telephone inquiries may be made by calling:
(972) 423-0090

Contents

Acknowledgments

Many thanks to the FileMaker community. Without you, this book would have never been written. We are extremely thankful for your support and kindness. We feel blessed that we have the opportunity to share with you something we feel so passionate about, and we look forward to hearing of your successes.

We would also like to thank Tim McEvoy of Wordware Publishing. Tim provided insight as to the inner workings of the publishing industry, as well as constant support throughout the entire process. Tim's enthusiasm for this book was contagious, and helped us all to enjoy the process.

Beth Kohler, Senior Editor of Wordware Publishing, is amazing. Beth is exceptionally organized and detailed and has led us through the editing process with amazing ease. She is exceptionally talented at asking questions that truly give life and meaning to the typed word. Thank you, Beth, for your professionalism and your sage advice!

We would also like to thank FileMaker, Inc., for developing such an amazing work of art. FileMaker continues to produce amazing software and provide numerous opportunities for developers and everyday users to grow. FileMaker truly puts its customers first. We would like to thank Kevin Mallon, Senior Public Relations Manager, for answering any questions that we had about FileMaker and Delfina Daves, Senior Manager FileMaker Developer Relations, for her constant support and knowledge of all things FileMaker.

Introduction

FileMaker and PHP — the Dynamic Duo

If you think FileMaker is a powerful database development program that enables individuals of all levels of expertise to develop relational database systems, you would be correct. If you were to add that it can power robust PHP web-based solutions, you would be correct again.

FileMaker is not the new kid on the block when it comes to manipulating and sharing data. FileMaker has an extremely successful history in the database market that has spanned more than 20 years. FileMaker began exploring web technologies starting with CDML and proprietary tag-based language and then progressed to XML and now to PHP.

The combination of PHP and FileMaker makes perfect sense. FileMaker is well-known for its ease of use, reporting, and business logic, and PHP is known for its power, speed, and rapid deployment capabilities. And now, with the new FileMaker API for PHP, you can quickly and easily deploy your FileMaker solutions to the web.

What Do I Need to Know to Get Started?

This book assumes that you have some basic knowledge of HTML and FileMaker. If not, it certainly is not the end of your glorious dream of becoming a professional FileMaker web developer.

There are chapters included in this book that cover basic HTML, CSS, and PHP to help you get started. If you want more in-depth coverage of any of these topics, we encourage you to purchase a beginners guide to HTML or visit one of the sites listed in Appendix B. Chapter 5 goes into quite a bit of detail as to how to set up your FileMaker database and recreate the blog sample database we include with this book.

Do I Need to Know FileMaker?

You do not need to know FileMaker, but it will certainly help. Wordware Publishing has a wonderful selection of FileMaker books available on its web site at http://www.wordware.com.

Do I Need to Know PHP?

A basic knowledge is certainly preferred, but definitely not necessary. This book does a great job of covering PHP basics in Chapter 8. That is not to say that intermediate and advanced users will not find this book to be a valuable resource. This book covers a new class of PHP written especially for FileMaker, and includes materials from basic to advanced topics.

What Do I Need to Use This Book?

This is an interactive book, meaning that we hope you will work through the exercises as you traverse the pages. What is required to do this? A web editor (several of which are listed in Appendix B), FileMaker Pro 8 or 9, and FileMaker Server Advanced or FileMaker Server 9. If you do not have Server 9 or Server Advanced, you can host your database at any of the FileMaker hosting companies listed in Appendix B and connect remotely.

The exercises are meant to teach you how to apply PHP to real-world applications. We encourage you to work step by step through the exercises, as each chapter builds on previous chapters.

Sample Files and Videos

Sample files for this book are available as downloads at both the Wordware web site (www.wordware.com/files/fmphpapi) and the FMWebschool web site (www.fmwebschool.com/wordware). Sample files are in folders that correspond to the chapter's title.

Screen capture movies of some of the chapters are available as well. These can be played on your browser, or downloaded and played on your computer.

Last Thoughts

Thank you for buying this book. In your hands lies the opportunity to become a virtual virtuoso of FileMaker web publishing. If you have not yet purchased this book, why are you waiting?

There are numerous benefits to learning custom web publishing with FileMaker and PHP. PHP is used world wide, and once you learn to use PHP with FileMaker, you can quickly begin applying it to other technologies as well. Learning PHP quickly adds to your ability to gain more clientele, and gives you the ability to expand the services you offer your current customers.

Learning FileMaker and PHP simply opens the door for many new possibilities and opportunities. So why are you waiting? Let's begin the exciting journey of web publishing!

Chapter 1

Introduction to Web Publishing with FileMaker

Few people will dispute that a presence on the web is quickly becoming one of the many requirements of running a successful business. With the increased accessibility of Internet technologies, communication between co-workers or between a business and its clients is now much more efficient than it was even 10 years ago. Companies are now looking at ways to enhance their users' experiences instead of simply filling a need. They are looking for an edge over their competition.

FileMaker has for years provided extremely flexible software that allows the creation of customized database solutions for a limitless variety of industries. As the need for a greater and more innovative presence on the web has grown, so has the search for the best solution for bringing FileMaker database content to the web in the most flexible and professional manner possible. With the marriage of FileMaker and PHP, that goal is closer now than ever before.

Why PHP and FileMaker?

Many companies are discovering that static web sites do not give them the ability to meet the changing needs of their customers. Combining FileMaker with PHP enables you to provide dynamic content for your web site.

PHP (PHP: Hypertext Preprocessor) is one of the most widely used and supported scripting languages available for web design. PHP support is available at most web hosting providers and is easy to install for those wishing to host their own web site. PHP is an open-source programming language that is supported by a vast and thriving online community of programmers through forums and email discussion groups. This supportive community provides a limitless resource for both novice and experienced programmers alike.

FileMaker Pro has won multiple Editor's Choice awards and combines a user-friendly interface with a wealth of developer tools to meet the needs of both entry-level users and professional developers. For many users the next logical step is to provide web access to their existing FileMaker Pro database. The FileMaker API for PHP allows that to be accomplished seamlessly by combining PHP and FileMaker technologies.

What's So Great about PHP?

PHP is a server-side scripting language. This means that the scripts are processed on the web server, not by the user's browser. This avoids the compatibility issues common to client-side scripting languages such as JavaScript. Scripts that query FileMaker Server are handled by the web server, and the returned data is sent to the client's browser as HTML. The details of the web server-to-FileMaker Server connection are within the PHP scripts and are not accessible to the client even when viewing the source.

Figure 1-1: User's browser-to-FileMaker Server process

PHP is cross platform, making it easy for you to move your site from one operating system to another. PHP is also one of the fastest scripting languages available, and provides thousands of built-in functions that allow you to communicate with other database systems such as MySQL. PHP also plays well with others in that it works well with common technologies such as HTML, CSS, JavaScript, and Ajax.

Requirements

Web publishing with the FileMaker API for PHP requires a web server, PHP, and FileMaker Server. The specifics of the requirements vary by operating system. FileMaker's API for PHP installation includes PHP 5.1.x. You may choose during the installation process to either install the packaged PHP or use your own version. You may want to use your own version if you already have PHP installed or if you will be using your web server for additional sites that do not use FileMaker.

Macintosh

- Apache or Personal Web Sharing (preinstalled Apache application)
- PHP version 4.3.x or greater
- Operating systems:
    - Mac OS X 10.4.x Workstation
    - Mac OS X 10.4.x Server
    - Mac OS X 10.5.x Workstation
    - Mac OS X 10.5.x Server

- Hardware:
    - Power Mac G4 or G5 computer, 1 GHz
    - 512 MB of installed RAM (1 GB or more recommended)
    - Hard disk with at least 1 GB of available disk space
    - CD or DVD drive

Windows

- IIS (Internet Information Services)
- PHP version 4.3.x or greater
- Operating systems:
    - Windows 2000 Server
    - Windows XP Professional
    - Windows 2003 Server
    - Windows Vista Server (Admin Console and web development tools only)
- Hardware:
    - Intel-compatible PC with a Pentium 4 or Xeon processor, 2 GHz
    - 512 MB of installed RAM (1 GB or more recommended)
    - Hard disk with at least 1 GB of available disk space
    - CD or DVD drive

Interface Differences

Beginning with FileMaker Server 9, the interfaces appear very similar and function the same in both Mac and Windows. This allows for easy management of systems on both platforms without having to learn two different methods.

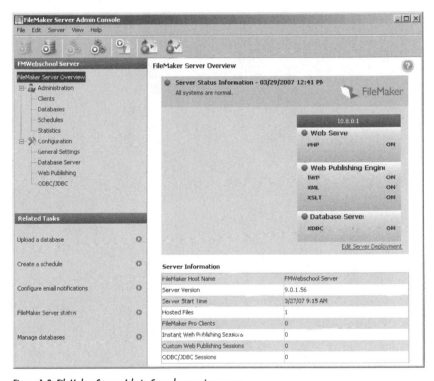

Figure 1-2: FileMaker Server Admin Console overview screen

Custom Web Publishing with PHP and XSLT are built into FileMaker Server 9. Because of this, FileMaker Server 9 Advanced is not required for PHP/FileMaker solutions.

Summary

Now that you have learned a bit about the potential of web publishing and what is involved in this exciting process, let's jump into it and get your system ready to take your application to the next level. We will start with setting up a web server, the heart of your dynamic pages.

Chapter 2

Setting Up Your Web Server

Web servers are responsible for taking in requests from web browsers and serving back both dynamic content such as PHP pages and static content such as images and movies. There are many different web servers on the market that work on many different operating systems, be it Windows, Mac OS, or Linux. Since the web server is vital to your success with web publishing, time and care should be taken to set it up properly for your operating system.

Deciding on a web server to use on your FileMaker Server machine couldn't be simpler. This is because FileMaker Server requires a specific web server for each operating system. If you are using a Windows operating system, you will need to install IIS. If you are using a Macintosh operating system, you will need to use Apache. Apache comes preinstalled on Mac OS X as Personal Web Sharing.

What You Need to Write and Test Your PHP Pages

Choosing a good PHP script editor can make your life much easier. There are many options available, including several free web editors. You can even use a plain text editor, although this should really only be an option if you are an experienced developer as text editors do not provide a graphical interface to immediately view the results of your work. In addition, some web editors color-code their code, which makes it easier to find and repair errors in your page.

If you choose to use one of your operating system's built-in text editors, make sure that the pages are saved with the required .php extension. Most operating systems hide common extensions by default. If the extensions are hidden, it may appear that you are saving your page as index.php when in fact you are saving as index.php.txt. When you attempt to access the index.php page in your browser, the page will not be found. Documents with an extension other than .php will not be processed by PHP and your scripts will fail.

Local or Remote Testing

Deciding whether to test locally or remotely may be determined by whether or not you have a copy of FileMaker Server. If you do not own a copy of FileMaker Server, you can use a FileMaker hosting company and access your database files remotely. Make sure that any hosting you use for your web files supports PHP. If you use a FileMaker hosting company, you may want to check before you begin to find out if it allows testing and development on the live server. If you own a copy of FileMaker Server and will be hosting the files yourself, the location of the FileMaker Server machine will determine whether you will be testing locally or remotely. See Appendix B for a list of FileMaker hosting companies.

Choosing a PHP Script Editor

Selecting a good script editor for your PHP pages will make building, testing, and editing your site much easier. Most web editors have evaluation versions of their software, so try them out before you purchase. You may find that a simple, free script editor is your best choice. Others may like the features available in a more expensive option.

Dreamweaver

Adobe Dreamweaver allows you to view your PHP pages in both design and code views. PHP scripts and other HTML elements are color-coded to help you spot errors quickly. More information, including a trial download, is available at http://www.adobe.com.

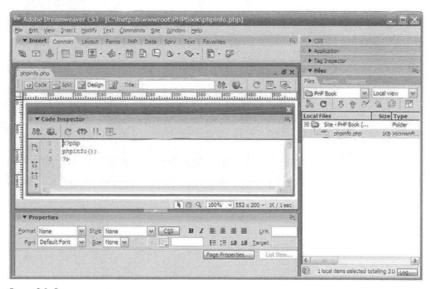

Figure 2-1: Dreamweaver

TextWrangler

TextWrangler from Bare Bones Software also has color-coded scripts; however, its lack of a design view can make it more difficult to use. TextWrangler can be found at http://www.barebones.com.

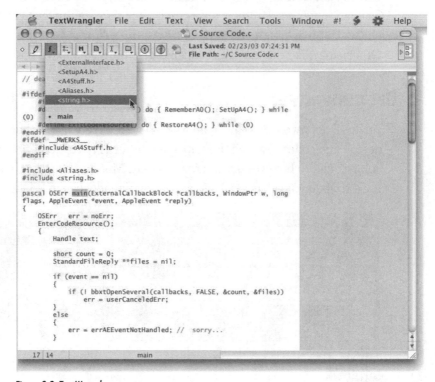

Figure 2-2: TextWrangler

Nvu

Nvu, available at http://www.nvu.com/, is an open-source web editor with both design and code view editing.

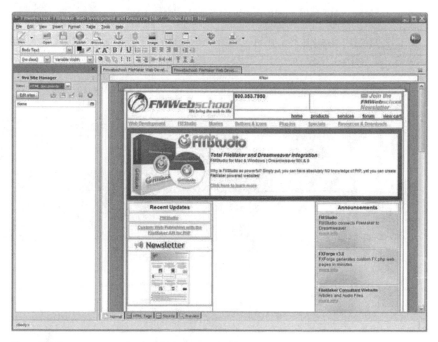

Figure 2-3: Nvu

Whichever editor you choose, take some time to familiarize yourself with the available features as they may greatly decrease your actual development time.

Setting Up IIS on Windows

IIS can be installed on Windows using an option under Add or Remove Programs and your Windows installation CD.

1. To install IIS, go to **Start > Control Panel > Add or Remove Programs**.

2. Next, select **Add/Remove Windows Components**.

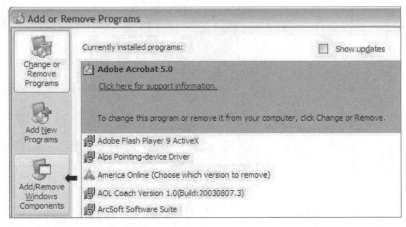

Figure 2-4: Add/Remove Windows Components option

3. Check **Internet Information Services (IIS)** and then click **Next.** This will walk you through the installation process. You may be asked to provide your Windows installation CD so that the necessary files can be copied.

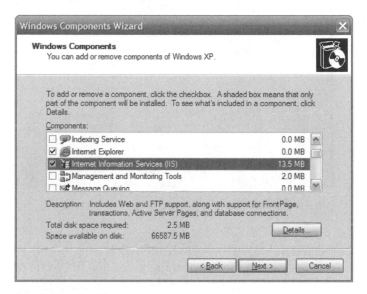

Figure 2-5: Installing IIS

4. Once IIS is installed, click **Finish** and close the Add or Remove Programs panel.

5. IIS can be started and stopped within the Services panel. To access this panel, go to **Start > Control Panel > Administrative Tools.** Select **Services.**

IIS Admin will be available in the list of services.

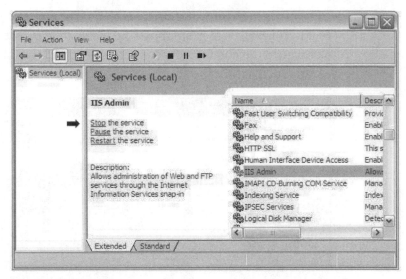

Figure 2-6: Choosing IIS Admin

Selecting IIS Admin from the Services list will allow you to stop, start, or restart the service. Right-clicking the name of the service provides access to all available options for the service.

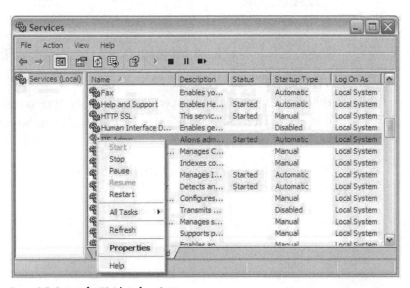

Figure 2-7: Options for IIS Admin from Services

Setting Up Apache on Mac

Apache comes preinstalled on Mac OS X.

1. To turn on Apache, go to **System Preferences > Sharing**.

2. Check **Personal Web Sharing** and click **Start**. This will enable Apache on your system.

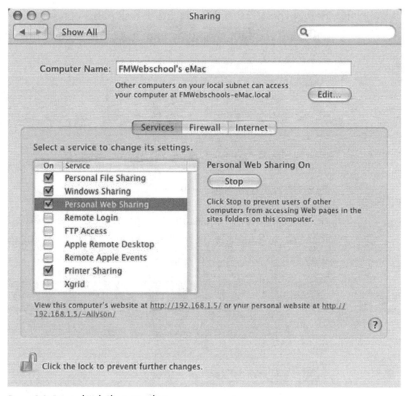

Figure 2-8: Personal Web Sharing in Sharing

PHP Installation Options

There are several ways to install PHP on your web server. There are installers available for both Mac and Windows that facilitate installation as well as provide access to optional extensions.

Windows users can download the latest installer from http://www.php.net/downloads.php.

1. Select the **PHP 5.2.3 installer** link. The version changes periodically, but the link should be similar to the second link in Figure 2-9.

Windows Binaries

- PHP 5.2.3 zip package [9,617Kb] - 01 June 2007
  md5: ff6e5dc212823009e68f26d66d85cbac
- PHP 5.2.3 installer [21,966Kb] - 01 June 2007
  md5: 4d042f649d9c264477e1b421c64c6435

Figure 2-9: Windows PHP installation options

2. Select a download location. The preferred download link for your location will usually be highlighted. Note that the available links may not exactly match what is shown in Figure 2-10.

	United Kingdom	
»	uk.php.net	Camel Network
»	uk2.php.net	Camel Network
»	uk3.php.net	Fubra
	United States	
»	us2.php.net	Hurricane Electric
»	us3.php.net	VersaServers
»	www.php.net	Yahoo! Inc.

Figure 2-10: PHP download locations

3. Once you have downloaded the PHP installer, double-click the installer, select the web server that you are using, and click **Next**.

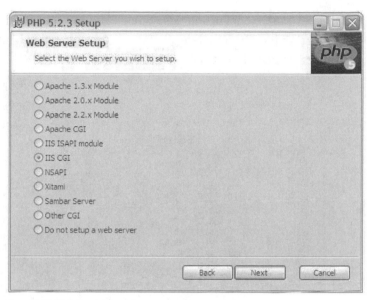

Figure 2-11: Web Server selection

Additional extensions can be installed by expanding the Extensions menu item.

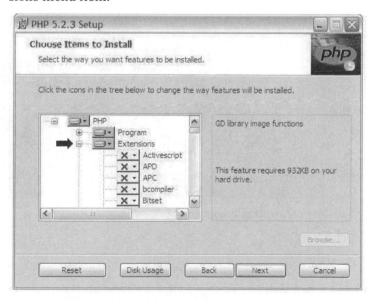

Figure 2-12: Installation options

4. Select an extension and then choose **Will be installed on local hard drive**. To complete all of the exercises in this book you will need to install the **Curl** and **GD** library items.

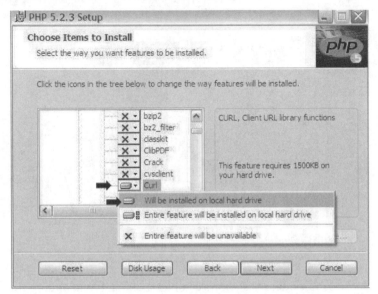

Figure 2-13: Extension installation options

Mac users can download a copy of Marc Liyanage's PHP Apache module at http://www.entropy.ch/software/macosx/php/. Again, the version changes periodically and may not exactly match Figure 2-14.

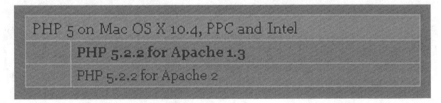

Figure 2-14: PHP installation downloads for Mac

Testing Your PHP Installation

Once you have installed and set up your web server and PHP, you should test that PHP is installed correctly on your server. A simple way to do this is to create a PHP page that contains a single PHP function. This function is phpinfo() and it returns the details of your PHP installation.

1. Create a new document using your script or web editor and name it **phpinfo.php**. Make sure that it has the .php extension.

2. Type the following at the top of the page:
   <?php
   phpinfo();
   ?>

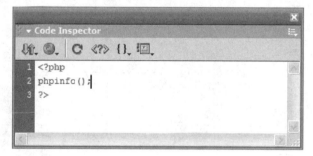

Figure 2-15: phpinfo() script

3. Save the page to the root level of your web server. The default locations for the root level of your web server are as follows:

   ■ Windows — C:\Inetpub\wwwroot\

   ■ Mac — HardDrive/Library/Web Server/Documents/

4. Open this page in your browser using your local address, which is
    usually **http://127.0.0.1** or **http://localhost**. The address to the
    phpinfo page would be either **http://127.0.0.1/phpinfo.php** or
    http://localhost/phpinfo.php. Your results should look similar to
    Figure 2-16.

PHP Version 5.2.3

System	Windows NT ALLYSONDESK 5.1 build 2600
Build Date	May 4 2006 10:30:29
Configure Command	cscript /nologo configure.js "--enable-snapshot-build" "--with-gd=shared"
Server API	CGI/FastCGI
Virtual Directory Support	enabled
Configuration File (php.ini) Path	C:\WINDOWS\php.ini
PHP API	20041225
PHP Extension	20050922
Zend Extension	220051025
Debug Build	no
Thread Safety	enabled
Zend Memory Manager	enabled
IPv6 Support	enabled
Registered PHP Streams	php, file, http, ftp, compress.zlib
Registered Stream Socket Transports	tcp, udp
Registered Stream Filters	convert.iconv.*, string.rot13, string.toupper, string.tolower, string.strip_tags, convert.*, consumed, zlib.*

Figure 2-16: PHP installation details

Summary

Now that your web server is up and running and PHP has been installed, you are ready to prepare your FileMaker database server for web publishing. With the web server configured, you can run a variety of PHP web-based software on your site such as forums, ticket support systems, and contact form scripts. Once the database server is configured, you will be ready to bring the power of FileMaker and web accessibility of PHP together and revolutionize your FileMaker solutions.

Chapter 3

Setting Up FileMaker Server

Previous versions of FileMaker required FileMaker Server Advanced in order to publish custom web sites. With the release of FileMaker 9, publishing FileMaker-driven PHP web sites requires only that your database is hosted with FileMaker Server 9. If you will be using Instant Web Publishing, ODBC, or JDBC, you will need to obtain a license key for FileMaker Server 9 Advanced.

Before installing FileMaker Server 9, make sure the following conditions are met:

- A previous version of FileMaker Server is not installed on the computer.

- IIS or Apache/Personal Web Sharing is installed and running on your computer.

- If you are installing FileMaker Server on multiple computers, make sure they are accessible via your network.

- Java Virtual Machine is installed on your computer.

- You have administrative privileges on the installation computer.

Single Computer Installation of FileMaker Server 9

Begin the installation process by inserting your FileMaker Server 9 CD into your CD drive.

1. Double-click the FileMaker Server 9 installation icon.

2. Windows users will be presented with a Welcome window, as shown in Figure 3-1. Click **Next** to continue with the installation. Mac users will not see this screen.

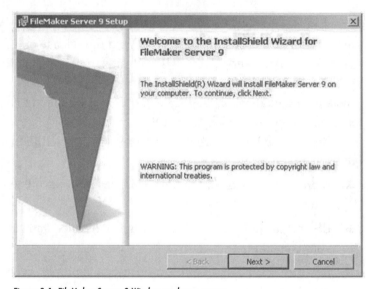

Figure 3-1: FileMaker Server 9 Windows welcome screen

3. Windows users should select **I accept the terms in the license agreement** and click **Next** to continue with the installation. Mac users should click **Continue** and wait for a prompt to accept or decline the license.

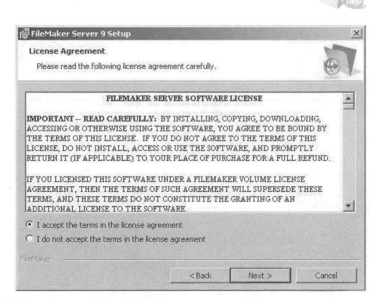

Figure 3-2: License Agreement screen

4. Select **Single Machine** for the installation type and then click
    Next. Mac users can also use this window to uninstall FileMaker
    Server. Windows users can uninstall the software by using Add or
    Remove Programs in the Control Panel.

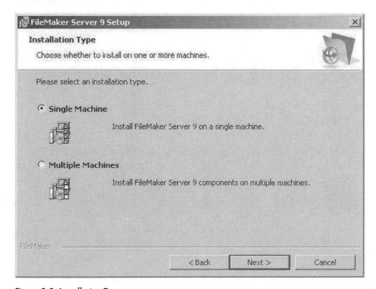

Figure 3-3: Installation Type screen

5. Enter your user name, organization name (this is optional), and license key. Windows users should click **Next**. Mac users should click **Install** to complete the installation.

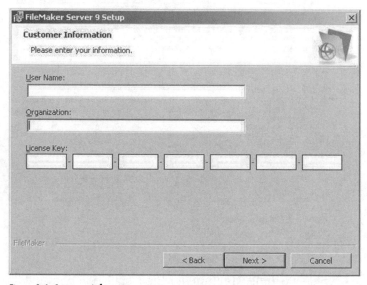

Figure 3-4: Customer Information screen

6. Windows users are now ready to complete installation. Click **Install** to install the application files.

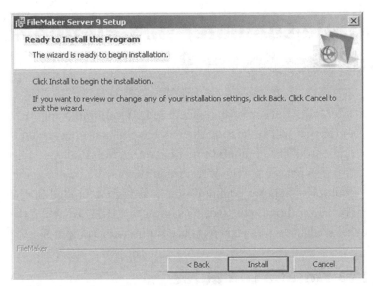

Figure 3-5: Starting the installation process in Windows

7.   Once the files are successfully installed, you will have the option
     to start the Deployment Assistant. Windows users can choose to
     start the Deployment Assistant and click **Finish**. The Deployment
     Assistant will open automatically for Mac users.

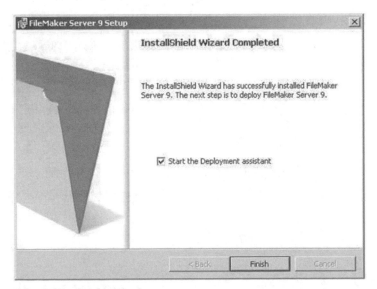

Figure 3-6: Installation completed

Multiple Computer Installation of FileMaker Server 9

FileMaker Server 9 can be installed on multiple computers. The computer that will be hosting the database files is considered the master computer. The computers that have the Web Publishing Engine and the web server are the worker computers. If you are going to use a multiple computer configuration, it is recommended that you install the application on the worker computers first. By doing this, they will be available when you configure the master computer.

The Worker Computer

Begin the installation process for the worker computer by inserting your FileMaker Server 9 CD into your CD drive.

1. Double-click the FileMaker Server 9 installation icon.

2. Windows users will be presented with a Welcome window, as shown in Figure 3-7. Click **Next** to continue with the installation. Mac users will not see this screen.

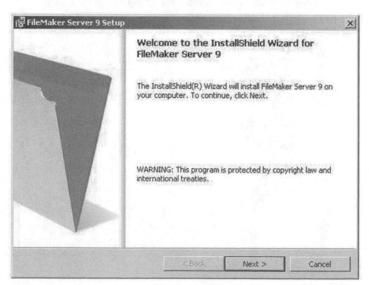

Figure 3-7: FileMaker Server 9 Windows welcome screen

3. Windows users should select **I accept the terms in the license agreement** and click **Next** to continue with the installation. Mac users should click **Continue** and wait for a prompt to accept or decline the license.

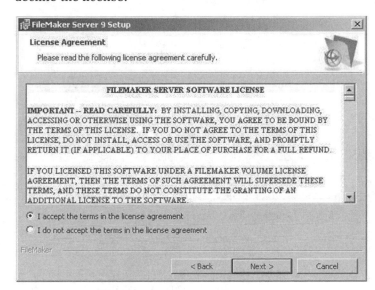

Figure 3-8: License Agreement screen

4. Select **Multiple Machines** for the installation type and then click **Next**. Mac users can also use this window to uninstall FileMaker Server. Windows users can uninstall the software by using Add or Remove Programs in the Control Panel.

Figure 3-9: Installation Type screen

5.   Configure the computer as a worker computer by choosing
     Worker and then clicking **Next** and **Install**.

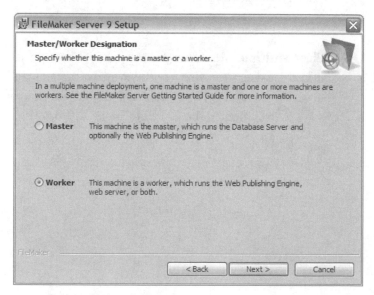

Figure 3-10: Master/Worker selection screen

The Master Computer

Begin the installation process for the master computer by inserting your FileMaker Server 9 CD into your CD drive.

1. Double-click the FileMaker Server 9 installation icon.

2. Windows users will be presented with a Welcome window. Click **Install** to continue with the installation. Mac users will not see this screen.

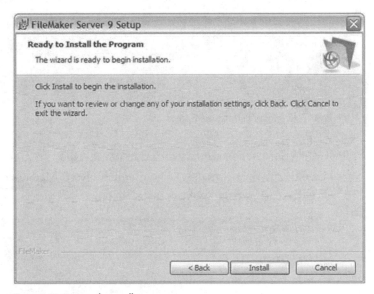

Figure 3-11: Starting the installation process

3. Configure the computer as a master computer by choosing **Master** and then click **Next**.

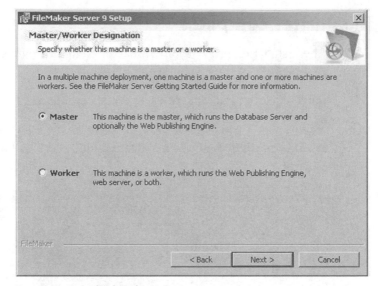

Figure 3-12: Master/Worker selection screen

4. Enter your user name, organization name (this is optional), and license key. Windows users should click **Next**. Mac users should click **Install** to complete the installation.

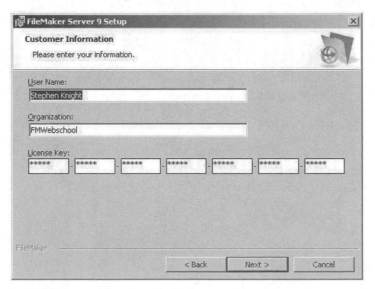

Figure 3-13: Customer Information screen

5. Select the deployment type depending on the number of machines
    on which you want to install the components, and then click **Next**.
    You may have up to three computers: one each for the Web Server,
    Web Publishing Engine, and Database Server.

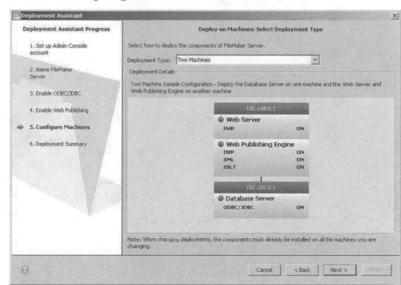

Figure 3-14: Deployment type selection screen

6. Select the web server to be used and click **Next**.

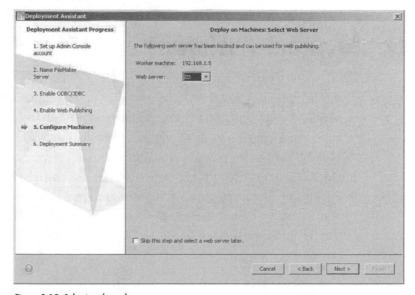

Figure 3-15: Selecting the web server

Once the application is configured, the deployment summary will
reflect a different computer for the Web Publishing Engine and the
Database Server.

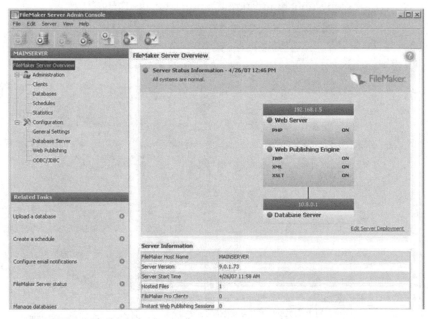

Figure 3-16: Deployment details showing installation on two computers

Deployment Assistant

The Deployment Assistant will help you set up and connect FileMaker
Server 9 on your computer. Once you have completed the installation
process, the Deployment Assistant will start.

FileMaker Server 9 uses Java Web Start to allow administration of
FileMaker Server through your web browser. This provides an interface with a common appearance on both Mac and Windows operating
systems. Java Web Start was created by Sun Microsystems to allow
Java application software to be started from a web browser.

</>

Figure 3-17: Starting the FileMaker Server 9 Admin Console

1. Create a user name and password for the Admin Console account and click **Next**.

Figure 3-18: Selecting a user name and password in the Admin Console

2. Enter a name and description for your server, enter the administrator's contact information, and click **Next**. This information can be used to contact the appropriate person in case of an issue or question regarding the server or database.

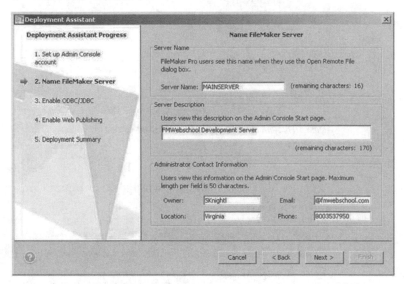

Figure 3-19: Naming the FileMaker Server

3. Decide whether or not you want to enable ODBC/JDBC. This option will not be available if you are using FileMaker Server 9 instead of FileMaker Server 9 Advanced. This is not required to use PHP with FileMaker. After you have made your choice, click **Next**.

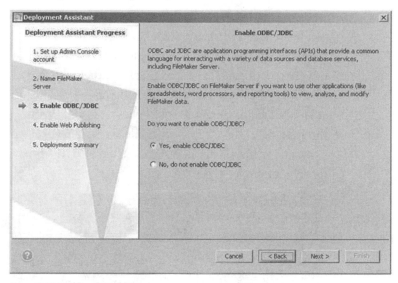

Figure 3-20: Enabling ODBC/JDBC

4. Decide whether or not you want to enable Web Publishing.
    Make sure your web server is enabled prior to turning on Web
    Publishing. Since you will be developing PHP pages that commu-
    nicate with FileMaker, you will need to select **Yes, enable Web
    Publishing**, then click **Next**.

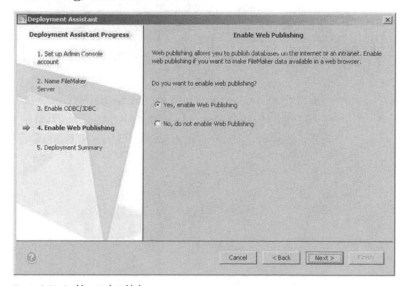

Figure 3-21: Enabling Web Publishing

5. Decide which web publishing technologies you want to enable. We will be using PHP with FileMaker Web Publishing in this book, so select **PHP.** The other technologies are optional. At this point, you can choose to install the PHP package that is included with FileMaker Server 9, or if you already have PHP installed you can select **No** and keep your existing installation. If you do not install the PHP 5.1.2 that comes with FileMaker Server 9, you will need to manually install the FileMaker API for PHP. After you have made your choices, click **Next.**

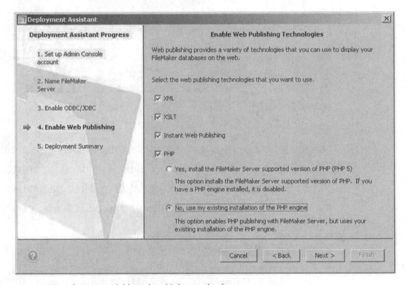

Figure 3-22: Selecting available Web Publishing technologies

6. Select the web server that you will be using with FileMaker Server 9. You will be presented with a list of available servers to make this an easy choice. Once you have chosen your server, click **Next.**

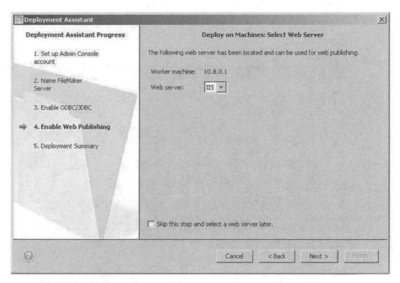

Figure 3-23: Selecting the Web Server

7. After you have completed all of the deployment tasks, you will be presented with the deployment summary. This summary will recap the options you selected. You can use the Back button to make any necessary changes. When you are satisfied with the choices you have made, click **Finish**.

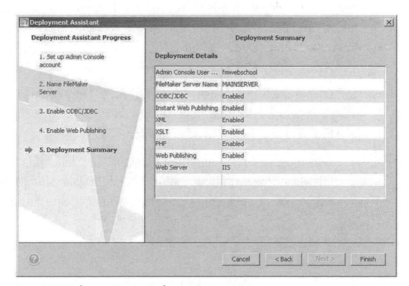

Figure 3-24: Deployment Assistant Deployment Summary screen

Once you have clicked **Finish**, the Deployment Assistant will set up
and configure your server.

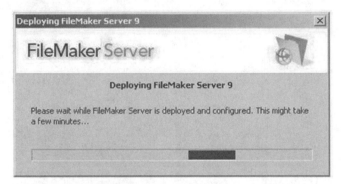

Figure 3-25: Deploying FileMaker Server 9

Manually Installing the FileMaker API for PHP

If you chose to use your own installation of PHP instead of the PHP
version provided with FileMaker Server 9, you will need to manually
install the FileMaker API for PHP prior to testing the FileMaker
Server 9 installation.

Follow these steps for a Windows installation:

1. Locate the FileMaker API for PHP files. They can be found at:
    C:\Program Files\FileMaker\FileMaker Server\Web Publishing\
    FM_API_for_PHP_Standalone.zip.

2. Decompress the file and then copy the FileMaker.php file and the
    FileMaker folder to C:\Program Files\FileMaker\FileMaker
    Server\Web Publishing\web-server-support\test\fmi-test\.

Follow these steps for a Mac installation:

1. Locate the FileMaker API for PHP files. They can be found at:
    HardDrive/Library/FileMaker Server/Web Publishing/
    FM_API_for_PHP_Standalone.zip.

2. Copy the FileMaker.php file and the FileMaker folder to
    HardDrive/Library/FileMaker Server/Web Publishing/web-server-
    support/test/fmi-test/.

Testing Your Installation

The first time you access the Admin Console, you will be presented
with options to register FileMaker Server or open a technology tests
page.

Figure 3-26: Registration and technology tests page links

The Technology Tests page allows you to test your access to the available technology options. If you need to come back to the Technology
Tests page, it can be accessed from the toolbar of the Admin Console.
FileMaker Server 9 installs a database named FMServer_Sample.fp7,
which has all of the available extended privileges enabled so that you
can test that each of your installation choices is functioning correctly.

In this book, we will be working with a FileMaker database as well as the API for PHP, so it is recommended that you test FileMaker Pro and PHP Custom Web Publishing. Testing FileMaker Pro will launch the FileMaker Pro application and open the test database that is included with FileMaker Server 9. You must have FileMaker Pro installed prior to launching this test.

Figure 3-27: FileMaker Server 9 Technology Tests page

A successful test of FileMaker Pro will open the database to the "Welcome To FileMaker Server" layout.

Figure 3-28: FileMaker Server 9 test database

Testing PHP Custom Web Publishing will open a sample PHP page in your browser. This will display a list of records from the FMServer_ Sample.fp7 database to confirm the proper configuration of FileMaker Server and PHP.

Figure 3-29: FileMaker Server 9 PHP Custom Web Publishing Test page

Summary

With FileMaker Server 9 ready to serve databases, it's time to configure the server for PHP access. You can already enjoy the advantages of
having FileMaker Server by opening your databases remotely from
multiple workstations using FileMaker Pro clients and collaborating on
database development with your colleagues. FileMaker Server even
allows you to use the database for data manipulation and at the same
time edit its data structure and layouts — a great way to do testing and
development simultaneously.

Chapter 4

Configuring FileMaker Server Admin Console

Now that you have installed FileMaker Server and tested PHP Custom Web Publishing, you can make changes to your server's configuration by accessing the Admin Console. The FileMaker Server Admin Console enables you to add additional settings that were not part of the initial setup when installing FileMaker Server 9.

To open the Admin Console, click on the Start Admin Console icon. The Admin Console will open as displayed in Figure 4-2.

Figure 4-1: FileMaker Server 9 Admin Console start page

FileMaker Server Admin Console

The FileMaker Server Admin Console is organized into several sections. In this book, we will only discuss the areas that are applicable to web publishing with PHP. The left-hand navigation panel displays a list of settings that can be further configured. As you click on each topic in the navigation panel, more details are displayed in the main area.

Two areas that are relevant for web publishing with PHP are Databases and Web Publishing.

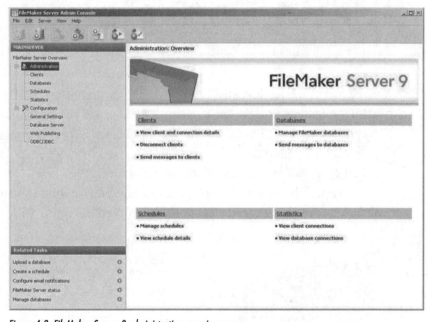

Figure 4-2: FileMaker Server 9 administration overview screen

Choosing the Databases selection in the navigation panel displays a list of all the databases hosted by FileMaker Server 9 as well as their privilege sets and the number of clients that are connected. The Actions drop-down menu enables you to perform a series of commands such as Send Message to all or Close All.

This screen is great as a quick overview of the connected databases so you can ensure that PHP is enabled for the database you are using.

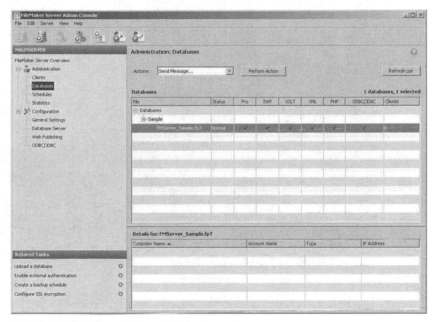

Figure 4-3: FileMaker Server database administration screen

Choosing Web Publishing in the navigation panel and selecting the General Settings tab displays a list of settings that allow you to enable logging and set the maximum number of simultaneous web publishing sessions. Logging can be valuable for tracking usage and errors.

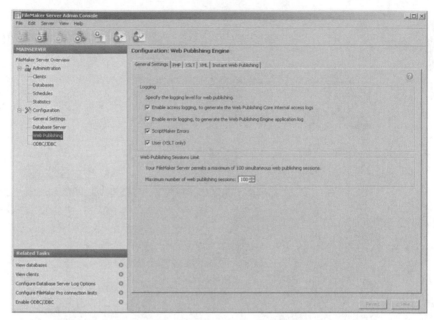

Figure 4-4: Web Publishing Engine General Settings tab

The PHP tab contains four sections for configuration:

■ PHP Publishing enables PHP web applications to access data using the FileMaker API for PHP.

■ Record Data Pre-Validations is FileMaker's own set of validation rules. We will actually leave this box unchecked, as we will be discussing validation in detail using Java Script and PHP in Chapter 10.

■ Default Character Encoding specifies the encoding to be used. You can leave this set to UTF-8.

■ Error Messages enables you to set the language that will be used when displaying error messages in PHP.

Once these settings are configured, it is unlikely that you will need to change them.

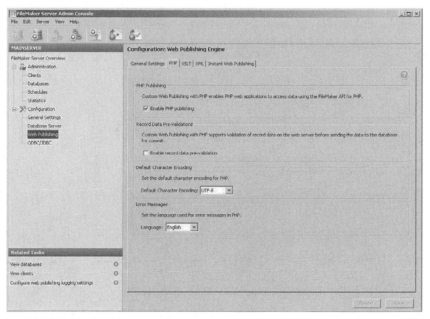

Figure 4-5: Web Publishing Engine PHP tab

Summary

Now that FileMaker Server is properly configured, you are ready to create and launch the database you will use for your PHP projects. In the next chapter, you will learn how to create and set up a basic database to be accessed by the FileMaker API for PHP.

Chapter 5

Preparing Your FileMaker Database for the Web

Blogs are a great way to communicate with many people at once. Businesses use them to discuss ongoing projects internally and to communicate with the public. Blogs can also be used to advertise your products and services, or just provide a vehicle to talk about your interests.

The project for this book is an exciting FileMaker-driven blog site. In this chapter you build the blog database. We have included a complete database with the user files for this book at www.wordware.com/files/fmphpapi and www.fmwebschool.com/wordware. We encourage you to work through this chapter to get a better understanding of how to build and optimize a simple database for the web.

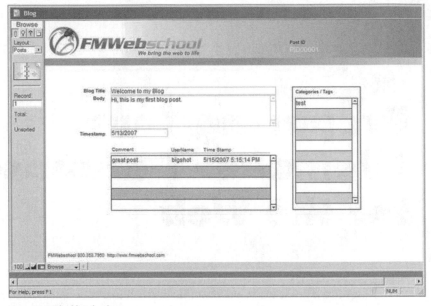

Figure 5-1: The blog database

Creating the Blog Database

Follow these steps to create the database:

1. Create a folder named **Blog** on your desktop and open FileMaker.

    If this is the first time you are creating a database with FileMaker, you will be presented with the FileMaker Quick Start window.

2. Select the **Create empty database** radio button, as shown in Figure 5-2, and then click the **OK** button.

3. You will be asked to create a name for the file and to save it. Name the FileMaker file **Blog.fp7**.

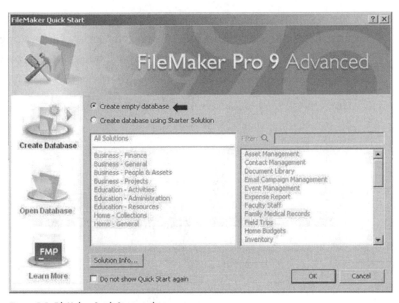

Figure 5-2: FileMaker Quick Start window

Creating the Tables

You will next need to create four tables to support the blog web site. Follow these steps:

1. Create a new table by selecting **File > Manage > Database**, and then select the **Tables** tab from the **Manage Database** window.

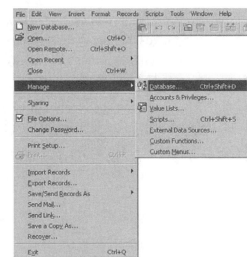

Figure 5-3: Opening the Manage Database window

For our blog project you will need to create the following tables: Posts, Commenters, Comments, and Categories. Since you named the FileMaker file Blog, the first table will automatically be named Blog.

2.   Change the first table name to **Posts** and then click the **Change** button as shown in Figure 5-4.

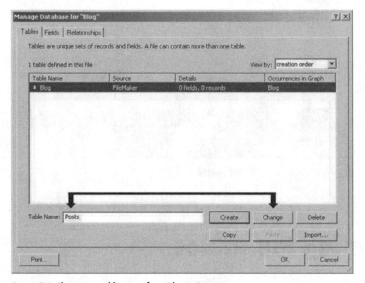

Figure 5-4: Changing a table name from Blog to Posts

3.   Create new tables named **Commenters**, **Comments**, and **Categories**. Simply type the name of the table in the Table Name text box and then click the **Create** button. Continue until you have created all four tables.

Once you have created the four tables, your Define Database window's Tables tab should look like Figure 5-5.

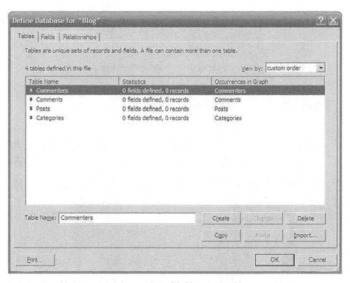

Figure 5-5: Table names and the number of fields in each table

Creating the Fields for Each Table

Once the individual tables are created, it is time to create the fields for each table.

The Posts Table

1. Select the **Fields** tab from the Manage Database window.

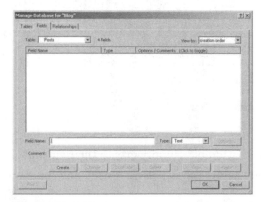

Figure 5-6: The Fields tab

56

Let's begin with the Posts table. The Posts table has these fields:

Figure 5-7: Fields for the Posts table

2. To create the timestamp field, enter **timestamp** in the Field Name box and choose **Timestamp** from the Type drop-down box as shown in Figure 5-8. Select **Create** to create the field.

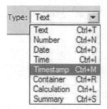

Figure 5-8: Selecting a field type

3. Select the **Options** button so you can set up the timestamp with the appropriate options.

4. In the Options for Field window, select the **Creation** check box in the Auto-Enter tab and choose **Timestamp (Date and Time)** from the drop-down. Then select the **OK** button to save your changes.

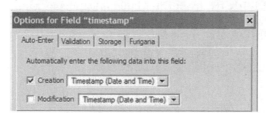

Figure 5-9: Setting timestamp options

5. To create the postId field, simply create the field and click **Options**. Then select the **Auto-Enter** tab and the **Serial number**

check box. Make sure the **Generate on creation** radio button is selected.

6. For the blog example, we set PID00001 as the next value of postId, and set the increment by value to **1**.

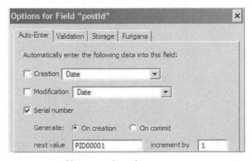

Figure 5-10: Adding a serial number

7. Create the title and body fields as simple text fields.

The Commenters Table

Next, you will need to create the fields for the Commenters table. The Commenters table contains the following fields:

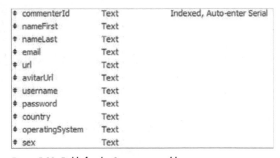

Figure 5-11: Fields for the Commenters table

1. The commenterId field will need to be set up as Indexed, Auto-enter Serial. You do this by creating commenterId as a text field and then clicking the **Options** button. Once again, select **Serial number** and select the **Generate on creation** radio button. Enter **UID00001** as the next value and set increment by to **1**.

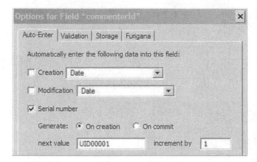

Figure 5-12: Adding a serial number with an incremental value of 1

2. Create each of the remaining fields as text fields.

The Comments Table

Next, you will need to create the fields for the Comments table. The Comments table contains the following fields:

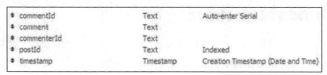

Figure 5-13: Fields for the Comments table

1. The commentId field will be a text field with an Auto-enter Serial value incremented by 1. In our example file, we are using CID00001 as the initial value.

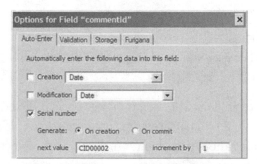

Figure 5-14: Setting options for the commentId field

2.   Create the timestamp field as an indexed timestamp.

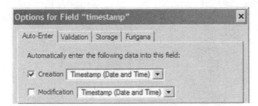

Figure 5-15: Setting options for the timestamp field

3.   Create three fields named comment, commenterId, and postId as text fields.

The Categories Table

Finally, you will need to create the fields for the Categories table. The Categories table contains the following fields, both of which are Indexed.

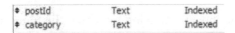

Figure 5-16: Fields for the Categories table

1.   Create both the postId and category fields as text fields.

The Relationships

Once the four tables have been created with their fields, you will need to define relationships. To create the relationships between the tables, simply click on the **Relationships** tab in the Manage Database window.

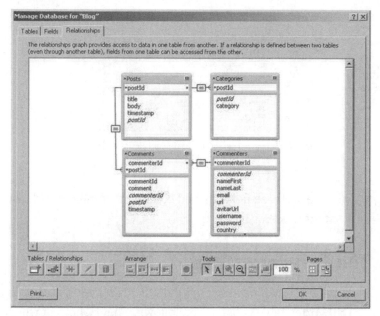

Figure 5-17: The Relationships tab

1. To visually facilitate adding relationships, arrange the four tables as shown in Figure 5-18.

2. Select **postId** from the Posts table and drag your mouse to **postId** in the Comments table. This will create a link between the two tables.

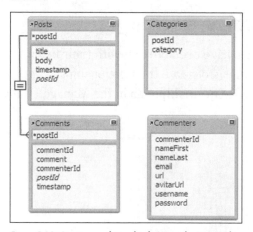

Figure 5-18: Creating a relationship between the Posts and Comments tables

3. Once you have created the connection between the two tables, edit the relationship by double-clicking on the square in the center of the link.

    The Edit Relationship window will appear. Make sure the correct fields are selected and check the following two boxes under Comments:

    ■ Allow creation of records in this table via this relationship

    ■ Delete related records in this table when a record is deleted in the other table

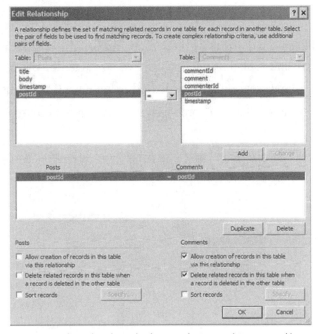

Figure 5-19: Editing the relationship between the Posts and Comments tables

4. Click **OK** when you are finished.

5. Next, select **postId** from the Posts table and drag your mouse to **postId** in the Categories table. This will create a link between the two tables.

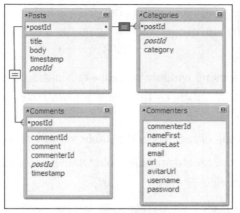

Figure 5-20: Creating a
relationship between the
Posts and Categories
tables

6. Edit the relationship by double-clicking on the square in the center
    of the link. Check the following two boxes under Categories:

    ■ Allow creation of records in this table via this relationship

    ■ Delete related records in this table when a record is deleted in
       the other table

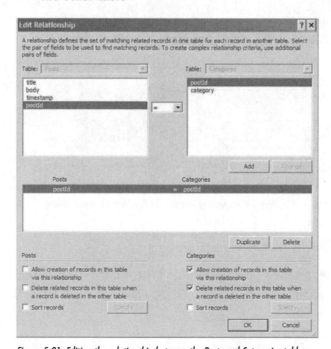

Figure 5-21: Editing the relationship between the Posts and Categories tables

7.   Click **OK** when you are finished.

8.   Next, select **commenterId** from the Comments table and drag your mouse to **commenterId** in the Commenters table. This will create a link between the two tables.

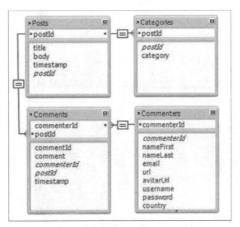

Figure 5-22: Creating a relationship between the Comments and Commenters tables

9.   Edit the relationship by double-clicking on the square in the center of the link. Check the following two boxes under Comments:

   ■   Allow creation of records in this table via this relationship

   ■   Delete related records in this table when a record is deleted in the other table

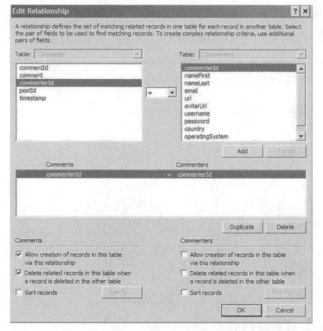

Figure 5-23: Editing the relationship between the Comments and Commenters tables

10. Click **OK** when you are finished.

That's it. The tables, fields, and relationships are ready. Now it's time to set up the FileMaker accounts to prepare the database for access by the API for PHP.

Adding Value Lists to the Database

Now you need to add a series of value lists to the database. You will be creating the following four value lists:

- Categories
- Countries
- OperatingSystems
- Sex

1. To create a value list, select **File > Manage > Value Lists**.

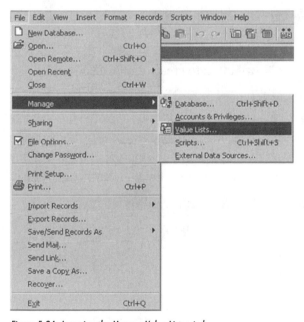

Figure 5-24: Accessing the Manage Value Lists window

The Manage Value Lists window will open.

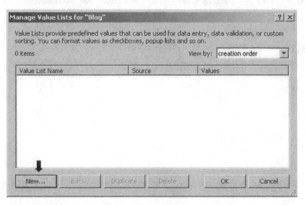

Figure 5-25: Creating a value list by clicking New

2.   Click the **New** button to create a new value list.

3.   Once New has been selected, the Edit Value List window will appear. This window enables you to name your value list, display values from a defined field, use a value list from another file, or create your own custom values by typing them into the space provided and separating each value with a carriage return.

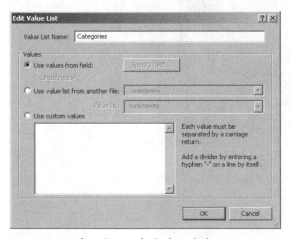

Figure 5-26: Specifying the type of value list to display

4. Name the first value list **Categories** and select **Use values from field**. Once this option is selected, the Specify Fields for Value List "Categories" window will open. Choose the table and field that contain the values you want to use. For our blog database, you will need to choose the **Categories** table and the **category** field. The Include all values radio button should be selected by default. Click **OK**.

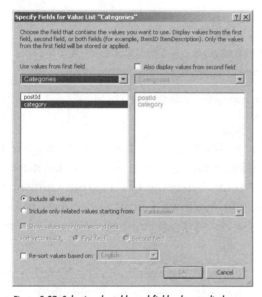

Figure 5-27: Selecting the table and field values to display

Congratulations. You have created your first value list.

5. Setting up the next three value lists is very simple. From the Manage Value Lists window, press **New**. Once the Edit Value List window opens, type the next value list name, **Countries**.

This time you will select the **Use custom values** radio button.

This selection enables you to type values directly into the text field. For this example, simply type in a few countries, and then click the **OK** button.

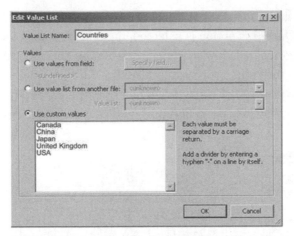

Figure 5-28: Entering custom values for the Countries value list

6.   From the Manage Value Lists window, click **New**. Once the Edit
     Value List window opens, type the next value list name,
     OperatingSystems. Select the **Use custom values** radio button
     and type **Mac OS**, **Windows**, **Linux**, each separated by a carriage
     return. Click **OK** once you are finished. We have one value list
     left.

7.   From the Manage Value Lists window, click **New**. Once the Edit
     Value List window opens, type the next value list name, **Sex**.
     Select the **Use custom values** radio button and type **Male** and
     Female, each separated by a carriage return. Click **OK** once you
     are finished.

     That's it! Now you will add the functionality of the value list to the
     proper fields. To make changes to the fields, we will need to be in
     Layout mode.

Layout Mode

You should have four layouts. To see the list of layouts, simply select the drop-down list under the word Layout on the status bar. In order to make changes to the layout, you will need to enter Layout mode.

To edit your layouts, select View > Layout Mode from the main menu, or select Ctrl+L on Windows or Cmd+L on the Mac.

Figure 5-29: Viewing the layouts

You will need to edit several of the layouts to display the correct data. To begin, select the Commenters layout and enter Layout mode. The Commenters layout should have 11 fields.

Move your cursor over the country field and right-click if you are on Windows or Ctrl+Click if you are using Macintosh. A list of menu options will appear. Select Field/Control > Setup from the menu.

 Note: There is also a keyboard shortcut that you can use to open the Field/Control Setup window — Crtl+Alt+F on Windows and Cmd+Opt+F on the Macintosh.

The Field/Control Setup window will open. Follow these steps to properly activate the value list with the country field.

Figure 5-30: Accessing the Field/Control Setup window

1. Make sure the Display data from drop-down shows **Current Table ["Commenters"]** and **country** is selected from the list of fields displayed.

2. Set Display as to **Drop-down List**.

3. Set Display values from to **Countries**.

4. Check the **Include arrow to show and hide list** box.

5. Select **Auto-complete using value list** and then click **OK**.

The Countries value list has now been added to the country field.

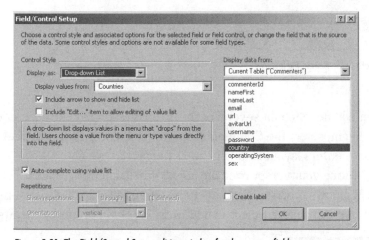

Figure 5-31: The Field/Control Setup editing window for the country field

To quickly test the Country field to make sure the value list has been applied, return to Browse mode, and then click on the field. The Country field should look like Figure 5-32.

Figure 5-32: Displaying the Countries value list

Next, move your cursor over the Sex field and right-click if you are on Windows or Ctrl+click if you are using Macintosh. Select Field/

Control > Setup from the menu. When the Field/Control Setup window opens, make the following changes:

1. Make sure the Display data from drop-down shows **Current Table ["Commenters"]** and **sex** is selected from the list of fields displayed.

2. Set Display as to **Radio Button Set**.

3. Set Display values from to **Sex** and click **OK**.

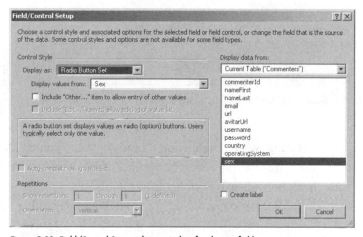

Figure 5-33: Field/Control Setup editing window for the sex field

The Sex field should now show the values Male and Female with a radio button beside each value. You will notice that you can only select one value at a time.

By now you should be comfortable setting up a value list for a specified field. We have one more value list left for this layout. Move your cursor over the operatingSystem field and open the Field/Control Setup window.

1. Make sure the Display data from drop-down shows **Current Table ["Commenters"]** and **operatingSystem** is selected from the list of fields displayed.

2. Set Display as to **Checkbox Set**.

3.   Set Display values from to **OperatingSystems** and click **OK**.

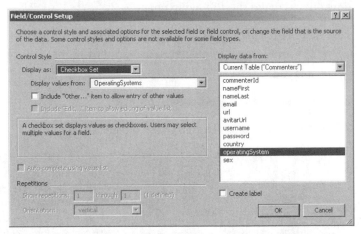

Figure 5-34: Field/Control Setup editing window for the operatingSystem field

The Operating System field should now show the values Mac OS, Windows, and Linux with a check box beside each value. You will notice with check boxes you can select multiple values.

When completed, the fields should look similar to Figure 5-33.

CommenterId	commenterId	
First Name	nameFirst	
Last Name	nameLast	
Email	email	
Country	country	⬅
Sex	○ Male ○ Female	⬅
URL	url	
Avitar URL	avitarUrl	
Username	username	
Password	password	
Operating System	☐ Windows ☐ Mac OS ☐ Linux	⬅

Figure 5-35: Value lists applied to the Country, Sex, and Operating System fields

Congratulations. You have just set up three different types of value lists on the Commenters layout.

The next layout you will work with is Posts. Posts requires both portals and value lists.

Portals

Portals enable us to view related data from other tables. The Posts layout will require you to create two portals, one to the Categories table and one to the Comments table.

Navigate to the Posts layout and enter Layout mode. The Portal tool is located on the status bar as shown in Figure 5-36.

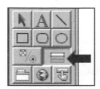

Figure 5-36: Portal
tool in the status bar

Select the Portal tool by clicking on it with your mouse. Then, using your mouse and holding down the mouse button, drag and draw a square on any unpopulated area of your layout. Don't worry if you make the portal too big the first time; you can easily resize it.

Once you have drawn the portal, the Portal Setup window will open.

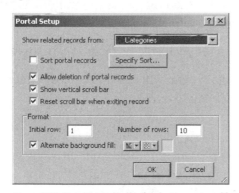

Figure 5-37: Portal Setup window for the Categories table

Follow these steps to set up your portal correctly:

1. Select **Categories** from the Show related records from selection.

2. Check **Allow deletion of portal records**.

3.   Check **Show vertical scroll bar.**

4.   Check **Reset scroll bar when exiting record.**

5.   Under Format, choose **1** for Initial row and **10** as the value for Number of rows.

6.   Choose **Alternate background fill** and select a light color to use as your background.

7.   Click **OK**. The Add Fields to Portal window will appear.

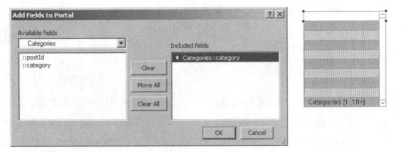

Figure 5-38: Add Fields to Portal window

This new window enables you to add the fields you want to display in the portal. Proceed through the following steps:

1.   Select **Categories** from the Available fields drop-down list.

2.   Double-click on **::category**; you will see Categories::category in the section titled Included fields.

3.   Click **OK**.

Your portal will now display the category field from the Categories table. We have one more item to add to this portal before it is complete. We need to apply a value list to the category field.

Double-click the category field inside the portal. In the Field/Control Setup window that opens, make the following selections:

1.   Be sure the Display data from drop-down shows **Categories** and **::category** is selected from the list of fields displayed.

2.   Choose **Drop-down List** from the Display as section.

3. Choose **Categories** from the Display values from section.

4. Check **Auto-complete using value list**.

5. Click **OK**.

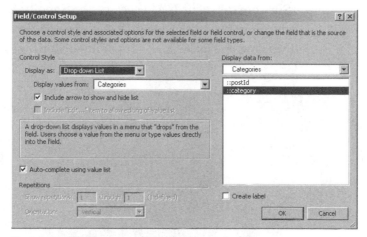

Figure 5-39: Editing the category field to display as a value list

Now that this is complete, the value list will display values from the Categories layout and the category field.

Next, you will need to set up a portal with multiple fields. This portal will need to be 350 to 375 pixels wide.

Select the Portal tool by clicking on it with your mouse. Then, using your mouse and holding down the mouse button, drag and draw a square on any unpopulated area of your layout. When you are finished drawing the portal outline, the Portal Setup window will open.

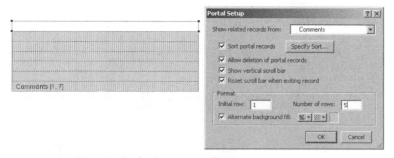

Figure 5-40: Portal Setup window for the Comments table

Perform the following steps to set up your portal correctly:

1. Select **Comments** from the Show related records from drop-down list.

2. Check **Sort portal records** and click on the **Specify Sort** button to open the Sort Records window. Double-click on **timestamp** in the left window, and make sure **Ascending order** is selected. Click **OK**.

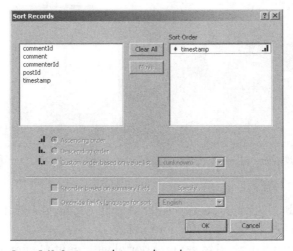

Figure 5-41: Sorting records in ascending order

3. Back in the Portal Setup window, check **Allow deletion of portal records**.

4. Check **Show vertical scroll bar.**

5. Check **Reset scroll bar when exiting record.**

6. Under Format, choose **1** for Initial row and **5** as the value for Number of rows.

7. Choose **Alternate background fill** and select a light color to use as your background.

8. Click **OK**. The Add Fields to Portal window will appear.

Proceed through the following steps to add fields to your portal:

1. Select **Comments** from the drop-down list.

2. Double-click on the **::comment** and **::timestamp** fields to add them to the Included fields section.

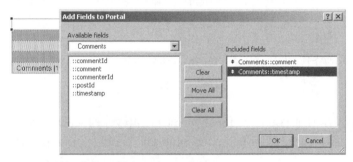

Figure 5-42: Adding fields to the Comments portal

3. Next, select **Commenters** from the Available fields drop-down list. A new set of fields will be displayed.

4. Double-click **::username** to add it to the other fields already present in the Included fields section.

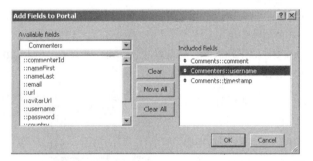

Figure 5-43: Adding fields to the Comments portal from the Commenters table

5. Click **OK** to add the three fields to the portal that you created.

Your new portal should look similar to Figure 5-44. The titles above each of the fields in the portal are simply text fields.

Comment	UserName	Time Stamp
great post	bigshot	5/15/2007 5:15:14 PM

Figure 5-44: Portal displaying the comment, username, and timestamp fields

Now that you have finished setting up your database, you will need to set up your FileMaker accounts that enable you to publish your database to the web.

Setting Up the FileMaker Accounts

Setting up FileMaker accounts and privileges is extremely important. FileMaker allows you to protect your database from unauthorized access as well as to define the privileges visitors have when they access your web site.

In order to use Custom Web Publishing with your blogging database, you will need to follow these steps:

1. Open the Manage Accounts & Privileges window by selecting **File > Manage > Accounts & Privileges**.

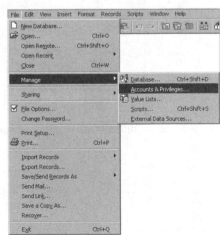

Figure 5-45: Opening the Manage Accounts & Privileges window

2. Selet the **Extended Privileges** tab and click the **New** button.

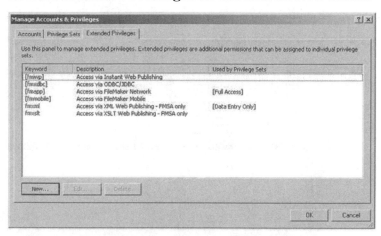

Figure 5-46: The Manage Accounts & Privileges window

3. In the Edit Extended Privilege window, define a new extended privilege set named **fmphp** to allow Custom Web Publishing with PHP.

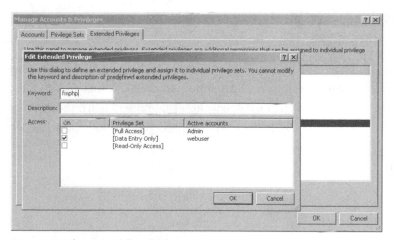

Figure 5-47: Defining extended privileges

4. Assign the extended privilege set to the proper privilege set (Data Entry Only).

5.   Click **OK**. You will now have a new extended privilege set named
     fmphp.

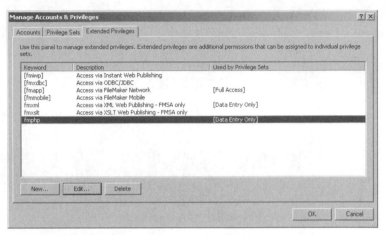

Figure 5-48: The fmphp privilege set defined

Summary

Congratulations! This concludes setting up the blog database. In this
chapter, you have learned how to create tables, fields, value lists, and
portals. In the next few chapters, you will learn the basics of HTML,
CSS, and PHP, which will prepare you for building a FileMaker-driven
PHP web site.

Chapter 6

HTML Basics

Working with FileMaker and web publishing requires a basic working knowledge of HTML. If you have never worked with web publishing, this is a great primer to give you the basics that you need onto which you can build a strong foundation. If you already have a strong background in HTML, you can skip this chapter and move forward to the CSS primer in Chapter 7.

HTML Review

HTML is a markup language that is interpreted by web browsers and enables you to display text and images in a uniform matter. Without HTML, your text and images would display haphazardly on your web page without any structure or consistency. HTML allows us to apply special tags to our web page content that enable you to change the way text and images are displayed and aligned on your page.

What Do I Need to Get Started?

HTML is truly nothing more than text on a page, saved with an .html extension. Of course, there are rules and proper tags that must be used, but to actually create HTML, you need nothing more than just a text editor. I use Notepad, the default text editor for Windows, for all of the examples in this book. Macintosh users can use TextEdit.

Note: Macintosh users — TextEdit can be used on the Macintosh to write your .html or .htm pages. However, there are a few steps you need to follow in order to make your pages work correctly. A help file for setup is available at http://www.fmwebschool.com/resources/textedit.pdf.

If you are already working with a web editor such as Dreamweaver or BBedit, then by all means, use those as you work through this chapter. Both Dreamweaver and BBedit offer trial versions of their software.

Note: Generally you should not use programs such as Microsoft Word as a web editor. Word processing programs tend to add invisible characters and strange formatting to your code. This can cause your web page to not render properly when deployed to the web. It is best to stick with a simple program such as Notepad or TextEdit or a professional web-editing program.

Website Folder Setup

Before we delve into the exciting world of writing HTML, we will need to create a home for our HTML pages and images. It's best to have a structured way of storing your HTML files and image files so they are easily accessible.

To begin, create a folder on your desktop, and name the folder **website**. Not very creative, but we will leave that for later. Open the website folder, and create a new folder inside that folder named

images. You will be saving all of the HTML pages that you create in the website folder, and all of the images in, you guessed it, the images folder. Now, open your text editor or web editor and let's begin creating your first HTML page.

Exercise 1 — Adding a Title

1. Open your editor, and begin by typing the following code:

```
<html>
<title>I am on my way to becoming a web guru</title>
</html>
```

2. Once you have typed this code, save this page to your website folder as **first.html**. By selecting Save As you can easily name your page with an .html extension. When you change the name of the file, you may receive the error shown in Figure 6-1. The warning simply lets you know that changing the extension from .txt to .html may make the file unusable. This does not apply to us in this example, so continue your saving process, and select **Yes** to change your file.

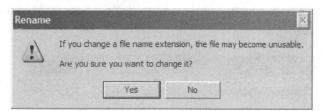

Figure 6-1: Warning about changing a file's extension

Once you change the file extension, your .txt file should look like an .html file. Your .html file will also look different depending on your default browser. In Figure 6-2, you can see that first.html is displayed as an Internet Explorer page. If you are using Firefox, the page would display as a Firefox page.

Figure 6-2: first.html
converted to a web page

3. Now that first.html has been created, double-click that file to open
    it in your default web browser.

 Note: You can also right-click the HTML page, select Open With,
and choose the Internet browser that you wish to use. On a
Macintosh, Ctrl+click on the HTML page and choose the Internet
browser of your choice.

Once first.html opens in your browser, you will notice that there is not
any text on the web page. Don't panic; that is the expected result. If
you look at the top of your browser window, you will see the text that
you typed between the <title> and </title> tags displayed in the
menu bar.

I am on my way to becoming a web guru - Microsoft Internet Explorer

Figure 6-3: Displaying text between <title> </title> tags

Exercise 2 — Working with Headers

Sometimes you will want to bring attention to certain sections of your
web page. Headers are a perfect way to accomplish this. There are six
commonly used header sizes. Header 1 is the largest and header 6 is
the smallest. In this exercise, we'll experiment with adding headers to
our web page.

Note: By now you have noticed that if you double-click on first.html it opens as a web page. So, how can you edit the page? You can simply open the document by right-clicking in Windows or Ctrl+clicking on the Macintosh and open the document with your text editor. You can also open the HTML page, choose View Source, make your changes to the document, and save it to your folder.

1. Open first.html and select **View Source**.

2. On the next row under the <title> tags, add the following tags: **<h1>** and **</h1>**.

3. Place your cursor between <h1> and </h1> and type **This row of text is formatted as a header 1 tag.**

4. Press **Return**, and on the next row, add **<h3>** and **</h3>** tags.

5. Place your cursor between the two tags, and type **This row of text is formatted as a header 3 tag.**

6. Save your page, and then open it in your browser. If you do not see the text, double-check your code and refresh your browser page.

   Your code should look like this:

   <html>
   <title>I am on my way to becoming a web guru</title>
   <h1>This row of text is formatted as a header 1 tag</h1>
   <h3>This row of text is formatted as a header 3 tag</h3>
   </html>

   Your web page should look like this:

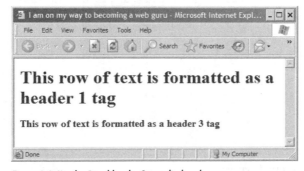

Figure 6-4: Header 1 and header 3 tags displayed

Chapter 6

Take the time to experiment with the different header sizes. You can easily change the size of any header by simply changing the numerical value of the tag. Headers are a great way of getting your visitors' attention.

Exercise 3 — Text Manipulation

Sometimes, plain text just isn't good enough, and it has to be manipulated somehow. That means learning more HTML tags!

Let's begin with the <body> and </body> tags. The <body> tag is used to identify the beginning of the main portion of your web page. Basically the <body> tags envelop the content of the web page. You will place all of your images, links, text, and forms between the <body> and </body> tags. The <body> tags are generally found under the heading tags.

Let's edit the code that we are currently working on.

1. Add the following tags in the next row underneath the <h3> and </h3> tags: **<body> </body>**.

2. Place your cursor between the <body> and </body> tags and type **HTML is so easy**.

3. Press **Return** and type one more line: **I will be teaching others HTML soon**.

4. Save your code. It should now look like Figure 6.5.

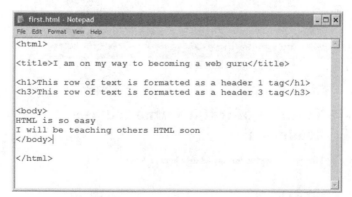

Figure 6-5: Using the <body> tags

5. Next, open the page in the browser. You will notice that the two
    lines you just typed are smashed together on the same line. To fix
    this, you can use either a <br> or a <p> tag at the end of each
    sentence.

    The <br> tag is different from the other tags we have worked
    with, as it does not require a closing tag. Use the <br> tag to
    enter blank lines. The <p> tag defines a paragraph.

Figure 6-6: The two sentences are on the same line and require more formatting.

    Insert the <br> tag after "HTML is so easy." The code now looks
    like this:

```
<body>
HTML is so easy <br>
I will be teaching others HTML soon
</body>
```

6. Save first.html, and open it in your browser. The two sentences
    should no longer be jammed together.

Figure 6-7: Formatting text with the <br> tag

If you want to add a paragraph return between the two sentences, you would simply add a <p> at the beginning of the sentence and a </p> at the end of the sentence. The code with a paragraph tag would look like this:

<body>
HTML is so easy
<p>I will be teaching others HTML soon </p>
</body>

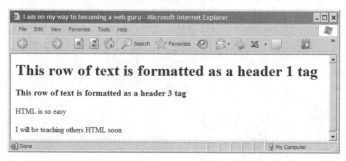

Figure 6-8: Formatting text with the <p> tag

Once you have more text on your page, you can separate the text by using the header tags <h1> through <h6> or the horizontal rule. The horizontal rule simply places a horizontal bar across your page. To insert a horizontal bar, you would use the <hr> tag.

If you wanted to place a horizontal bar between these two lines of text:

HTML is so easy
I will be teaching others HTML soon

you would add the <hr> tag after the first line of text. The <hr> tag is similar to the <br> tag, as it also has no end tag.

**HTML is so easy
**
<hr>
I will be teaching others HTML soon

7. Add the <hr> tag to your first.html page, save it, and then view it in the browser. The code for first.html is displayed below. The screenshot of the browser is in Figure 6-10.

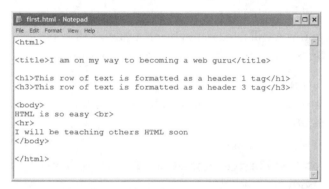

Figure 6-9: Adding a horizontal line with the <hr> tag

Figure 6-10: Formatting text with the <hr> tag

Notice that the horizontal line is displayed between the two sentences. Take a few minutes now and work with the tags that you have learned. I'll wait.

Exercise 4 — Adding Emphasis

Before you begin working with new HTML tags, let's simplify the
first.html page.

1. First, you will need to remove the lines with the <h1>, <h3>,
    <hr>, and <br> tags so your code looks like this:

    <html>
    <title>I am on my way to becoming a web guru</title>
    <body>
    HTML is so easy
    <p>I will be teaching others HTML soon<p>
    </body>
    </html>

2. Save your page once you have made the changes.

    The <em> and </em> tags are used to add emphasis to a certain
    word or sentence. In the next chapter, "CSS Basics," you will see
    that we are able to apply much richer effects using style sheets.

3. Let's add the <em> tags to the two sentences between the
    <body> tags so your code looks like this:

    <body>
    <em>HTML is so easy</em>
    <p>I will be teaching others <em>HTML</em>
    soon</p>
    </body>

4. Save your page once you have added the <em> tags and then
    view the page in your browser.

Figure 6-11: The first sentence and "HTML" in the second sentence are affected.

5. Another powerful phrase element is the <strong> tag. Replace the <em> tags in the second sentence with the <strong> tags. The <strong> tag will bold your text. Save your page and view the changes in your browser.

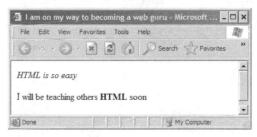

Figure 6-12: The <strong> tag applied to the word "HTML"

Exercise 5 — Formatted Lists

Creating lists with HTML is very simple. Lists help you present your page in an organized manner. To create a list on the web, you use the <li> tag in conjunction with <ul> and <ol> tags. The <li> tag defines the start of a list item, the <ul> tag indicates an unordered list, and the <ol> tag indicates an ordered list.

1. Open your text editor, create a new document, and name this document **ulist.html**. Make sure you save this page in the website folder.

2. The code in Figure 6-14 uses <ul> and <li> tags. Add the code to your ulist.html page.

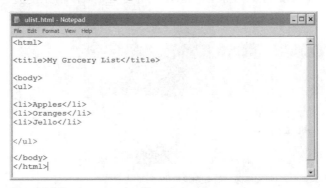

```
ulist.html - Notepad
File  Edit  Format  View  Help
<html>

<title>My Grocery List</title>

<body>
<ul>

<li>Apples</li>
<li>Oranges</li>
<li>Jello</li>

</ul>

</body>
</html>
```

Figure 6-13: Creating an unordered list with the <ul> tag

3. Once you have finished adding the code, save your page, and view it in the browser. Your page should look like Figure 6-14.

    If your web page does not look like the example, check your HTML code for errors. One of the most common errors is forgetting to include the </> closing tag.

Figure 6-14: Unordered list displayed in browser

4. Now that you are an expert with unordered lists, let's try ordered lists. Simply change the <ul> tags to <ol> tags. You do not need to change the <li> tags.

```
<ol>
<li>Apples</li>
<li>Oranges</li>
<li>Jello</li>
</ol>
```

5. Save your changes, and then view ulist.html in your browser. You will see that the bullet list is now replaced with a numbered list.

Figure 6-15: Ordered list displayed in browser

6. Since you are doing so well, let's create a numbered list with sub-categories. To keep things simple, create a new page named **numbers.html** and save it in your website folder.

7.   Open numbers.html, and add the following code:

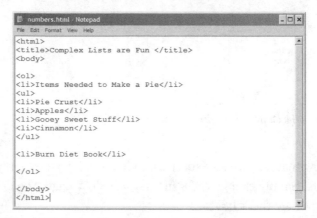

Figure 6-16: Numbered list with subcategories

8.   Once you have completed typing the code, save your page and open it in your browser. Your page should look like Figure 6-17.

Figure 6-17: Numbered list with subcategories displayed in browser

Now that you have mastered the fine art of adding lists to your web pages, take a few minutes to practice before moving on to the next exercise.

Exercise 6 — Images

What would a web page be without some kind of visual enhancement? When used intelligently, images can add an air of professionalism to your web site. Images can be used as wonderful navigation tools or to display a visual representation of the products and services that you offer.

A good rule of thumb when working with images is to use JPEGs for photographs and to use GIF and PNG formatting for graphic art involving flat areas of color, lines, and text.

The images used for this chapter are in the Chapter 6 folder of the companion files. Copy the following images into the images folder, located in your website folder. You will need these images to complete the exercises in the rest of this chapter.

- Coffee.jpg
- Envelope.gif
- Bullet.jpg

The first image we will work with is the coffee image. This image is 202 pixels wide by 132 pixels high, which is written in HTML code as:

```
<img src="images/Coffee.jpg" width="202" height="132"
alt="I love to drink coffee">
```

Let's break down this line of HTML into smaller, bite-sized pieces.

- The src attribute names the file, and the "images" text tells the browser that the file is in the images folder.
- The width and height attributes provide the dimensions of the image.

- The "alt" text is used by search engines, as well as people that cannot see your page. When you mouse over an image, the <alt> tag will display a string of text describing the image. If an individual is blind, their browser can use special software to read this text to them. The script above will display "I love to drink coffee" when you mouse over the Coffee.jpg image.

1. Let's go ahead and create a page named **coffee.html**. Add the code shown below:

```
<html>
<title>Coffee is Great</title>
<body>
<img src="images/Coffee.jpg" width="202" height="132"
alt="I love to drink coffee">
</body>
</html>
```

2. Once you are finished, save this page in your website folder and then open it in your web browser. You should now have the Coffee.jpg image on the web page, and if you slowly mouse over the image, you should see the text "I love to drink coffee."

Figure 6-18: Image with the "alt" text displaying

 Note: If you are using Firefox, the text will not show on mouse over as in other browsers. Firefox uses the <alt> tag as an alternative to the image if it doesn't load. That is, if the image file gets moved or is named incorrectly, the <alt> tag will display the text in the image's place.

What if you can't see the image? There are several reasons why this could be happening. First, check to make sure that the Coffee.jpg image is actually in the images folder inside your website folder. Also, check your code and make sure there are no misspellings.

3. Now that you have the image displaying on your web page, wouldn't it be neat if you could have it link to another page? You can accomplish this amazing feat using the <a> tag. The <a> tag defines an anchor. Anchors can be used to create a link to another document or to create a bookmark inside the document. You will learn how to apply both of these techniques in this chapter.

To create a link to another document, you use the href attribute. A typical link looks like this:

<a href="mywebpage.html">Stephen Knight's page</a>

The page that is being called by the <a href> is mywebpage.html. The text that will appear on the page, usually underlined in blue, is "Stephen Knight's page." Go ahead and add this code to your web page. Remember to add either a paragraph return (<p>) or a line break (<br>) after the line beginning with <img src>, or all of the text and images on your web page will be clumped together. Once you have added the new code, save the page and view it in your web browser.

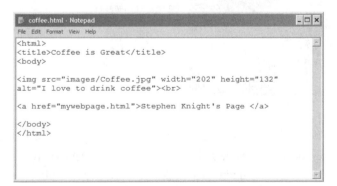

Figure 6-19: Code used to link to another web page

Figure 6-20: Blue link
displayed under the
image

Stephen Knight's Page

4. You can easily link to another web site by adding the full address
    between the <a> tags:

    **<a href="http://www.fmwebschool.com">FMWebschool
    Website</a>**

    You can also make the image into a hyperlink by using an <a
    href> tag and including a URL. Replace this line of code on your
    web page:

    **<a href="http://www.fmwebschool.com">FMWebschool
    Website</a>**

    with this code:

    **<a href="http://www.fmwebschool.com"> <img
    src="images/Coffee.jpg" alt="I love to drink coffee"></a>**

5. Save the page, and then view it in your browser.

Figure 6-21: Image as
a link

6. When you view the image on your web page, you will notice that a
    blue border surrounds it. The blue border lets visitors to your site
    know that the image is a clickable link. If you'd like, you can
    remove the blue border.

To remove the blue border, simply add **border="0"** to your code:

<a href="http://www.fmwebschool.com"> <img src="images/Coffee.jpg" alt="I love to drink coffee" border="0"></a>

After adding the new code, save your page and view it in your web browser. The blue outline will be gone.

7. You have added links to text and to images, but you can also make a button a link using the form commands. To do this, place the outlined code shown in Figure 6-22 below the <a href> code you typed earlier. Be sure to add the <p> and </p> tags so the lines are not on top of each other. Here is how the code should look. Once you have finished typing the code, save the page and view it with your web browser.

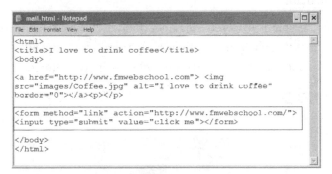

Figure 6-22: Code to make a button a link

Figure 6-23: Clicking the button will open up http://www.fmwebschool.com in your browser window.

Forms will be discussed more thoroughly later in this chapter and in Chapter 9.

Exercise 7 — Sending Emails with a Link

You can also add an email link on your web site that will enable visitors to email you using their default email client.

1. Create a new page, and name it **mail.html**. Type the following code onto the new page and save it in your website folder:

```
<html>
<title>Emailing is Delightful</title>
<body>
<a href="mailto:stephen@fmwebschool.com">Stephen
Knight</a>


</body>
</html>
```

2. Once you have saved the page, open it with your web browser. When you click the Stephen Knight link, your default email client will open, ready to send an email to stephen@fmwebschool.com.

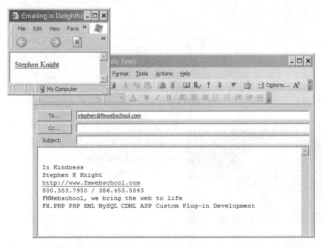

Figure 6-24: Opening the default email client by clicking on a link

3. You can also use an image as an email link. Make sure Envelope.gif is in your images folder. Then change the <a href> line of code that you just typed to:

<a href="mailto:stephen@fmwebschool.com"><img border="0" src="images/Envelope.gif"></a>

4. Save this new code and then open the page with your web browser. You should now have an envelope image that opens your default email client when clicked.

Figure 6-25: Click the envelope to send an email.

 Note: When you mouse over the envelope image, you will see the "mailto" address at the bottom of the web page. In Figure 6-25, it says "mailto:stephen@fmwebschool.com."

 Note: When sending an email from your browser, your default email application will execute. Depending on your email client, your browser may display messages such as "another program is attempting to send an email." There are ways to configure your email application so it will not display this message. See the "Sending Emails from the Web" section later in this chapter.

Exercise 8 — Anchors Aweigh!

Anchors are used to connect text and images to a specific location on a page. For example, imagine a web site with dozens of paragraphs, each discussing a different animal. At the top of the page is an index of the animals. When you click on any of the animals in the index, you are automatically taken to the paragraph discussing that animal. This is done using anchors.

1. Create a new web page named **anchors.htm**, and save it in your website folder. You are about to do a lot of typing, so you may want to stretch your fingers.

2. Type the code shown in Figure 6-26, and save your page.

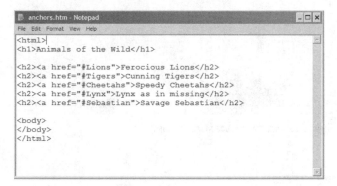

Figure 6-26: Header 2 links with anchors added

So far, you have added an <h1> tag as the main descriptive title of the page. The next few lines of code are the ones that contain the anchors.

Usually a link looks like this:

<h2><a href="anchors.html">Ferocious Lions</a></h2>

But since the link is going to an anchor and not a page, you would use the "#" sign followed by the anchor name instead, like this:

<h2><a href="#Lions">Ferocious Lions</h2>

To add the anchor, you simply add <a name=""></a> to the location in your document that you want the link to jump to. "name" is
the name of your anchor. When you click on the link **<h2><a
href="#Lions">Ferocious Lions</h2>**, you will be taken to
the paragraph on Ferocious Lions. Let's see how this works by
adding the rest of the code to the page.

3. Type the following paragraph between the <body> tags:

   **<p><a name="Lions"></a>Lions can be ferocious if they
   so desire. I personally have never met a lion outside of a
   zoo, and I hope that I never have to meet one in the wild,
   considering I live in a very quiet neighborhood, and this
   would be most unusual. I'm not sure how you should react if
   you see a lion in your neighborhood. Do you stop, drop, and
   roll? You certainly cannot outrun a lion...and they can climb
   trees, right?</p>**

4. Once you have typed the above code, duplicate it four more times,
   and add it to the page. You can simply copy and paste each time.
   When you are finished, you should have five paragraphs. Save your
   page, as you still have a little more editing to perform.

5. You will notice that each paragraph begins with **<p><a
   name="Lions"></a>Lions can be ferocious if they so
   desire.** That is fine for the first paragraph, but we need to make
   changes to the other paragraphs so the anchors work correctly.

   ■ Change the beginning of the second paragraph to read **<p>
     <a name="Tigers"></a>Tigers can be ferocious**

   ■ Change the beginning of the third paragraph to read **<p><a
     name="Cheetahs"></a>Cheetahs can be ferocious**

   ■ Change the beginning of the fourth paragraph to read **<p>
     <a name="Lynx"></a>Lynxes can be ferocious**

   ■ Change the beginning of the fifth paragraph to read **<p><a
     name="Sebastian"></a>Sebastian can be ferocious**

6.   Save the page once you have completed copying and pasting and
      making changes to the first line in the four paragraphs. Once you
      save your page, open it in your web browser and minimize it so
      that it is about half or one-third the size at which you would nor-
      mally view the web page.

When you click on one of the links at the top of the page, the page
will scroll to the paragraph that is connected to that anchor. For
instance, if you were to click on "Savage Sebastian," the page will
jump down to the paragraph with the anchor set to <a name=
"Sebastian">. You can see how this would be very useful if you had
a page with numerous paragraphs. There is an example of the
anchors.htm page in the Chapter 6 folder.
      You can also link an anchor to an image. The code is very
simple:

<img src="images/Coffee.jpg"><a name="coffee"></a/>

Take some time to review using anchors with both text and images.

Exercise 9 — Tables

You may have noticed that the pages we are creating are not very
structured. Yes, we are using <br> and <p> tags to separate sentences, but we really don't have a lot of control as to where the content
will display on the page. This is where tables enter the picture. Tables
provide a simple way to organize the content of your pages by enabling
us to add alignment, background colors, borders, cell padding, cell
spacing, and more.
      Tables are made up of horizontal rows and vertical columns. Each
row and each column has a table cell.
      Tables consist of one or more rows of table cells. The <table> tag
defines a table.

1.   Create a new page named **table.html** and save it in your website
      folder.

Let's create a couple of very simple tables.

2. To create a one-column table with a border of 1, copy this code and
    then save your page:

    ```
    <html>
    <body>
    <table border="1">
    <tr>
    <td>one column</td>
    </tr>
    </table>
    </body>
    </html>
    ```

    Open table.html with your web browser. You will see a one-column
    table with a border of 1.

    | one column |

    Figure 6-27: One-column table with a border of 1

3. To create a table with one row and three columns, you can simply
    add two more lines of code under "<td>one column</td>."

    ```
    <html>
    <body>
    <table border="1">
    <tr>
    <td>three column</td>
    <td>three column</td>
    <td>three column</td>
    </tr>
    </table>
    </body>
    </html>
    ```

    | three column | three column | three column |

    Figure 6-28: Three-column table with a border of 1

4.　Now that you've created a single row with multiple columns, you're probably wondering how to create two rows. You can do this by simply duplicating the section between the `<tr>` and `<td>` tags, as shown in Figure 6-29.

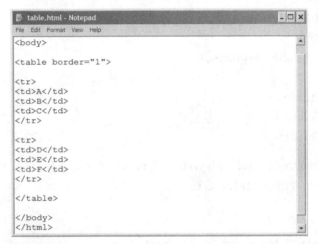

Figure 6-29: Adding a second table row

Figure 6-30: Second table row added

5.　Now that you have the hang of creating simple table rows, let's add a few more table elements. Open your table.html page, and delete everything between the `<body>` tags. Your page should look like this now:

`<html>`
`<body>`
`</body>`
`</html>`

6. Make sure you save your page once you have finished editing. Then copy the code in Figure 6-31. I will explain each line once you are finished.

```
table.html - Notepad
File  Edit  Format  View  Help
<html>
<body>

<table width="200" border="1">
<caption> <strong>Employees</strong></caption>

<tr>
<th>Name</th>
<th>Title</th>
</tr>

<tr>
<td>Jill</td>
<td>President</td>
</tr>

<tr>
<td>Robert</td>
<td>Vice President</td>
</tr>

<tr>
<td>Becky</td>
<td>Marketing</td>
</tr>

</table>

</body>
</html>
```

Figure 6-31: Code for multi-row table with table headers

The first line of code begins with the <table> command. This lets the browser know that you are about to create a table. In this example, the table has a set width of 200 pixels. You can adjust the size of the table by changing the numerical value. The border is set to 1, and you can also adjust the border size by changing the numerical value. If you do not want to display a border, set the border equal to 0.

<table width="200" border="1">

The next line of code adds a bold table title or caption above the table. This is not required, but it is an easy way to let your visitors quickly ascertain the contents of the table.

<caption><strong>Employees</strong></caption>

Adding <strong> tags around the word "Employees" makes that word appear as bold text.

The <tr> tag is used when you want a new table row to begin. The <tr> tag also has a closing tag (</tr>) Make sure you add this to the end of your table row.

<tr>
</tr>

The <th> tag stands for table header. Generally the table header is used for the first row of text in a table. The table header is like the title of a column. The <th> tag will bold the text in that table cell. Table headers also have a closing tag (</th>).

<tr>
<th>Name</th>
<th>Title</th>
</tr>

The <td> tag denotes table data. This tag needs to go in front of every piece of information you want to appear in a table cell.

<tr>
<td>fill me with info</td>
<td>fill me with info</td>
</tr>

This is the completed table opened in my web browser.

Employees

Name	Title
Jill	President
Robert	Vice President
Becky	Marketing

Figure 6-32: The completed table

Manipulating Cell Data

If you look at the table that you just created, you will notice that all of the information displayed between the <td> and </td> cells is left aligned. The table also uses a fixed pixel width. In this section, you will learn how to manipulate table data and table structure.

 Note: It can be terribly confusing to use table width and percentages. Think of your web page as having a width of 100%. When you create a table at 60%, this means it is 60% of the width of the page.

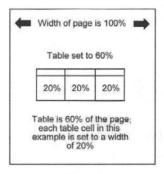

Figure 6-33: Table widths using percentages

1. Let's continue working with tables. Create a new web page, name it **table2.html**, and save it in the website folder. In this example, we will write code that will enable you to align text in a table using the align attribute as shown in Figure 6-34. Here, we use left, center and right alignment.

Figure 6-34: Aligning text left, center, and right

2. Type the following code into table.html.

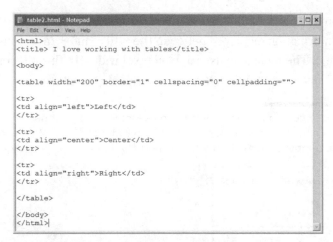

Figure 6-35: HTML code for aligning text in a table

In the code above, you created a table with three rows. Each row has text that enables you to set alignment:

<td align="left">
<td align="center">
<td align="right">

3. You can also add cell padding to the cell to give the text more space, so it isn't nestled up against the wall of the cell. Cell padding is the interior padding of the cell; it adds space between the cell content and its border.

To add cell padding with a value of 10, use this line of code:

<table width="200" border="1" cellpadding="10">

Let's look at an example of setting cell padding to 1, 5, and 10.

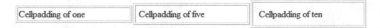

Figure 6-36: Cell padding with increments of 1, 5, and 10

4. Cell spacing separates the distance between table cells. To add cell spacing, you use cellspacing="", placing a numerical value between the quotes.

<table width="200" border="1" cellspacing="5">

Cellspacing of ten	Cellspacing of five	Cellspacing of one

Figure 6-37: Cell spacing with increments of 1, 5, and 10

5. The width attribute allows you to define the width of the table using either percentages or pixels. The percentage represents the amount of space between the page margins.

Figure 6-38 shows a table width set at 60%. The code to set the width of the table to a percentage is: **<table width="60%">**

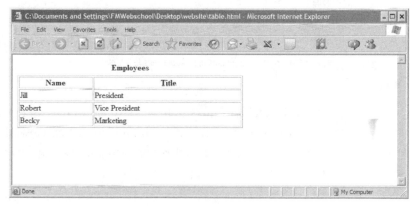

Figure 6-38: Table set to a width of 60%

Creating Clickable Links in a Table

Creating clickable links in a table cell is extremely easy.

1. Create a new page, name it **table3.html**, and save it in your website folder.

2. Next, type the following code to create the table and links.

Figure 6-39: HTML code for adding clickable links to a table

This code includes links to a web site, as well as an email link. Figure 6-40 shows how the table should look when viewed in your browser. As you can see, it is very simple to add a series of links to your tables.

FMWebschool
FileMaker
Stephen Knight

Figure 6-40: Links added to a table

Adding Images to Tables

In this section, you will learn how to add images to tables. Here, we will use the Bullet.jpg image shown in Figure 6-41.

Figure 6-41: Image inserted into a table cell

1. Create a new document named **table4.html** and save it in your website folder.

2. Add the following code to insert the image into the table:

```html
<html>
<body>
<table width="200" border="1">
<tr>
<td align="center"><img src="images/Bullet.jpg"></td>
</tr>
</table>
</body>
</html>
```

Notice that by simply adding <img src="images/Bullet.jpg"> you are able to add an image to any table cell. You will also notice that images follow the same alignment rules as text. You can align images using <td align=" "> and simply add the words left, center, or right between the quotes.

Figure 6-42: Images aligned left, center, and right in a table

Note: When working with tables, you need to put a
<td> </td> tag in the code if you have an empty cell. What
is   ? This is the code used to represent a non-breaking space.
It is essentially a standard space, with the primary difference being
that a browser should not break or wrap a line of text at the point
where " " is. (Most professional web editors such as
Dreamweaver automatically insert this code for you.)

Figure 6-43 shows two tables. The first table is missing the " ",
while the second table has the " ". You will notice that the last
cell in that table did not collapse as it did in the other table.

Allyson Olm	FMWebschool
Stephen Knight	FMWebschool
Eric Estrada	

Allyson Olm	FMWebschool
Stephen Knight	FMWebschool
Eric Estrada	

Figure 6-43: First table without " " and second table with " "

The code to insert " " is:

```
<tr>
<td>I have content</td>
<td> </td>
</tr>
```

Working with <rowspan> and <colspan>

In this example, you will be working with the <colspan> and
<rowspan> tags.

The <colspan> tag enables you to create a cell that spans multiple columns.

Column Span Example			
Cell 1	Cell 2	Cell 3	Cell 4

Figure 6-44: <colspan> across four columns

As you can see, the top row spans four columns.

1. Let's create a new HTML document. Name it **span.html** and save it in the website folder.

2. Copy the code below into span.html, save the page, and then view it with your browser.

```
span.html - Notepad
File  Edit  Format  View  Help
<html>
<body>

<table width="300" border="1">
<tr align="center">
<td colspan="4">Column Span Example <td>
</tr>
<tr>
<td>Cell 1</td>
<td>Cell 2</td>
<td>Cell 3</td>
<td>Cell 4</td>
</tr>
</table>

</body>
</html>
```

Figure 6-45: <colspan> set to "4"

The <colspan="4"> line of code tells the cell to span four columns. If I had specified <td colspan="3">, it would have only spanned three columns.

<td colspan="4">Column Span Example</td>

Now let's look at the <rowspan> tag in action. The <rowspan> tag enables you to span a single cell across many rows. In the following example, the cell spans three rows.

Figure 6-46: <rowspan> across three cells

Let's take a look at the code used to generate this table.

```
span.html - Notepad                                        _ □ ×
File  Edit  Format  View  Help
<html>
<body>

<table width="250" border="1" cellspacing="1" cellpadding="5">
<tr align="center">
<td rowspan="3">This is the Rowspan Example</td>
<td>Cell</td>
</tr>
<tr>
<td>Cell</td>
</tr>
<tr>
<td>Cell</td>
</tr>

</table>

</body>
</html>
```

Figure 6-47: <rowspan> set to "3"

Now that you have learned how to use numerous table elements, let's use them to create a complex table. Figure 6-48 shows what the table will look like when completed. Figure 6-49 displays the code used to create this table. Try to recreate the table without looking at the code.

Quarterly Sales	Regional Offices		
	East Coast	West Coast	Totals
1st Quarter	$5M	$11M	$16M
2nd Quarter	$6.2 M	$12.8M	$19M

Figure 6-48: Table using multiple elements

```
multitable.html - Notepad
File Edit Format View Help
<html>
<body>

<table width="80%" border="1" cellpadding="10">
<tr>
<th rowspan="2" align="center"> Quarterly Sales </th>
<th colspan="3" align="left"> Regional Offices </th>
</tr>

<tr>
<th align="center">East Coast</th>
<th align="center">West Coast</th>
<th align="center">Totals</th>
</tr>

<tr>
<td align="center">1st Quarter</td>
<td align="center">$5M</td>
<td align="center">$11M</td>
<td align="center">$16M</td>
</tr>

<tr>
<td align="center">2nd Quarter</td>
<td align="center">$6.2 M</td>
<td align="center">$12.8M</td>
<td align="center">$19M</td>
</tr>
```

Figure 6-49: Code used to create complex table

Thus far, you have mostly worked with tables as a whole. We have described table dimensions as multiple rows and columns, and you have adjusted the width of the table numerically and by percentages. In the next few exercises, you will work with table cells.

Many times you will find that when you create a table, the table cells will collapse onto themselves as shown in Figure 6-50 unless they are given an absolute width.

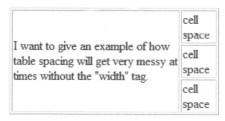

Figure 6-50: Table with cells collapsed

You can easily set the width of the individual cells so that they will accommodate the text and display it properly. Notice that the table in Figure 6-51 looks much better.

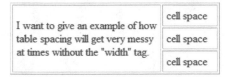

Figure 6-51: Table with set width applied to individual cells

You can easily apply table width by using width="" and placing a number or percentage between the quotes.

```
collapse.html - Notepad
File  Edit  Format  View  Help
<html>
<body>
<table width="300" border="1" cellpadding="5">
<tr>
<td width="200" rowspan="3">I want to give an example of how table
spacing will get very messy at times without the "width" tag.</td>
<td>cell space</td>
</tr>

<tr>
<td>cell space</td>
</tr>

<tr>
<td>cell space</td>
</tr>

</table>
</body>
</html>
```

Figure 6-52: Table code with cell width set to 200

Nested Tables

Many times you will need to put a table inside another table. This is not difficult to do.

1. Create a new HTML page, name it **table5.html**, and save it in your website folder.

2. Next, add the HTML code shown in Figure 6-53 to table5.html.

Figure 6-53: Table inside a table

Here is what a table inside a table looks like when opened in the browser:

The cell next to this one contains another table	Second Table	Second Table

Figure 6-54: Browser view of a table inside another table

The first table has a width of 600 and contains two columns. The first cell is set to 200. Since the table is set to 600, this means the next cell defaults to 400. The second table, with a width of 350, is placed inside the second cell of the first table.

Changing Text and Background Colors of Cells

You can easily change the color of text and table cells. The code that you use to change the font color is <font color="#XXXXXX">, where the "#" sign is followed by a series of six letters and numbers. Colors are defined on the web using a series of six digits that represent a combination of red, green, and blue. The series can be all numbers, all letters, or a combination of both.

For example, <FFFFFF> is the color white, and <A52A2A> is the color brown. There are numerous color charts on the web that display all of the web-safe colors that are cross-platform compatible. One such site is www.w3schools.com/html/html_colors.asp. FMWebschool also has a FileMaker color converter for finding matching colors when working with the web at www.fmwebschool.com/fmcolorpro.php.

To create background colors for each cell, you use the bgcolor command. If you would like to change the background color of a particular cell, simply add bgcolor="#color goes here". To change the font color, you simply add the code <font color="font color goes here">. Let's break apart the code to see how this works.

1.   Create a new HTML page, name the page **colors.html**, and save it in your website folder.

2.   Add the **<html>** and **<body>** tags to the top of the page.

3.   Next we will create a table with three cells. Each cell will be a different color, and the text in each cell will also be a different color.

Figure 6-55: Table with different background colors and font colors

Begin by creating a table with the following code:

<table width="300" border="1" cellpadding="10" cellspacing="2">

You are creating a table with a width of 300 pixels.

4.   Next we will add the first cell:

**<tr>
<td bgcolor="#3366CC"><div align="center"><font color="FFFFFF">White Text</font></div></td>**

In the above lines of code, we set the background color to blue using the hex code that is equal to blue. Starting with **<div align="center">**, we are setting the alignment of this cell to "center" to center the contents of this cell. The next section of code beginning with **<font color="FFFFFF">** sets the font color to white.

5. Add this line of code:

    **<td bgcolor="#FFCC66"> <font
    color="3366CC">Blue Text</font> </td>**

    The line **<td bgcolor="#FFCC66">** adds a background color of
    orange, and **<font color="3366CC">** adds blue text.

6. Now, add this line of code:

    **<td bgcolor="#CCFF99"> <font
    color="FF9900">Orange Text</font> </td>**

    The line **<td bgcolor="#CCFF99">** adds a background color of
    green, and **<font color=" FF9900">** adds orange text.

7. Now add your closing tags.

    </tr>
    </table>
    </body>
    </html>

8. Save your page, and then view it in the browser. You should now
    have a table with multiple colored cells and different colored fonts.
    Figure 6-56 shows the completed code.

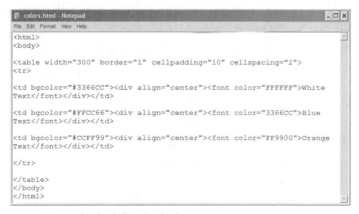

```
colors.html - Notepad

File  Edit  Format  View  Help

<html>
<body>

<table width="300" border="1" cellpadding="10" cellspacing="2">
<tr>

<td bgcolor="#3366CC"><div align="center"><font color="FFFFFF">White
Text</font></div></td>

<td bgcolor="#FFCC66"><div align="center"><font color="3366CC">Blue
Text</font></div></td>

<td bgcolor="#CCFF99"><div align="center"><font color="FF9900">Orange
Text</font></div></td>

</tr>

</table>
</body>
</html>
```

Figure 6-56: Completed code for colors.html

I Never Meta Refresh I Didn't Like

Have you ever gone to a web site, and all of a sudden you were taken to another web site? This is known as redirection, or a meta refresh. A meta refresh allows you to refresh and reload the current page you are on or enable you to automatically move to another web page after a period of time.

To have your web page refresh every 5 seconds, you would use this code:

> **<meta http-equiv="refresh" content="5">**

You can also perform a meta refresh that takes you to another web page. This is commonly done if the web site has moved or if the page you are visiting is outdated. The code below performs a meta refresh after 2 seconds and sends you to another web page:

> **<meta http-equiv="refresh" content="2;**
> **URL=http://www.newpage.com">**

This code tells the browser to refresh the page after 2 seconds and that the new URL should be http://www.newpage.com. You can add any URL link here.

If you wanted the new web page to load instantly, you would simply change the refresh time to "0".

This is a simple example with some additional text notifying your visitors that they will be redirected to another page in 5 seconds.

1. Create a new HTML page, name it **meta.html**, and save it in your website folder.

2. Type the code shown in Figure 6-57 into meta.html and save the page when you have finished.

Figure 6-57: Code to refresh a page after 5 seconds and redirect the user to
http://www.fmwebschool.com

3. Open meta.html in your browser and wait 5 seconds.

Adding meta refresh to your own pages is very simple. Practice changing the time of the refresh, as well as sending the page to other web
sites.

Sending Emails from the Web

Earlier in the chapter we discussed sending emails using your web
browser and default email client. Internet Explorer displays the message shown in Figure 6-58, warning you that you are about to send
your email address to a recipient and that the information you are
sending is not encrypted. For the sake of this exercise, click **OK**.

Figure 6-58: Internet Explorer alert informing you that your
email address and content will be sent unencrypted

If you are using Outlook Express as your email client, you will be informed that a program is attempting to send the following email message on your behalf.

Figure 6-59: Outlook Express warning

You can turn this feature off in Outlook Express by doing the following:

1. Select **Tools > Options**.

2. Select the **Security** tab.

3. Deselect the check box that says **Warn me when other applications try to send mail as me**.

4. Click **Apply** and then **OK**.

Now, when you send emails, the Outlook Express warning will no longer appear. This will also allow you to send emails automatically from FileMaker without having this warning appear.

The above technique works for Outlook Express but not for Outlook. If you have Outlook, there is a free software program that you can run in the background that will solve the alert box problem. The program, named Express ClickYes, is available for download at http://www.contextmagic.com.

Summary

Congratulations on completing this chapter on HTML basics. This chapter was not meant to be a total immersion into HTML but a brief overview of the language and techniques you will need to know to work with PHP. There are several great resources available online and hundreds of books written on HTML that can provide further study and insight into the HTML language. The next chapter will teach you about the power of cascading style sheets (CSS) in managing the design elements of your entire web site.

Chapter 7

CSS Basics

Cascading Style Sheets

CSS stands for cascading style sheets. CSS works in conjunction with HTML by adding features that are not available with HTML, giving you the ability to control fonts, margins, size, boldness, colors, etc. CSS allows you to make global changes to a web site by editing one line of code.

If you examine the typical HTML page, you will notice numerous font tags throughout the page. Imagine that your page has 30 of these font tags set for Verdana, and your boss says, "Verdana is a nice font, but Helvetica looks more fun. I want you to change all of the pages to Helvetica." What if your site has 15 pages? Now you have 450 font tags to change. This is great if you love mind-numbing repetitive work! There is, of course, an easier way, which is why I am introducing you to CSS. Just one simple line of code will make the necessary changes you need for all of your web pages. Sound good?

There are two different styles of CSS: external and internal. Internal simply means that the style sheet is contained within the HTML document. Your CSS code will go between the <style></style> tags, which reside between the <head></head> tags.

An external style sheet is a set of style rules saved as a .css file. A reference to the file's location is placed between the <head> tags of your HTML document. This CSS file can be linked to a single page, or can control the look and feel of your entire web site. You will also find that using external style sheets saves tremendous amounts of file space and allows your pages to load faster. In this book, we will be focusing on external style sheets.

Below is an example of a link to an external style sheet:

```
<html>
<head>
<link href="stylesheet.css" rel="stylesheet"
type="text/css">
</head>
```

Let's delve right into our first CSS page. You will be using the same website folder you created in Chapter 6. Open the companion folder for this chapter, and copy the **images** folder into the website folder. The path should look like this:

website/images

The images folder contains all of the images we will be using throughout this chapter.

1.   To begin with CSS, you first need to create a CSS document, name it **stylesheet.css**, and save it in your website folder. It is very important that you save the file using **.css**, as this extension tells the browser that it is reading CSS code.

2.   Open this document with your text editor, and enter the following lines of code:

```
h2 {
font-family: Arial, Helvetica, sans-serif;
font-size: 18px;
color: #000066;
}
```

Be sure to save **stylesheet.css**.

3.   Next, create an HTML page named **cascading.html** and save that document in your website folder as well. Type the code shown in Figure 7-1 into **cascading.html**, save the page, and view it in your browser.

```
cascading.html - Notepad
File  Edit  Format  View  Help
<html>
<head>
<title>CSS Example</title>
<link href="stylesheet.css" rel="stylesheet" type="text/css">
<h1>The next line will be blue</h1>
</head>

<body>

<h2>I told you...see I'm blue</h2>

<p>The default color of the text is black, but because we applied style
to "h2", only "h2" will be affected.</p>

<h3>I'm not affected</h3>

</body>
</html>
```

Figure 7-1: Calling an external style sheet that affects the <h1>, <h2>, and <h3> tags

The code **<link href="stylesheet.css" rel="stylesheet" type="text/css">** tells the browser that you will be using an external style sheet.

```
CSS Example - Microsoft Internet Explorer
File  Edit  View  Favorites  Tools  Help

The next line will be blue

I told you...see I'm blue

The default color of the text is black, but because we applied style to "h2", only "h2" will be affected.

I'm not affected

Done                                          My Computer
```

Figure 7-2: cascading.html viewed in the browser

The CSS code in step 1 is set to change the text surrounded by the <h2> tags to blue. Recall from the previous chapter that there are several different header tags. When you apply header tags to text, they change the size of the text.

Also, in the code above, we only have one <h2> tag. If I had added more <h2> tags, the CSS code would automatically turn all of the text surrounded by the <h2> tags blue.

Let's discuss constructing a style rule using our example from above.

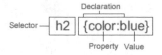

Figure 7-3: Description of a style rule

Each style rule consists of two main parts: the selector and the declaration. The selector specifies what component of the HTML document is to be styled. In the above example, we see that it is h2 that is to be styled. The next part, the declaration, goes between a set of curly braces { }. The style rule declaration consists of two parts: the property and the value.

You can include multiple properties and values for a single selector, but be sure to separate them with a semicolon.

A property is the characteristic that you want to change, like "color" in the above example. A value is what you want the property to be. In this example, we used a value of "blue."

Note: In the above example, we used the color blue. If you wish to specify an exact color, you may want to use hexadecimal coding. In that case, the above example would read: h2 {color:0000F0}

If you wanted to include multiple declarations, the style rule would look like this:

h2 {color:blue; background:black}

Notice a colon separates the property and value, and a semicolon separates each declaration.

Just as you can claim multiple declarations, you can have multiple selectors affected by a declaration as well. For example, the following code will make both h1 and h2 blue:

h1, h2 {color:blue}

Your style rule can become a bit confusing if it has multiple declarations. You can add a space between the property and the value after the colon as shown below.

h2 {color: blue; background: gray}

4. Let's build a simple page with multiple declarations. Open your style sheet, and edit the code to look like Figure 7-4.

```
stylesheet.css - Notepad
File  Edit  Format  View  Help
h1 {
font-family: Arial, Helvetica, sans-serif;
font-size: 18px;
color: green;
background: orange;
}

h2 {
font-family: Arial, Helvetica, sans-serif;
font-size: 18px;
color: blue;
background: gray;
}|
```

Figure 7-4: Working with multiple declarations in stylesheet.css

Note: When typing font-size, you cannot have a space between the number value and the "px" or "pt" value. Your values must look like 18px or 18pt.

5. Go ahead and save your style sheet. Now open up **cascading.html** in your browser. Your results should match Figure 7-5, where the first line has an orange background with green text, and the second line has a gray background with blue text.

Figure 7-5: stylesheet.css opened in browser with orange and gray backgrounds

Before we move on, let's take a closer look at the style sheet so we can see what's going on.

We have learned that the value that appears before the curly braces ({) is called the selector. The selector specifies what component of the HTML document is to be styled.

h2 {

The next line begins with the property "font-family" with a value of Arial, Helvetica, sans-serif. Why are so many fonts listed? The fonts are listed from the most desired font to, well, the least desired font. Not everyone's computer will have all of the fonts that you desire to use, so you must give those computers an option of using another font.

font-family: Arial, Helvetica, sans-serif;

The next line of code shows the font-size property with a value of 18px. You can change the pixel value to just about any size you want…well, within reason. This determines how large the font will appear on the web page.

font-size: 18px;

The color property has a value of blue. You could have also used the hexadecimal value for blue, or for any color.

color: blue;

The background property has a value of gray. You could have also used the hexadecimal value for gray, or for any color.

background: gray;

Don't forget to add your closing tag!

}

The h1 declaration below is pretty much the same as the h2 declaration, except for the different colors used.

h1 {
font-family: Arial, Helvetica, sans-serif;
font-size: 18px;
color: green;
background: orange;
}

Fonts

Let's style both h2 and p text. We will use two separate font families. The list of fonts starts with the most desired font family and ends with a generic option. In this example, I have added Tahoma, Arial, and sans-serif to the h2 declaration, and I have added Times New Roman and serif to the p declaration.

1. To make these changes, we will need to first open **stylesheet.css**. Edit the code in your style sheet so it looks like the code displayed in Figure 7-6.

```
stylesheet.css - Notepad
File  Edit  Format  View  Help
h1 {
font-family: Arial, Helvetica, sans-serif;
font-size: 18px;
color: black;
}

h2 {
font-family: Tahoma, Arial, sans-serif;
font-size: 18px;
color: black;
}
```

Figure 7-6: Editing stylesheet.css to add fonts

Once you have made the changes to your code, create a new style rule that looks like this:

```
p {
font-family: Times New Roman, serif;
font-size: 12px;
color: black;
}
```

Once you have added these changes to your style sheet, save your style sheet.

2. Next, open **cascading.html** with your text editor. Highlight all of the code between the <body></body> tags and delete it. Also delete the <h1> line of code in the head section of the page. Then type the code below between the <body> tags and save your changes:

```
<h1>"h1" defaults to Arial</h1>
<h2> "h2" Will default to Tahoma, Arial, sans-serif</h2>
<p>"p" Will default to Times New Roman, serif</p>
<h3>"h3" will not be affected</h3>
```

3. Open **cascading.html** in your web browser. Your results should reflect those shown below.

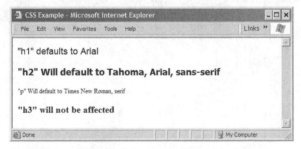

Figure 7-7: Font changes applied to <h1>, <h2>, and <p> tags

Pretty easy, eh?

Font Size

You can designate font sizes by using either "px" for pixel or "pt" for point size. The decision is entirely up to you as to which one you decide to use. Just remember that you cannot have any space between the numerical value and the "pt" or "px." Your values must look like 24pt, with no space, rather than 24 pt.

Font Weight

Font weight refers to the actual lines that make up the individual font. The font weight system uses a numerical value from 100 to 900, with 100 being the lightest and 900 being the heaviest.

Check out the example below. I've added a font weight of 100 to the <h2> tag and a font weight of 900 to the <p> tag.

"h2" Will default to Tahoma, Arial, sans-serif

"p" Will default to Times New Roman, serif

Figure 7-8: <h2> with a font weight of 100 and <p> with a font weight of 900

Now let's change the font weight order and apply 900 to the h2 declaration and 100 to the p declaration.

"h2" Will default to Tahoma, Arial, sans-serif

"p" Will default to Times New Roman, serif

Figure 7-9: <h2> with a font weight of 900 and <p> with a font weight of 100

That's a big difference!

You can make changes to the font weight by simply adding this line of code:

font-weight: 900;

Here is what the code looks like inside the h2 declaration:

```
h2 {
font-family: Tahoma, Arial, sans-serif;
font-size: 18px;
font-weight: 900;
color: black;
}
```

Open up your style sheet, and add **font-weight: 900;** to your code. Save your page and open **cascading.html** in your browser. Take some time to play with font weight by using different numerical values.

Font Style

The next category we should cover is font styles. There are three different kinds of font styles: normal, italicized, and emboldened. Normal is the default value. To add a font style, you can simply add this line of code to your declaration.

```
font-style: italic;
```

I have added the font-style property to the h1 code below:

```
h1 {
font-family: Arial, Helvetica, sans-serif;
font-size: 18px;
font-weight: normal;
color: black;
font-style: italic;
}
```

Go ahead and add this line of code to your style sheet as well. Save **stylesheet.css** and then open **cascading.html** in your browser. You will notice that the text with the <h1> tag is now in italics.

 Note: I like to add a semicolon after the last value just in case I want to add another property. This way I won't forget to add the semicolon.

Margins

Cascading style sheets give you the ability to determine all four margins on a page: top, bottom, left, and right. You do have limited abilities with HTML as far as margins are concerned. You can use the <blockquote> tag to affect the left margin (basically giving you more indentation). But using <blockquote> in your HTML pages does not even come close to providing you with the capabilities cascading style sheets offer.

Let's see how we can apply <blockquote> to our CSS code.

1. Let's go ahead and create a new HTML page. Name the page **margins.html** and save it in the website folder.

   You do not need to create another style sheet, as one external style sheet can control an entire web site. Simply remember to include your link to the external style sheet in the <head> section of your web page: **<link href="stylesheet.css" rel="stylesheet" type="text/css">**.

2. Open **margins.html** with your text editor, and enter the following code:

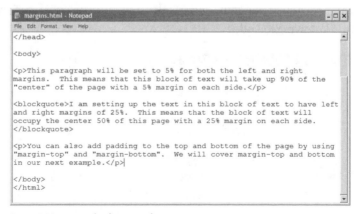

Figure 7-10: margins.html source code

3. Save this page into the website folder.

4. Next, you will need to make some additions to your style sheet. Open **stylesheet.css** with your text editor, and find the declaration that starts with "**p {**". Then add this line of code: "**margin-left: 5%;margin-right: 5%;**". The code should look like this:

    p {
    font-family: Times New Roman, sans-serif;
    font-size: 12px;
    color: black;
    margin-left: 5%;margin-right: 5%;
    }

5. Next, create a declaration called **blockquote**, and add it to your style sheet.

    blockquote {
    font-size: 14px;
    color: black;
    margin-left: 25%;margin-right:25%
    }

6. Save your document.

Let's go ahead and view the results in your browser. Then, we will break down the code.

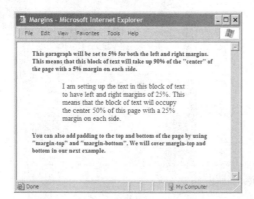

Figure 7-11: margins.html with different margin dimensions applied

In the above example, we have set the p element equal to 5% and we have set blockquote equal to 25%. The percentage values are applied to both left and right margins.

Top and Bottom Margins

Note: For this example I am going to use "em" instead of a percentage. The reason is this: Different fonts have different heights. If you were to use different fonts on your page, or if a visitor to your site does not have a particular font on their computer, things could get really ugly. "em" equals the line height of a particular font and is therefore more exact.

Let's add some padding to the block of text in the center of our web page.

1. Open **stylesheet.css**, and edit the blockquote code so it looks like this:

    **blockquote {
    font-size: 14px;
    color: black;
    margin-left: 25%;margin-right:25%;
    margin-top: 5em;
    margin-bottom: 5em;
    }**

2. Go ahead and save your changes. Now, open **margins.html** in your web browser.

Figure 7-12: margins.html edited using em for precise settings

Notice the difference in the amount of space above and below the blockquote text?

You can use one line of code to set the top and bottom, and left and right margins in one fell swoop. The important thing to remember when doing this is that the top and bottom margins are set first, and that the left and right margins are set next. If we wanted to code the above example in one line, it would look like this:

margin: 5em 25%;

The whole blockquote declaration would then look like this:

blockquote {
font-size: 14px;
color: black;
margin: 5em 25%;
}

 Note: There is no comma between the two values; simply separate them with a space.

What if I wanted to apply different values to each margin? You can easily do this by using what we have learned above:

blockquote {
font-size: 14px;
color: black;
margin: 5em 25% 15em 20%;
}

In this example, the top margin is set to 5, the right margin is set to 25%, the bottom margin is set to 15, and the left margin is set to 20%. The pattern goes in a clockwise circle around the block of text.

Alignment

The alignment property used with CSS allows you to change the text values of a page. You can set this to left, right, center, and justify. The text-align property is very similar to the <align> element used in HTML, but it is much more powerful. Let me demonstrate.

1.   Create a new HTML page, name it **alignment.html**, and save it in the website folder. Add the code shown in Figure 7-13, and save the page.

```
alignment.html - Notepad
File  Edit  Format  View  Help
<html>
<head>
<title>Alignment</title>
<link href="stylesheet.css" rel="stylesheet" type="text/css">
</head>

<body>

<h1>This is h1 and I am not centered</h1>
<h2>I am h2, and I am centered</h2>
<h3>I am h3 and I am not centered</h3>
<h2>I am also h2 and I am centered as well</h2>

</body>
</html>
```

Figure 7-13: Code for alignment.html

2. Next, open up **stylesheet.css**. We will need to make a few
    changes to the code. Find the **h2** block of code, and make changes
    so it looks like the code below:

    h2 {
    font-family: Tahoma, Arial, sans-serif;
    font-size: 18px;
    font-weight: 900;
    color: black;
    text-align: center;
    }

3. Make sure you have saved your changes to both **stylesheet.css**
    and **alignment.html**. Open **alignment.html** in your browser. You
    will notice that both lines of text that begin with h2 are centered
    on the page.

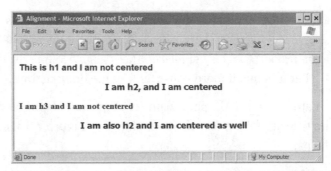

Figure 7-14: Browser view of alignment.html

I know this is not tremendously amazing, since you learned how to do
this with HTML. The difference is this. Let's say that I want to also
center the h3 headers. With HTML, I would have to add the align
value to the h3 headers. With CSS, I can simply add h3 right into my
style rule. Also, since we are using external style sheets, we can apply
this style sheet to every page in our web site with one line of code.
Our one style sheet would change our entire web site for us instantly.

```
h2,h3 {
font-family: Tahoma, Arial, sans-serif;
font-size: 18px;
font-weight: 900;
color: black;
text-align: center;
}
```

Now any time h3 is present in my HTML code, the text will be centered. Go ahead and try it out. Your web page should look like Figure 7-15.

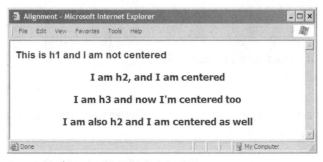

Figure 7-15: Alignment added to multiple headers

Text Decoration

Text decoration enables us to add different elements to our page by applying none, underline, overline, and line-through to our text. The none value is usually set as the default and generally isn't required. Links, of course, are an exception. We'll discuss this later in this section.

1. Open **stylesheet.css**. You will need to make some simple coding changes to demonstrate text decoration. Edit the code so it is the same as that shown in Figure 7-16. I have only listed the declarations that will need to be changed.

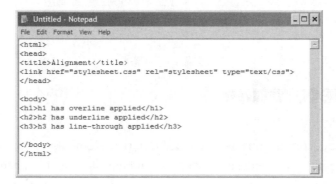

Figure 7-16: Editing stylesheet.css to use text decoration

2. Save your changes, and then open **alignment.html**. Change align-
    ment.html to look like the code in Figure 7-17.

Figure 7-17: alignment.html source code

3. Save **alignment.html** and then view the page in your browser.

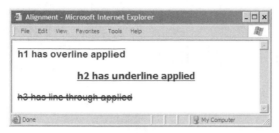

Figure 7-18: Alignment.html displayed in the browser

Earlier I implied that "none" was kind of a boring default value that is just there when needed. This is not altogether true. One of the most important roles "none" can play is to remove underlines that are automatically added to text on our pages. A great example is a link to another web site. You can use the following code line to get rid of those pesky underlines.

> **text-decoration: none;**

Commenting Your Code

Our style sheet has become pretty busy. We've made quite a few changes, and it now contains numerous declarations. You can organize your style sheet by adding comments to the code. This is common practice, especially if someone else may be working on the web site with you. Comments quickly give you and the other coder a quick understanding of the code. Comments in style sheets are indicated by /* and */, as in:

> **/* add comment here */**

Figure 7-19 shows how comments look in your style sheet.

```
/* h2 is the only style rule that will use the Tahoma font */

h2 {
font-family: Tahoma, Arial, sans-serif;
font-size: 18px;
font-weight: 900;
color: black;
text-align: center;
text-decoration: underline;
}

/* h1 has an overline text decoration added */

h1 {
font-family: Arial, Helvetica, sans-serif;
font-size: 18px;
font-weight: normal;
color: black;
text-decoration: overline;
}

/* h3 has a line-through text decoration added */

h3 {
font-family: Arial, Helvetica, sans-serif;
font-size: 18px;
font-weight: normal;
color: black;
text-decoration: line-through;
}
```

Figure 7-19: Examples of commenting code

Code surrounded by /* and */ is not processed. You can actually comment out entire style rules just by adding /* in front of the first line of code and */ after the last line of code to be skipped.

Backgrounds

You can change the background color of your page by adding style to the body element. The code is:

body {background-color: any color goes here;}

1. Open **stylesheet.css** with your text editor, and create a new style rule by entering the following:

    body {
    background-color: gray;
    }

2. Save this change, and then open **alignment.html**. Your page should look like Figure 7-20.

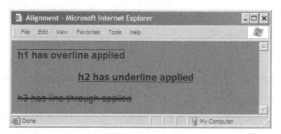

Figure 7-20: Gray background applied to alignment.html

Remember, there is a plethora of colors to choose from. Instead of entering a color name, such as gray, red, blue, etc., it's more accurate to use the hexadecimal code for the color value instead.

Background Images

The colored background is great, but what if you want to add an image to the background instead? It's actually quite easy. Inside your images folder for this chapter, you should have an image titled background.jpg. If not, please make sure you add it to your images folder; you will need it for this exercise.

1. Open **stylesheet.css** with your text editor. Navigate to:

body {
background-color: gray;
}

2. Let's make a couple of changes to the code. First, change the background-color to **#FFFFFF**. Next, add this line of code under the background-color line: **background-image: url(images/background.jpg);**. The last line of code will add background.jpg as the background of your web page.

```
body {
background-color: #FFFFFF;
background-image: url(images/background.jpg);
}
```

Notice that the last line of code has an addition that we have not
used in any of the previous examples. We use "url" to specify the
path to the image and the name of the image. The image resides in
the images folder, so we must include that before the name of the
image.

3. Go ahead and save the changes to stylesheet.css, then open **align-
ment.html** in your web browser. It should now resemble Figure
7-21.

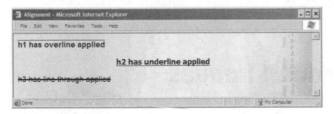

Figure 7-21: Using a background image

 Note: Before we go into a lot of detail about images, let me add
that the body element should include a default font-family as well. I
have not included it in the next several exercises as we are working
with images, but you should add it to your code when building web
pages.

Fixed Background Images

If you have an HTML document that is longer than a single page, and
it requires scrolling to get to the bottom of the page, you can create a
page where the image stays put, and the text moves over the image.

To create this effect, simply add **background-attachment: fixed** to your style rule as shown below:

```
body {
background-color: white;
background-image: url(images/background.jpg);
background-attachment: fixed;
}
```

Note that #FFFFFF and white are equivalent.

Repeating Background Images

1. Let's go ahead and create a new html page named **cssexample.html**. We will be doing a lot of image manipulation in this section and it will help to start with a clean page.

2. Go ahead and add this code to **cssexample.html**, and then save your page.

```
<html>
<head>
<title>CSS Example</title>
<link href="stylesheet.css" rel="stylesheet"
type="text/css">
</head>
<body>
</body>
</html>
```

A problem you may come across when you use a background image is that your image tiles across the page. Images tile across the page in a left-to-right, top-to-bottom pattern. This can be quite annoying if you want a single fixed image as the background of your page. Figure 7-22 demonstrates tiling with a background image that is 250 x 250 pixels.

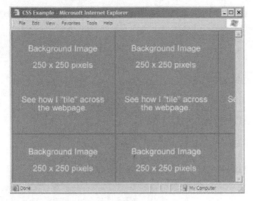

Figure 7-22: Example of image tiling

We can stop this from happening by adding **background-repeat: no-repeat;** to the style rule:

```
body {
background-color: white;
background-image: url(images/tile2.jpg);
background-repeat: no-repeat;
}
```

Most of the time, you will use the above code with larger images.

Repeat-x

Another background value is "repeat-x," which displays the background image in a single horizontal line across the page. I have included an image titled repeat_x.jpg in the companion files. Please make sure this image is in your images folder.

1. Open **stylesheet.css** and add the following changes to your style sheet. You will need to change the image name from **background.jpg** to **repeat_x.jpg**, and you will need to add **background-repeat: repeat-x;** to your code.

```
body {
background-color: white;
background-image: url(images/repeat_x.jpg);
background-repeat: repeat-x;
}
```

2. Once the changes have been made, save your style sheet and open **cssexample.html** in your browser. The repeat_x.jpg image will tile horizontally across the page as shown in Figure 7-23.

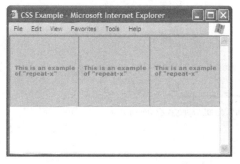

Figure 7-23: background-repeat: repeat-x demonstrated

Repeat-y

This example is very similar to the previous one except that repeat-y tiles the image in a vertical column. In this example I am using an image titled repeat_y.jpg, and the last line of code now reads background-repeat: repeat-y;.

1. Open **stylesheet.css** with your text editor, and make the necessary changes.

```
body {
background-color: white;
background-image: url(images/repeat_y.jpg);
background-repeat: repeat-y;
}
```

2.   Save this page and open **cssexample.html** in your web browser. Your display should look like Figure 7-24.

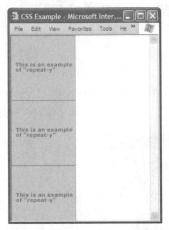

Figure 7-24: background-repeat: repeat-y demonstrated

Background Position

You also have control over the background position. The background position defaults to the left, but you can use "right" and "center" as well. If you wanted the background position to display on the right side of your page, you would add the line **background-position: right;** to your style sheet, as shown below.

```
body {
background-color: white;
background-image: url(images/repeat_y.jpg);
background-repeat: repeat-y;
background-position: right;
}
```

Figures 7-25 and 7-26 show background-position right and center. Try changing the background position in your style sheet. Save the changes, and open cssexample.html in your browser. Your changes should reflect the examples displayed below.

Figure 7-25: background-position: right   *Figure 7-26: background-position: center*

Vertical Alignment

Vertical alignment enables you to set image values as "top," "bottom," and "center." The code below sets the background position to bottom and uses the image v_bottom.jpg. If you want the background to tile across the bottom of the page, your code would look like this:

```
body {
background-color: white;
background-image: url(images/v_bottom.jpg);
background-repeat: repeat-x;
background-position: bottom;}
```

In your style sheet, try the bottom, center, and top positions. Make sure you save your style sheet every time you change your code. Open cssexample.html in your browser to view the results.

*Figure 7-27:
background-position:
bottom*

*Figure 7-28:
background-position:
center*

Figure 7-29:
background-position:
top

Combining Vertical and Horizontal Alignment

It is actually extremely easy to combine vertical and horizontal alignment. The following example uses an image named Coffee.jpg and the instruction **background-position: bottom right** to place the image in the lower-right corner of the page.

```
body {
background-color: white;
background-image: url(images/Coffee.jpg);
background-repeat: no-repeat;
background-position: bottom right;
}
```

Go ahead and make the above changes to your style sheet. Then open **cssexample.html** in your browser. The coffee image should appear in the lower-right corner of your page.

Notice that a space separates the two values "bottom" and "right." You do not need to add a comma, as the simple space between the two values will suffice.

Figure 7-30:
background-position:
bottom right

When using both vertical and horizontal values, the vertical value will always come first. Remember, vertical values are top, bottom, and center, and horizontal values are left, center, and right.

Background Property

This code will create multiple rows of coffee cups along the right side of the page.

```
body {
background-color: white;
background-image: url(images/Coffee.jpg);
background-repeat: repeat-y;
background-position: right;
}
```

You can use the background property to set all of the above values in one declaration. Here is the code:

```
body {background: white url(images/Coffee.jpg) repeat-y right;}
```

If you want to create a column rather than a row, you will need to use repeat-x. Be sure to practice with images of different sizes.

There are some great programs such as Adobe Photoshop and Adobe Fireworks that enable you to create some great images for the web.

Below is a simple square with a line and gradient added using Adobe Fireworks. The image name is bar.jpg.

Figure 7-31: Gradient created with Adobe Fireworks

By adding the following simple line of code, I can tile this image down the right side of my web page to look like one continuous bar:

body {background: white url(images/bar.jpg) repeat-y right;}

Figure 7-32: Image made to look like one continuous bar

Multiple Style Sheets

Why would you need multiple style sheets? A good example is if you have a web site with an order form. You would probably want your order form to look different from an informational page. Don't worry; adding an additional style sheet is extremely easy.

1. Make three simple HTML pages. Name the pages **page1.html**, **page2.html**, and **page3.html**. Copy the code below into each page and save each page into the website folder once you are finished.

```
page1.html - Notepad
File Edit Format View Help
<html>
<head>
<title>Page 1</title>
</head>
<body>

<h2 align="center"> I'm a big header</h2>
<h2 align="center"> I'm a big header too</h2>
<a href="page2.htm"> I connect to page 2</a>
<a href="page3.htm"> I connect to page 3</a>

</body>
</html>
```

Figure 7-33: Code for page1.html, page2.html, and page3.html

2. Next, create a new style sheet, and name it **multi.css**. Add the following code to **multi.css** and save the page.

   h2 {
   font-family: Tahoma, Arial, sans-serif;
   font-size: 12pt;
   font-weight: 700;
   color: green;
   }

3. Now, link this style sheet to the three html pages you just created by typing this line of code between the header tags in each page:

   <link rel="stylesheet" href="multi.css" type="text/css">

4. Make sure you save all of your html pages. Then open each page in your browser to make sure that multi.css is linked properly. The text on the pages should be centered and green.

Figure 7-34:
page1.htm viewed in
the browser

5. Create another style sheet, and name it **multi2.css**. Copy the h2 style rule below and save your page:

   h2 {color: gray;}

6. Copy the code below, and add it to **page1.html** under the first style rule. Do not add it to any of the other pages.

   <link rel="stylesheet" href="multi2.css" type="text/css">

7. Save **page1.html** after you have added the new line of code. The source code for page1.html should now look like this:

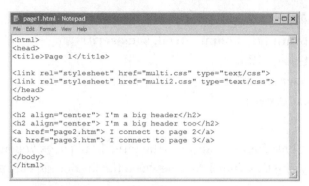

Figure 7-35: Source code for page1.html

You will notice that we now have two external links to different style sheets on this page. The only difference between the two lines of code is the name of the style sheet.

8. Let's go ahead and open **page1.html** in your browser. Notice that h2 is now gray and not green. This is because the second style sheet, multi2.css, has overridden the color property of multi.css.

Figure 7-36:
Connecting to multiple
style sheets

9. Click on the links that connect to page2.html and page3.html. You will see that their text is still green and that they are unaffected. There is no effect on the pages not linked to the multi2.css style sheet.

Figure 7-37: page2.html; the text has not changed

Figure 7-38: page3.html; the text has not changed

If you had changed the order of the style sheet links, the original style sheet would overrule the gray coloring.

Cascading works top to bottom. The first style sheet is loaded, and then the second one overrides and inherits from the first. You could actually have more than two style sheets; just remember that the last style sheet will override the previous style sheet.

Summary

This concludes your look into the basics of CSS. I hope that by reading this chapter and working through the examples you can see the power of cascading style sheets. A great online resource for gaining more knowledge on CSS can be found at http://www.w3schools.com/css/. In the next chapter you will learn about the basics of PHP, which will prepare you for publishing your FileMaker data to the web.

Chapter 8

PHP Basics

PHP is a server-side scripting language that is processed before the page is sent to the client's browser. Any page whose extension is registered as containing PHP scripts is sent through the PHP engine first. By default, this extension is usually .php. Other extensions may be added to the wcb server's MIME types to also be processed for PHP scripts.

PHP Scripts

When the PHP engine scans a page for PHP scripts, it is looking for the opening PHP tag, which is:

<?php

The PHP engine continues to process the script until it reaches either an error in the code or the closing PHP tag, which is:

?>

Make sure that all of your PHP code is within PHP script tags, or the code will be interpreted as text. Failing to have a closing PHP script tag will result in an error.

Displaying Text

Data, including text and numerical data, can be displayed on the page using **echo** or **print**, as follows.

> **<?php**
> **echo 'It is such a beautiful Spring day today.';**
> **?>**

and

> **<?php**
> **print 'It is such a beautiful Spring day today.';**
> **?>**

Save one of these examples with a .php extension and load it in your browser. The result should be a simple text display for either example, as shown in Figure 8-1.

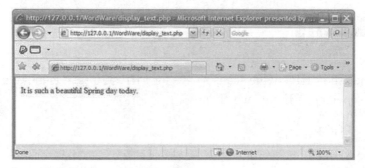

Figure 8-1: Printing text to the page

Notice that the echo and print lines end with a semicolon. The semicolon is to PHP what a period is to a sentence. It defines the single statement. When you are writing PHP scripts, conclude each line with a semicolon.

Variables

Variables are useful for storing several types of data including numbers, characters, strings, Booleans, arrays, and objects. A variable is denoted by a preceding dollar sign ($). Variable names can be made up of letters, numbers, and underscores, but can only begin with a letter or underscore. They are case sensitive, so a variable named $myVariable is different from one named $myvariable. Variable names cannot contain spaces.

Values are assigned to a variable with the equal sign (=).

```
$textMessage = 'This is a text string.';
$numberValue = 3;
$calcValue = 1 + 3;
$newValue = $currentValue + 1;
```

Hip Hip Array

Often you will need to store more than just a simple string or numerical value. Arrays allow you to store multiple values with an index or a key. An index is a numerical label starting from zero and continuing in order. A key is a unique text label given to each value. Data is also returned from FileMaker databases as arrays, and so it is helpful to know how to create and manipulate array data. Let's look at several ways to create and modify arrays.

Creating a Simple Array

The first array we will work with is a simple array with a series of text values using the array() function.

1. Create a PHP script and a variable to hold the array.

    <?php
    $birds
    ?>

2. Set the variable equal to the array() function.

    $birds = array();

3. Add elements to the array in the parentheses and separate each with a comma. Text values will need to be enclosed in single quotes.

```
1 <?php
2 $birds = array('Cardinal', 'Bobwhite', 'Blue Jay', 'Mallard', 'Pelican', 'Osprey');
3 ?>
4
5
```

Figure 8-2: A simple array

4. Arrays must be printed to the page using the print_r() function. Below the array, add **print_r()** and include the variable name within the parentheses. Follow the array with two line breaks.

```
1 <?php
2 $birds = array('Cardinal', 'Bobwhite', 'Blue Jay', 'Mallard', 'Pelican', 'Osprey');
3 print_r($birds);
4 echo '<br><br>';
5 ?>
```

Figure 8-3: Printing a simple array with print_r()

5. Save the page and preview the results in your browser. You will see the array that was created and the index for each element.

Figure 8-4: Browser view of a simple array

Each element in the array can be accessed by its index number. The indexes start at zero. A specific element can be accessed using the name of the array variable followed by the index in square brackets, like this: $arrayname[1].

6. After the line breaks, echo the array element for Blue Jay.

Figure 8-5: Code view of printing a specific array element

You should get the following result:

Figure 8-6: Printing an array element in the browser

7. Save the page and preview in your browser. Other elements in the array can be printed by changing the index.

Creating an Array with Keys

Arrays can also be created with a specific key in place of the index. This can be done using the association symbol (=>).

1. Create a PHP script and a variable to hold the array.

    <?php
    $mammals
    ?>

2. Set the variable equal to the array() function.

    $mammals = array();

3. Add elements to the array in the parentheses in the following format:

    'key' => 'value'

    Be sure to separate each key/value pair with a comma.

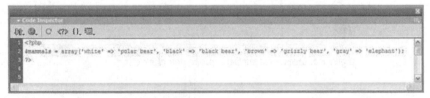

Figure 8-7: Creating an array with custom keys

4. Print the array using print_r() and then add two line breaks.

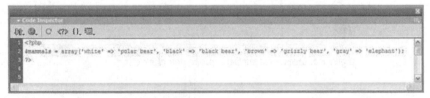

Figure 8-8: Printing the array using print_r()

5. After the line breaks, echo the array element for grizzly bear using this format: $arrayname['key'].

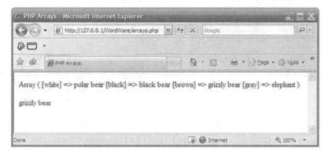

Figure 8-9: Printing an array element using the associated key

6. Save the page and preview the results in your browser.

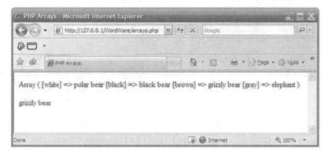

Figure 8-10: Printing the full array and a single element by key in the browser

Creating an Array by Specifying Each Index

Arrays can also be created by specifying the index of the element in the array as part of the initial variable, like this: $variable_name[0] = 'the value';.

1. Create an array similar to the one in Figure 8-11 by specifying each element and the element's position in the array. Then print the array with print_r().

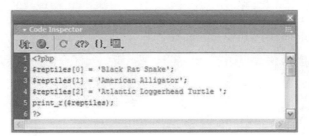

Figure 8-11: Creating an array by specifying the position of each element in the array

2. Save the page and preview the results in your browser.

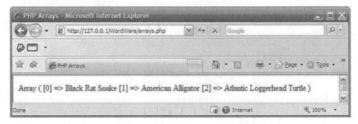

Figure 8-12: Browser view of individually created array elements

Replacing an Element in the Array

Specific elements in the array can be changed by setting a new value equal to the location of the element to be replaced

1. Define an array similar to the following with several values, and print the array.

```php
<?php
$birds = array('Cardinal', 'Bobwhite', 'Blue Jay', 'Mallard', 'Pelican', 'Osprey');
print_r($birds);
echo '<br><br>';
?>
```

Figure 8-13: Creating a simple array

2. Change the element in the fourth position to a new value using this format: $variable[3] = 'new value';. Then print the new array.

Figure 8-14: Changing a specific element in the array

3. Save the page and preview the results in your browser.

Figure 8-15: Browser view of changing an array

Adding an Element to the End of the Array

An element can be added to the end of an array using the array_push() function.

1. Define an array with several values and print the array.

2. Then use the array_push() function to add an element to the end of the array and print the new array.

Figure 8-16: Adding an element to the end of an array using array_push()

3.   Save the page and preview the results in your browser.

Figure 8-17: Browser view of adding an element to the end of an array

Another way to add an element to the end of an array is to use the variable name followed by an opening and closing square bracket, like this: $variable[] = 'new value';.

Figure 8-18: Adding an element to the end of an array using $variable[]

Removing an Element from the End of the Array

An element can be removed from the end of an array using the array_pop() function.

1. Define an array with several values and print the array.

2. Then use the array_pop() function to remove an element from the end of the array and print the new array.

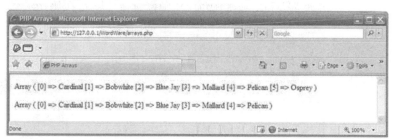

```php
<?php
$birds = array('Cardinal', 'Bobwhite', 'Blue Jay', 'Mallard', 'Pelican', 'Osprey');
print_r($birds);
echo '<br><br>';

array_pop($birds);
print_r($birds);
?>
```

Figure 8-19: Removing an element from the end of the array using array_pop()

3. Save the page and preview the results in your browser.

Array ([0] => Cardinal [1] => Bobwhite [2] => Blue Jay [3] => Mallard [4] => Pelican [5] => Osprey)

Array ([0] => Cardinal [1] => Bobwhite [2] => Blue Jay [3] => Mallard [4] => Pelican)

Figure 8-20: Browser view of removing an element from the end of the array

Removing an Element from the Beginning of the Array

An element can be removed from the beginning of an array using the array_shift() function.

1. Create a simple array and print the array to the page using print_r().

2. Use the array_shift() function to remove the first element of the array.

3. Print the new array using print_r().

```php
<?php
$birds = array('Cardinal', 'Bobwhite', 'Blue Jay', 'Mallard', 'Pelican', 'Osprey');
print_r($birds);
echo '<br><br>';

array_shift($birds);
print_r($birds);
?>
```

Figure 8-21: Removing an element from the beginning of the array using array_shift()

4. Save the page and preview the results in your browser.

Array ([0] => Cardinal [1] => Bobwhite [2] => Blue Jay [3] => Mallard [4] => Pelican [5] => Osprey)

Array ([0] => Bobwhite [1] => Blue Jay [2] => Mallard [3] => Pelican [4] => Osprey)

Figure 8-22: Browser view of removing an element from the beginning of the array

Adding an Element to the Beginning of the Array

An element can be added to the beginning of an array using the array_unshift() function.

1. Create a simple array and print the array to the page using print_r().

2. Use the array_unshift() function to add an element to the beginning of the array.

3. Print the new array using print_r().

```php
<?php
$birds = array('Cardinal', 'Bobwhite', 'Blue Jay', 'Mallard', 'Pelican', 'Osprey');
print_r($birds);
echo '<br><br>';

array_unshift($birds, 'Turkey');
print_r($birds);
?>
```

Figure 8-23: Adding an element to the beginning of the array using array_unshift()

4. Save the page and preview the results in your browser.

Figure 8-24: Browser view of adding an element to the beginning of the array

Sorting an Array Ascending Alphabetically

Arrays can be sorted in ascending order using the sort() function.

1. Create a simple array.

2. Use the sort() function to sort the records, adding the array variable between the parentheses.

3. Print the array using print_r().

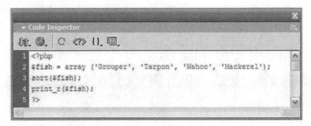

Figure 8-25: Sorting an array ascending alphabetically

4. Save the page and preview the results in your browser.

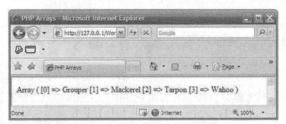

Figure 8-26: Browser view of sorting an array in ascending order

Sorting an Array Descending Alphabetically

Arrays can be sorted in descending order using the rsort() function.

1. Create a simple array.

2. Use the rsort() function to sort the records, adding the array variable between the parentheses.

3. Print the array using print_r().

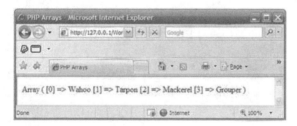

```php
<?php
$fish = array ('Grouper', 'Tarpon', 'Wahoo', 'Mackerel');
rsort($fish);
print_r($fish);
?>
```

Figure 8-27: Sorting an array descending alphabetically

4. Save the page and preview the results in your browser.

Array ([0] => Wahoo [1] => Tarpon [2] => Mackerel [3] => Grouper)

Figure 8-28: Browser view of sorting an array in descending order

Separating and Printing the Array Elements as a Text String

Array elements can be separated and joined into a string with the implode() function. The implode() function replaces the comma in the array with whatever value you enter as the first parameter. The format is:

> **implode(' divide value ' , $arrayvariable)**

1. Create a simple array.

2. Set a new variable equal to implode().

3. Separate each array value with ' and ' and enter the array variable as the second parameter.

4. Print the new variable using echo.

```
<?php
$fish = array ('Grouper', 'Tarpon', 'Wahoo', 'Mackerel');
$string = implode(' and ', $fish);
echo $string;
?>
```

Figure 8-29: Using implode() to separate an array

5. Save the page and preview the results in your browser.

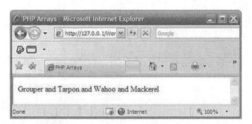

Figure 8-30: Browser view of the new text string

PHP Functions

Functions are frequently used in PHP to facilitate development. A function is simply a section of PHP code that can be used by referring to the function name and any associated parameters. There are over 1,500 functions built into PHP, and you can easily add your own or use any of the thousands of functions available online.

Let's take a look at how to create a few simple functions of your own:

1. First, use the word **function** to define a new function.

2. Next, give the function a name following the same rules as naming a variable; for example: **function myFunction()**.

3. Then use curly braces to enclose the code for your function.

   function myFunction() {
   echo 'This is my first function and it was a huge success. My parental units are so proud.';
   }

4. Calling the function will cause the code contained within the function to be evaluated.

   myFunction();

   The completed script would look like this.

```
1 <?php
2 function myFunction() {
3 echo 'This is my first function and it was a huge success.  My parental units are so proud.';
4 }
5 myFunction();
6 ?>
```

Figure 8-31: Completed code of a basic function

5.   Save this page with a .php extension and load it in your browser
     using the address of your web server; for example:
     http://127.0.0.1/myfunction.php.

Parameters can also be sent to a function to be evaluated. If you want
to send a color to a function from the main script, enter the value in
the parentheses following the function name. When the function is
defined, specify a variable name for the parameter passed. The variable can then be used in the function.

Figure 8-32: Sending a parameter to a function

*Figure 8-33: Results of sending a parameter to a
function*

Conditions

When working with PHP, you will often need to determine whether or
not a condition is true before proceeding. This enables you to determine in which direction the script should continue based on
information already available. For instance, you may want users to log
in to the same page and then direct them to appropriate pages or
records within the site based on their predefined access level.

The if statement in this case will be formatted as:

if(the situation you wish to evaluate) {
what to do if the situation is true
}

When evaluating a condition, you can use a comparison operator. The available comparison operators are:

==	equal
!=	not equal
===	identical
>	greater than
>=	greater than or equal to
<	less than
<=	less than or equal to

For example:

```php
<?php
$today = 'Monday';
if($today == 'Monday')
{
echo 'Today is the first day of a great week!';
}
?>
```

In some cases, you need to not only test for a condition to be met but also give an alternative. This can be done by using else in addition to if.

```
if( the situation you wish to evaluate ) {
what to do if the situation is true
}else{
what to do if the situation is false
}
```

Includes

PHP has an easy way to add repeating code and common scripts to your web pages. This can be useful in many different situations such as including common navigation elements or often used PHP scripts. When working with PHP and FileMaker, you will be using this functionality to include the files necessary to use the FileMaker API for PHP.

There are a few functions available for including external files. These are include(), include_once(), require(), and require_once(). The include() and require() functions work the same unless the file you are trying to include does not exist. If the file is missing and you are using include(), an error warning will be returned, but the remainder of the page will attempt to load. If the file is missing and you are using require(), it will return a fatal error and the rest of the page will not attempt to load.

You may want to consider using require() for files that are essential to the rest of the page and using include() for files that are relatively independent and won't harm the page if they do not load. The remaining two functions, require_once() and include_once(), perform exactly like the shorter versions except that they will only load the page once. The shorter versions can be loaded multiple times. This should also be considered when deciding which version to use.

This is a great way to include common navigation or logos in your web pages. If you need to update your web site, you will only have to make the change once, and any pages where you have the file included will be automatically updated.

Let's take a look at how to include a simple text string in a page.

1. Create a new document and name it **text_string.php**.

2. Type a text message into the page. Make sure that the page only includes the text string and no other HTML tags.

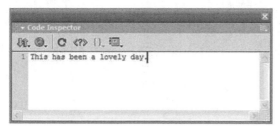

Figure 8-34: text_string.php with a simple sentence

3. Save the page.

4. Create a new document and name it **includes.php**. This page will include the basic HTML tags.

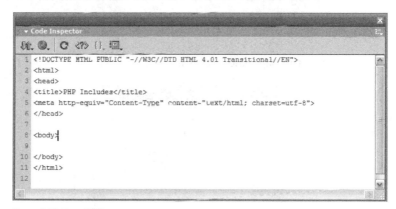

Figure 8-35: Basic HTML tags

5. Between the <body> tags, enter a string of text followed by a line break (**
**).

6. Add a PHP script and include the text_string.php page using
    include_once().

Figure 8-36: Including a separate file using include_once()

7. Save the page and load it in your browser.

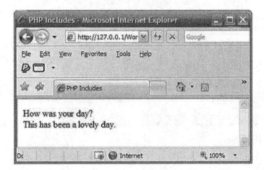

Figure 8-37: Browser view showing both static text and the included file

Comments

While you are developing and making changes to your web pages, it is useful to leave comments in your code for yourself or anyone else who may be editing your scripts in the future. Commenting your code is easy to do, but you need to remember that the comments must be added within the PHP script tags or they will display as text on your page and in your source code.

A single line comment can be added by using either two forward slashes (//) or a pound symbol (#) before the line.

//This is a single line comment
#This is also a single line comment

A multiple-line comment can be added by using a forward slash followed by an asterisk (/*) at the beginning of the comment and an asterisk followed by a forward slash at the end of the comment (*/).

/*   This is
a multi
line comment
*/

Comment tags are also helpful for temporarily disabling PHP code while developing and testing.

```
<?php
/*
function myFunction() {
echo 'This is my first function and it was a huge success.  My parental units are so proud.';
}
*/
// myFunction();
?>
```

Figure 8-38: Commenting out PHP code

Quotes

Whether you use single or double quotes depends on the type of information you want to display. Single quotes output the contents as literal text. Double quotes interpret variables for their contained value instead of as literal text.

Let's take a look at how single and double quotes behave.

1. Create a new document and name it **quotes.php**.

2. At the top of the page before the HTML tags, add a PHP script and set a variable **$name** equal to **Sally Smith**.

Figure 8-39: Setting a variable above the HTML tags

3. Within the <body> tags, create a new PHP script.

4. Use echo to display the following sentence with single quotes:

    '$name will be teaching the course.'

5. Use echo to add a line break with **'
'**.

6. Use echo to display the same sentence with double quotes:

"$name will be teaching the course."

```
1  <?php
2  $name = 'Sally Smith';
3  ?>
4  <!DOCTYPE HTML PUBLIC "-//W3C//DTD HTML 4.01 Transitional//EN">
5  <html>
6  <head>
7  <title>Quotes</title>
8  <meta http-equiv="Content-Type" content="text/html; charset=utf-8">
9  </head>
10
11 <body>
12
13 <?php
14 echo '$name will be teaching the course.';
15 echo '<br>';
16 echo "$name will be teaching the course.";
17 ?>
18 |
19 </body>
20 </html>
```

Figure 8-40: Completed quotes.php

7. Save the page and load it in your browser.

Notice the differences in the way that the single and double quotes display the sentence. The second sentence using the double quotes will replace the $name variable with the value "Sally Smith."

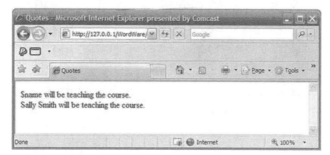

Figure 8-41: Browser view of quotes.php

Special Characters

There may be special characters that you want to use that could be misinterpreted by PHP. Individual characters can be skipped by using a character escape (\) before the character to be skipped. Suppose we want to echo a sentence that contains a quoted statement and also contains a variable to be replaced, such as:

$name said "This class will begin promptly at 9 AM".

We would need to escape the two quotes. The echo would look like this;

echo "$name said \"This class will begin promptly at 9 AM\"."

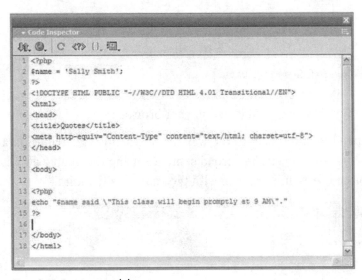

Figure 8-42: Escaping special characters

When viewed in your browser, this will display the value of the $name variable and the desired quotes.

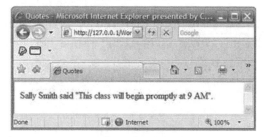

Figure 8-43: Browser view of escaping special characters

If you do not escape the extra quotes, the code will produce an error. This is because when the PHP engine reaches the second quote, it expects the text string to end and some other character to either append the string or end the line.

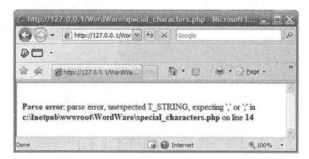

Figure 8-44: Error produced if extra quotes are not escaped

Summary

Now that you know the basics of using PHP, you are ready to start integrating PHP with commonly used links and forms. This will allow you to provide comprehensive navigation and a seamless user experience.

Chapter 9

Links and Forms

Long gone are the days of single-page web sites. Because many web sites span numerous pages, users need easy and intuitive ways to navigate through a site as well as within a page. Database-driven web sites also need a way to pass existing and user-entered data through the site. Two of the most common ways to deliver this functionality are with links and forms.

What Type of Navigation Should You Use?

Determining the type of navigation to use will often depend on what kind of data you need to send to the link or form destination. Links allow data to be sent in a key/value pair format that does not include user input. Forms allow you to send static data as well as user-entered data in the form of text and value lists.

GET and POST

You can use either GET or POST as the method of your forms. In a GET request, the key/value pairs are sent in the URL, meaning that the pairs will display in the user's address bar. In a POST request, the key/value pairs are sent in the header instead of the URL.

The GET method is limited to a maximum key/value pair character length of 2,048 characters. The GET method does have its advantages, though. If you want your users to be able to bookmark a page and save search results, you must use GET.

Links

Links used in their simplest form contain a single page name without any additional data. The page can be listed as a relative link or an absolute link. Regardless of the type of link you will be using, the format is the same.

A link is formed using an <a href> tag. The "a" stands for anchor and "href" stands for hypertext reference. Use the following format to create a link:

<a href="pagename">The Text for the Link</a>

The name of the destination is placed between the quotes following "href=." The text or image item that will be active as the link is placed between the opening and closing <a href> tags.

There are two types of links, relative and absolute. Which one you use depends on the location of the destination page in relation to the current page.

Relative Links

A relative link is used when the destination is located within the same site. The relative link gives instructions for accessing the destination from the location of the current page.

If the destination page is in the same directory as the current page, then the link only needs to include the destination page name. No additional directory or http address is needed.

- Page in same directory:

  <a href="about.htm">About Us</a>

If the destination page is in an additional directory, then the link needs to also include the directory name along with the destination page name.

- Page one directory down:

  Current page is at: **http://www.yourwebsite.com/index.php**

  Destination page is at: **http://www.yourwebsite.com/common/about.php**

  Then the link to about.php from index.php would be:
  <a href="common/about.php">About Us</a>

If the destination page is in an additional directory back, then you will need to add ".../" for each directory that you need to go back before the destination page name.

- Page one directory back:

  Current page is at: **http://www.yourwebsite.com/common/about.php**

  Destination page is at: **http://www.yourwebsite.com/index.php**

  The link would be: **<a href="../index.php">About Us</a>**

Absolute Links

An absolute link can be used from any page or site. It is the complete web address of the destination, like this:

<a href="http://www.mywebsite.com/about.php">About Us</a>

Sending Data in a Link

Data can be sent as part of a link in the form of key/value pairs. These pairs are formatted as "key=value." Data sent as part of a link are sent with the GET method:

color=blue

Multiple values can be sent by separating the pairs with an ampersand:

color=blue&number=17

These key/value pairs are appended to the destination with a question mark (?):

<a href="destination.php?color=blue&number=17"> Link Text </a>

Forms

Forms are widely used in HTML and PHP pages. A form can be used for user input or to pass hidden data. A form simply passes information to the response page. The response page processes any sent data.

All forms begin and end with opening and closing <form> tags. All form elements need to be within the <form> tags or they will not be included when the form is submitted. Neglecting to include a closing <form> tag will cause the form to fail. If you were to click the Submit button on a form without a closing <form> tag, nothing would happen.

The opening <form> tag looks like this:

<form action="form_response.php" method="POST">

The form action is the name of the destination page, and the method can be either post or get. Note that the form action is case sensitive, and the form method is case insensitive.

The closing <form> tag is:

</form>

The method for a form can be either **post** or **get**.

Form tag with POST method:

<form action=" form_response.php" method="post">
</form>

Form tag with GET method:

<form action=" form_response.php" method="get">
</form>

Each form also needs a "submit" input line in order to send the form. The submit line creates a clickable button that can either be the browser's default image or a custom image you provide.

A "submit" line using the browser's default button:

<input type="submit" name="submit" value="Submit this form">

A "submit" line using a custom image for the Submit button:

<input type="image" name="submit" src="images/submit.gif">

Types of Form Elements

There are several types of form elements to choose from when submitting data with a form. All of the form elements including input lines and select lists need to be within the <form> tags.

The available form elements include:

- Text
- Hidden
- Radio button
- Check box
- Select list
- Text areas

Let's create a form and examine the different form elements that are available.

1. Open a new document and place the <form> tags between the <body> tags. It is always a good idea, and many web editors will automatically do this, to create the closing tag as soon as you create the opening <form> tag. This prevents the common mistake of forgetting to close the form.

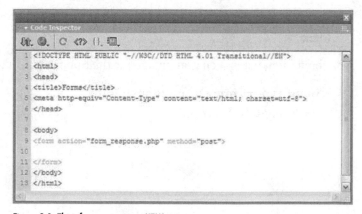

Figure 9-1: The <form> tags in an HTML page

2. Add a submit link to the bottom of the form that uses an image as the button.

```
▼ Code Inspector
1  <!DOCTYPE HTML PUBLIC "-//W3C//DTD HTML 4.01 Transitional//EN">
2  <html>
3  <head>
4  <title>Forms</title>
5  <meta http-equiv="Content-Type" content="text/html; charset=utf-8">
6  </head>
7
8  <body>
9  <form action="form_response.php" method="post">
10
11 <input type="image" name="submit" src="images/submit.jpg">
12 </form>
13 </body>
14 </html>
```

Figure 9-2: Adding the Submit button

3. Save the document as **form.php**.

Text

An editable text box can be displayed in the browser by using a "text" input type. There are two other parameters in the <input> tag, name and value. name is the label given to the value, and value is the data that is in the text box. The value can contain predefined data or it can be blank. If the starting value is blank, you can omit the value parameter.

4. Add two input lines to allow users to enter their first and last names. Be sure to add these between the <form> tags. They can be placed in any order, either before or after the Submit button.

<input type="text" name="first_name" value="">
<input type="text" name="last_name" value="">

The name given to the input line will not display in the browser, so make sure that you give your user an adequate description of the data to be entered.

5. Label each input line so that the users know what they are to
    enter. Add a line break (<br>) after each text box so that they
    align one on top of the other instead of in a straight line across the
    page.

Figure 9-3: Two text boxes with labels and line breaks

6. Save the page and preview the results in your browser.

Figure 9-4: Browser view of two text boxes and an image Submit button

If your form does not display cleanly in the browser or if part of the
source code displays, double-check your code for misplaced tags.

Hidden

Sometimes you will want to send through information that is not user entered and is not displayed, such as the type of user or the source of the original page. This hidden information can be sent as type="hidden".

7. Create a hidden value for user_type with a value of "**Commenter**":

    <input type="hidden" name="user_type" value="Commenter">

```
  5  <meta http-equiv="Content-Type" content="text/html; charset=utf-8">
  6  </head>
  7
  8  <body>
  9  <form action="form_response.php" method="post">
 10  <input type="hidden" name="user_type" value="Commenter">
 11
 12  First Name: <input type="text" name="name_first" value=""> <br>
 13  Last Name:  <input type="text" name="name_last" value=""> <br>
 14
 15  <input type="image" name="submit" src="images/submit.jpg">
 16  </form>
 17  </body>
 18  </html>
```

Figure 9-5: Adding a hidden value

8. Save the document and preview the results in your browser.

Notice that the hidden line does not display in the browser. The value is visible to the user only if the page source is viewed.

Radio Buttons

Another input type that is available is the radio button. Radio buttons allow users to select a single value from a group. All items with the same name value are considered part of the group.

9. Add three radio buttons for the group "name='user_level'." Use the values **Beginner, Intermediate**, and **Advanced.**

10. Add labels to each of the radio buttons so that users know what they are selecting. Include line breaks after each line so that the radio buttons line up nicely on the page.

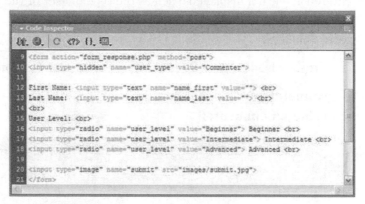

Figure 9-6: Adding radio buttons

11. Save the page and preview the results in your browser.

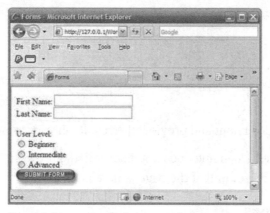

Figure 9-7: Browser view of radio buttons in the form

The radio buttons should be lined up under the User Level label.

Check Boxes

If you have a list of choices where the user may need to select more than one option, then check boxes are probably the best solution. Just like radio buttons, check boxes with the same name value belong to the same group; however, unlike radio buttons, multiple values may be selected. The multiple values submitted will need to be collected into an array. To add the selected values to an array, append the name with an opening and closing square bracket, like this:

> **<input type="checkbox" name="operating_system[]" value="Windows">**

12. Add three check boxes, one each for **Windows**, **Mac OS**, and **Linux**. Label each so that users know what they are selecting, and follow each line with a line break.

```
20 What operating system do you use? <br>
21 <input type="checkbox" name="operating_system[]" value="Windows"> Windows <br>
22 <input type="checkbox" name="operating_system[]" value="Mac OS"> Mac OS <br>
23 <input type="checkbox" name="operating_system[]" value="Linux"> Linux <br>
24
```

Figure 9-8: Adding check boxes to the form

13. Save the page and preview the results in your browser.

The check boxes should be lined up under the question "What operating system do you use?".

Select Lists

Another type of form element is the select list. Select lists are made up of two different HTML tags, the <select> tags and the <option> tags. The <select> tag specifies the name for the values just as in the input lines.

> **<select name="country">**
> **</select>**

The <option> tag specifies the values available in the list just as the value element did for both radio buttons and check boxes. The <option> tags are placed between the <select> tags. The value that actually displays is listed between the opening and closing <option> tags.

<option value="submit value">Display Value</option>

14. Add a select list to your form for entering a country. Include a few sample countries to test.

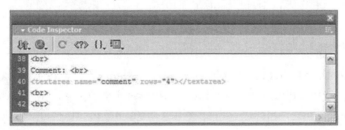

Figure 9-9: Adding a select list to the form

15. Save the page and preview the results in your browser.

Text Areas

If you need to allow your user to enter more than just a simple word or phrase, then you will want to use a textarea. It is formatted like this:

<textarea name="comment" rows="4"></textarea>

16. Add a textarea to your form for users to enter comments.

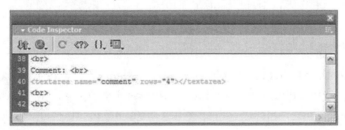

Figure 9-10: Adding a text area to the form

After adding all of the different form elements, your page should look similar to Figure 9-11.

```
<!DOCTYPE HTML PUBLIC "-//W3C//DTD HTML 4.01 Transitional//EN">
<html>
<head>
<title>Forms</title>
<meta http-equiv="Content-Type" content="text/html; charset=utf-8">
</head>

<body>
<?php echo $message; ?>
<form action="form_response.php" method="post">
<input type="hidden" name="user_type" value="Commenter">

First Name: <input type="text" name="name_first" value=""> <br>
Last Name:  <input type="text" name="name_last" value=""> <br>
<br>
User Level: <br>
<input type="radio" name="user_level" value="Beginner"> Beginner <br>
<input type="radio" name="user_level" value="Intermediate"> Intermediate <br>
<input type="radio" name="user_level" value="Advanced"> Advanced <br>
<br>
What operating system do you use? <br>
<input type="checkbox" name="operating_system[]" value="Windows"> Windows <br>
<input type="checkbox" name="operating_system[]" value="Mac OS"> Mac OS <br>
<input type="checkbox" name="operating_system[]" value="Linux"> Linux <br>
<br>
Country<br>
<select name="country">
    <option value="Canada"> Canada </option>
    <option value="Mexico"> Mexico </option>
    <option value="USA"> United States </option>
</select>
<br>
Comment: <br>
<textarea name="comment" rows="4"></textarea>
<br>
<br>
<input type="image" name="submit" src="images/submit.jpg">
</form>
</body>
</html>
```

Figure 9-11: Completed form with all elements

17. Save the page and view the results in your browser.

Figure 9-12: Browser
view of completed
form with all elements

Now that the form is complete, it is time to build the response page
and actually interact with the passed values.

The Response Page

The response page handles all of the processing of any passed values. It is possible to have a single page that acts as both the submission and response page, but for now let's keep things simple.

1. Create a new page and name it **form_response.php**. Type a simple text message within the <body> tags. This will allow you to test your form before you start adding a PHP script.

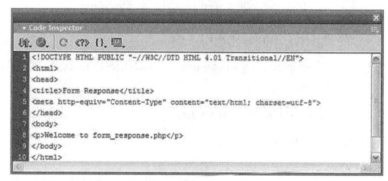

Figure 9-13: Response page with text message

2. Save the file and open **form.php** in your browser (for example, http://127.0.0.1/ form.php).

3. Enter the requested information into the form and select the **Submit Form** button. You should see the text message that you typed into form_response.php.

Figure 9-14: Browser view of response page with text message

If the text message appears correctly, you are ready to create a PHP script on the response page.

4.   At the top of form_response.php, create a PHP script.

Each form value will be in a $_POST variable. The values can be accessed by the $_POST variable followed by the name value in square brackets and single quotes.

$_POST['name_first']

If the form uses the GET method or if the values are sent in a link, you would use $_GET instead of $_POST.

$_GET['name_first']

Alternatively, you can use $_REQUEST for both POST and GET values.

$_REQUEST['name_first']

5.   Create a variable for each of the form values, as shown in Figure 9-15.

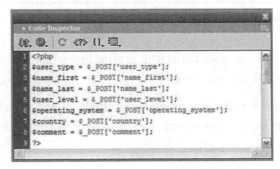

Figure 9-15: Saving the posted values as variables

Viewing the Passed Data

To allow you to see that the information is actually being passed and available on form_response.php, let's print the new variables under the text message in the body of the page.

6. Add a PHP script to the body of the page under the text message.

7. Use echo to print each of the variables except $operating_system.

8. Add a line break after each variable to separate the values.

9. The $operating_system variable contains an array, so use print_r() to print the array.

    print_r($operating_system);

```
Code Inspector                                              X
16  <body>
17  <p>Welcome to form_response.php</p>
18  <?php
19  echo $user_type.'<br>';
20  echo $name_first.'<br>';
21  echo $name_last.'<br>';
22  echo $user_level.'<br>';
23  echo $country.'<br>';
24  print_r($operating_system);
25  ?>
26  </body>
```

Figure 9-16: Script to print the variables

10. Save your changes and open form.php in your browser. Enter the requested information and select **Submit Form**.

The response page should display the values submitted in the form.

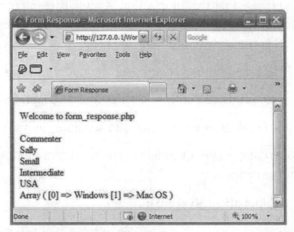

Figure 9-17: Printing the variables

Summary

Links and forms are the key to a seamless database-driven web site. Armed with the knowledge of how to create, submit, and access link and form passed values, you are ready to begin working with database interaction. In the next chapter we will look at ways to validate form data to ensure that the user is following the correct paths and submitting valid data.

Chapter 10

Validation

When web sites contain forms that allow users to enter their own data, there is always the risk that improper data will be entered. Whether this improper data is accidental or intentional, steps should be taken to ensure that the data entered is what is expected. One of the most common issues is that the user has not entered any data at all. Other potential problems are users entering letters where numbers should be or entering invalid email addresses. Let's take a look at a few examples using the form.php and form_response.php pages from Chapter 9.

1. Open **form.php** in your web editor. We will need to add a few more input lines to adequately test validation scenarios.

2. At the bottom of the form before the submit line, add the following lines. This will allow us to test numerical and expected character lengths.

   **Age: <input type="text" name="age" value="">
**
   Postal Code: <input type="text" name="postal_code"
   **value="">
**
   **
**

3. Save the page.

Before we test for specific conditions, it is important to test that the form variables actually exist.

Validating the Existence of a Form Value

The first validation to perform is the actual existence of an expected form variable. If you assume a nonexistent form variable exists and attempt to access it, you will often be presented with an undefined index error, as shown in Figure 10-1.

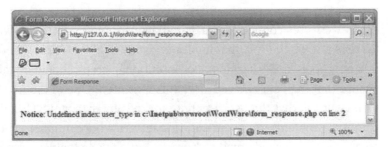

Figure 10-1: Undefined index error

A simple way to check for the existence of a form variable is to use the function isset(). This function checks to see if a variable exists. Alternatively, you can use !isset() to determine if the variable does not exist. In this case, if the variable is missing you would redirect the user and discontinue processing the current page using die().

1. Open **form_response.php**.

```php
1  <?php
2  $user_type = $_POST['user_type'];
3  $name_first = $_POST['name_first'];
4  $name_last = $_POST['name_last'];
5  $user_level = $_POST['user_level'];
6  $operating_system = $_POST['operating_system'];
7  $country = $_POST['country'];
8  ?>
9
10 <!DOCTYPE HTML PUBLIC "-//W3C//DTD HTML 4.01 Transitional//EN">
11 <html>
12 <head>
13 <title>Form Response</title>
14 <meta http-equiv="Content-Type" content="text/html;
   charset=utf-8">
15 </head>
16 <body>
17 <p>Welcome to form_response.php</p>
18 <?php
19 echo $user_type.'<br>';
20 echo $name_first.'<br>';
21 echo $name_last.'<br>';
22 echo $user_level.'<br>';
23 echo $country.'<br>';
24 print_r($operating_system);
25 ?>
26 </body>
27 </html>
```

Figure 10-2: The starting form_response.php page

2. Create an if() statement at the top of the first PHP script above the
    variable declarations.

```php
1  <?php
2  if(){
3
4  }
5  $user_type = $_POST['user_type'];
6  $name_first = $_POST['name_first'];
7  $name_last = $_POST['name_last'];
8  $user_level = $_POST['user_level'];
9  $operating_system = $_POST['operating_system'];
10 $country = $_POST['country'];
11 ?>
```

Figure 10-3: Creating an if() statement at the top of the page

3. Next use the !isset() function to check for one of the form
    variables.

```php
<?php
if( !isset($_POST['user_type']) ){

}
$user_type = $_POST['user_type'];
```

Figure 10-4: Using !isset() to check for the existence of a form variable

If the form variable does not exist, you will need to decide what
action to take. For this example, let's set a $message variable
equal to an error message. Then we will load the original form
page and quit the script.

4. Between the curly braces of the if() statement, set a variable
    $message equal to an error message.

5. Load the original form page using include_once().

6. Quit the script and current page with die();.

```php
<?php
if( !isset($_POST['user_type']) ){
$message = 'Please complete the form.';
include_once('form.php');
die();
}
```

Figure 10-5: Instructions if the form value does not exist

This will load the form.php page with a text message in the $mes-
sage variable if the anticipated form variable is absent. Next, we
need to make a couple of additions to the form.php page to display
the message.

7. Open the form.php page you created in Chapter 9.

8. Create a PHP script at the top of the page. We will use this script to determine if a $message variable already exists or if we need to create one.

```
Code Inspector                                              X
⚙. ◉.  C  <?>  {}. ▣.
1  <?php
2  if( !isset($message) ){
3  $message = 'Please complete the following form.';
4  }
5  ?>
6
7  <!DOCTYPE HTML PUBLIC "-//W3C//DTD HTML 4.01 Transitional//EN">
8  <html>
9  <head>
10 <title>Forms</title>
11 <meta http-equiv="Content-Type" content="text/html; charset=utf-8">
12 </head>
```

Figure 10-6: Instructions if the form value does not exist

Next, we need to display the $message variable in an appropriate place on the page. Since the message gives instructions to fill out the form, the $message variable should be placed above the form.

9. Print the $message variable to the page above the form.

```
Code Inspector                                              X
⚙. ◉.  C  <?>  {}. ▣.
13
14 <body>
15 <?php echo $message; ?>
16 <form action="form_response.php" method="post">
17 <input type="hidden" name="user_type" value="Commenter">
```

Figure 10-7: Printing the $message variable above the form

This solution will display the appropriate message when the user views the form. This will also prevent a user from going straight to the form response page and skipping the form entry page.

Now let's look at ways to validate that the form variables are not sent through with empty values.

Validating Empty Form Values

Once you are sure that the form has actually been submitted by con-firming that at least one form variable does exist, the next step is to check that any required values were completed by the user. For most form elements, you can use the empty() function to make sure that the variable is not empty. Let's start with the name_first value.

1. Create an if() statement after the first if() statement using empty() to check for a value in $_POST['name_first'].

```php
<?php
if( !isset($_POST['user_type']) ){
$message = 'Please complete the form.';
include_once('form.php');
die();
}

if( empty($_POST['name_first']) ){

}
```

Figure 10-8: Checking for an empty $_POST['name_first'] variable

2. Assign an appropriate message to the $message variable.

3. Load the form.php page to allow the user to try again.

4. Exit the page with die().

```php
<?php
if( !isset($_POST['user_type']) ){
$message = 'Please complete the form.';
include_once('form.php');
die();
}

if( empty($_POST['name_first']) ){
$message = 'Please complete all of the form fields.';
include_once('form.php');
die();
}
```

Figure 10-9: Instructions if the form variable is empty

This will check for a single empty value, but what if you want to check more than one form value? You can easily combine multiple conditions to check within the same if() statement using "and" or "or." In this example, we would want to reject the form if any of the required fields were empty.

5. Add an additional empty() function to the same if() statement to check for an empty value for $_POST['name_last'].

```
1  <?php
2  if( !isset($_POST['user_type']) ){
3  $message = 'Please complete the form.';
4  include_once('form.php');
5  die();
6  }
7
8  if( empty($_POST['name_first']) or empty($_POST['name_last']) ){
9  $message = 'Please complete all of the form fields.';
10 include_once('form.php');
11 die();
12 }
```

Figure 10-10: Checking for two empty $_POST[""] variables

6. Add two more checks for $_POST['user_level'] and $_POST['country'].

```
1  <?php
2  if( !isset($_POST['user_type']) ){
3  $message = 'Please complete the form.';
4  include_once('form.php');
5  die();
6  }
7
8  if(    empty($_POST['name_first'])
9     or empty($_POST['name_last'])
10    or empty($_POST['user_level'])
11    or empty($_POST['country']) ){
12 $message = 'Please complete all of the form fields.';
13 include_once('form.php');
14 die();
```

Figure 10-11: Checking for multiple empty $_POST[""] variables

The last user input value is for operating system. This value is treated slightly differently since it contains an array instead of a single value. If no value is selected in the check boxes, then the POST variable is not even created. Because of this we need to check for the existence of the variable instead of whether or not it is empty. This can be done using the !isset() function.

7. Add a fifth condition to the if() statement to check if $_POST['operating_system'] is not set.

```
Code Inspector

8  if(     empty($_POST['name_first'])
9      or empty($_POST['name_last'])
10     or empty($_POST['user_level'])
11     or empty($_POST['country'])
12     or !isset($_POST['operating_system']) ){
13 $message = 'Please complete all of the form fields.';
14 include_once('form.php');
15 die();
16 }
```

Figure 10-12: Checking that the $_POST['operating_system'] variable exists

With these checks the entire form is validated for at least some value.

Validating Numbers

Form variables can be validated for numerical characters only by using the is_numeric() function. Let's validate the age field for a valid numerical value.

1. After the empty validations, create a new if() statement. Use the not symbol (!) combined with the is_numeric() function to test if the age is not a number.

2. As with the empty checks, set a message for the $message variable between the curly braces of the if() statement.

3. Include the original form page and then quit the page with die().

```
Code Inspector
if (!is_numeric($_POST['age'])) {
$message = 'Age must be a number.';
include_once('form.php');
die();
}
```

Figure 10-13: Checking that $_POST['age'] is a number

This will return the message "Age must be a number" if any character other than a number is entered by the user.

Validating String Length

Another popular validation is to check the character length of a string. In some instances you may want to check that a string is a minimum or maximum character length or both. This can be done by using the strlen() function.

1. After the empty validations, create a new if() statement. Use the strlen() function to test if postal_code is at least five characters long.

2. Set a message for the $message variable between the curly braces of the if() statement.

3. Include the original form page and then quit the page with die().

```
Code Inspector
if (strlen($_POST['postal_code']) < 5) {
$message = 'The Postal Code you entered is too short to be valid.';
include_once('form.php');
die();
}
```

Figure 10-14: Checking the character length of a string

This will return the message "The Postal Code you entered is too short to be valid." if the string contains fewer than five characters.

You may want to also check that a string is between two character lengths. In this case you would need to specify both limits.

4. Extend the if() statement by adding OR and then an additional strlen(). Set the second condition to check if the $_POST['postal_code'] variable character length is longer than 10 characters.

```
24 if (strlen($_POST['postal_code']) < 5 or strlen($_POST['postal_code']) > 10) {
25    $message = 'The Postal Code you entered is too short or too long to be valid.';
26    include_once('form.php');
27    die();
28 }
```

Figure 10-15: Checking that character length of a string is between two values

This will return the message "The Postal Code you entered is too short or too long to be valid." if the string contains fewer than five characters or more than 10 characters.

Validating Email Format

Since email addresses are commonly used in web forms, it can be helpful to validate that at least the format is correct. This will not confirm that the entered email address is a valid address, but it will check for a valid format and allow the user to make changes if it was entered by mistake.

The standard email format can be evaluated using the ereg() function. This function compares a given pattern to a string pattern. In this case, we will construct a comparison pattern and compare that with the $_POST['email'] variable.

1. Create a new if() statement using the not symbol (!) combined with the ereg() function.

   The ereg() function has two parameters. The first parameter is the pattern you are looking for and the second parameter is the string that you are checking.

   ereg(test pattern , string)

   The test pattern for checking the format of an email address is:

   ^([a-zA-Z0-9])+([\.a-zA-Z0-9_-])*@([a-zA-Z0-9_-])+ (\.[a-zA-Z0-9_-]+)*\.([a-zA-Z]{2,6})$

   The string that you will be checking is $_POST['email'].

2. Enter the email test pattern as the first parameter and the $_POST['email'] variable as the string to be checked.

3. Sct a message for the $message variable between the curly braces of the if() statement.

4. Include the original form page and then quit the page with die().

```
▼ Code Inspector
₰. ◉.  C  <?> {},  ▦.
30  if (!ereg('^([a-zA-Z0-9])+([\.a-zA-Z0-9_-])*@([a-zA-Z0-9_-])+(\.[a-zA-Z0-9_-]+)*\.([a-zA-Z]{2,6})$', $_POST['email'])) {
31  $message = 'The Email Address you entered is not valid.';
32  include_once('form.php');
33  die();
34  }
```

Figure 10-16: Validating the format of an email address

This will return the message "The Email Address you entered is not valid." if the email address does not match the given format.

Summary

Form validation is a great tool to help ensure consistent data is sent to the database. Using validation will prevent unanticipated and accidental errors from occurring during the user's experience. This will also save you many headaches trying to track down errors in submitted information. Data validation is one case where an ounce of prevention is definitely worth a pound of cure.

In the next chapter you will learn all about the FileMaker API for PHP and prepare to begin interacting with your FileMaker data on the web with PHP.

Chapter 11

What Is the API for PHP?

Now that you are familiar with PHP and have had a chance to play around with this web publishing technology, it is time to introduce the long-awaited star of this book. It is a library of code that has changed the way people think of web publishing with the FileMaker database — none other than the FileMaker API for PHP.

What Is an API?

This cryptic name usually invokes in seasoned programmers a torrent of mixed feelings and memories that include lengthy manuals and frustration with strange functions. The term "API" stands for "application programming interface," which means a layer of code that allows two applications to exchange information in a standard and predictable manner. In this case, the two applications are FileMaker Server and PHP, where PHP is the application using the API to communicate with FileMaker Server.

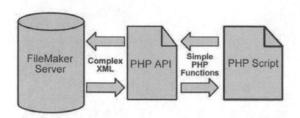

Figure 11-1: PHP API layer between FileMaker Server and PHP

The application programming interface is structured to provide a set of methods and properties to the programming language that will remain constant throughout the lifetime of the product. That means that if the application changes its own internal structure to provide new features, optimizations, or any other big architectural changes, the programming interface should generally remain the same and be compatible with a whole range of product versions. This provides a tremendous advantage to the programmer, since the code written for one version of the application will be able to communicate with newer versions of that application without any modification to the source code. The power of using an API when writing applications can be easily seen within any Windows application. For example, an application that was written in the age of Windows 95 can in most cases run without any modifications or patches on Windows 2000, Windows XP, and even Windows Vista. In each version of Windows, the internal code to create objects such as application windows and menus has changed and evolved, while still allowing old applications to use the set of services originally provided by Windows 95. However, as new features are introduced, some newer applications decide to take advantage of those features, making them only forward compatible from the version of the API that they used — such as many new applications that can only be used on something newer than Windows XP.

The FileMaker API is no different in its philosophy to retain future compatibility of code written for its API now. Therefore, it is very likely that the applications you write for FileMaker 9 with PHP will be compatible with future releases of FileMaker software. While newer features of FileMaker that will come along will not be implemented by your software without an update, the old set of functions provided by the FileMaker API today will still behave the same years from now. This also means that you will be able to use the knowledge derived from this book for years to come as long as FileMaker, Inc., keeps releasing the FileMaker API for PHP for its future products.

A Little Bit of History

Before the FileMaker API for PHP was developed by FileMaker, Inc., there were a number of solutions used to perform web publishing with FileMaker and PHP. Originally, FileMaker used CDML as one option to publish data on the web; however, this limited developers to using a single language on the web. FileMaker also has an ODBC interface that allows communication with a FileMaker database using the SQL language and a special communication driver, but this limited FileMaker to just data with no access to information about the layouts within the database. Then FileMaker, Inc., introduced XML and XSLT web publishing, a complicated method to access and format information. With the XML interface, many programming environments could now access FileMaker data, and PHP was no different. Using the XML interface, a PHP class was introduced under the name FX.php, which allowed easy access to FileMaker data from PHP. As FileMaker features have evolved, FX.php was not developed further to support newer features and currently lacks the capability for direct editing of portal records — a feature vital in many applications that requires numerous workarounds to implement with PHP. With such an uncertain and varied world of web publishing, FileMaker, Inc., decided to step in and develop a standardized method of accessing FileMaker data from PHP, and the FileMaker API for PHP was born.

Anatomy of the FileMaker API for PHP

The FileMaker API provides a relatively small number of functions with which to interact with a FileMaker database, greatly simplifying the number of functions that you have to remember when working with it. Generally, the interaction with the FileMaker API can be broken down into the following five steps:

■ Create an instance of a FileMaker object with your database settings.

■ Ask the FileMaker object for a new command object.

■ Modify the command object with properties such as field values.

■ Execute the command object to perform the action on the database.

■ Process the results from the command object.

This section will briefly review each one of those steps, and the remainder of this book will focus on the details of each step and how to implement it to achieve the desired result. This section provides an overview of the workflow that will be used throughout your PHP applications, hence it is very abstract and does not include any specific code or examples. As you read it, try to visualize each step of the process and see how it fits into the overall interaction with the database. With no further ado, let's look at the first step: creating an instance of a FileMaker object.

Creating an instance of the FileMaker object involves including the correct FileMaker libraries into your PHP script and then using the PHP new operator to create a FileMaker object. When creating an object, you supply the host name or IP address of your FileMaker Server, the database name, and the credentials for the connection. Once this action has been performed, the next step is to select a command to perform on the FileMaker database.

Interaction with your FileMaker database is performed through a series of command objects. The command objects include find, edit, add, and delete. Creating one of those command objects involves using your previously created FileMaker object by calling a function on it in the form of newTypeCommand, where Type is a type of command such as newFindCommand or newEditCommand. When calling one of these functions, you normally supply the FileMaker layout name on which the operation will be performed. If operating on an existing record, the record ID is also supplied at this stage. Once you have one of the command objects, it is time to set some properties to it before using it with the database.

Setting parameters to the command object is done through a series of functions that will be thoroughly explained in this book. At this stage you would be setting find criterions for a find object, or field values for new or edited records. You can also limit the number of records returned as well as assign the number of records to skip; this is essential functionality for systems that have multiple pages of data to page through. Once the command has been personalized for your query and has all the needed information, it is time to execute your command.

Executing a FileMaker command is the step at which interaction with the database actually happens. Up to that point, changes and operations on the command object are only temporarily recorded as PHP variables. Executing the command involves calling the execute method on it and storing the result in a variable. This result should then be checked for errors, such as failed data validations or missing fields on your layout. If the result contains a set of records such as a new record or a found set of data, you would proceed to the next step of extracting the data into your PHP application.

A successfully executed command will typically return either a single record object or a set of records, allowing PHP to process the results. The API provides very easy functions to loop through the set of records, and then access each record in the set. Once a record is accessed, it is possible to extract field values from it, acquire information about fields such as value lists, and access related portal records.

While this process might seem long and complicated, it only takes a couple of PHP lines to implement and immediately access your database. Once the technical details of those steps are introduced as we build the blog application, using this process to perform all the actions within your database will become second nature.

Summary

Now that you know a little bit more about the way the FileMaker API for PHP fits into web publishing, you are ready to start exploring the exciting world of FileMaker publishing on the web. First, we'll cover the basics, which include connecting to a FileMaker database, finding a few simple records, manipulating data, and finishing with a complete system that manipulates all aspects of a FileMaker database from within a web browser. This is the time to leave the powerful FileMaker back-end interfaces and reports behind, and dive into the exciting world of user-centered web publishing.

Chapter 12

Creating the Blog and Performing a Simple Query

At this stage, your PHP servers should be set up and hopefully you are familiar with the basic PHP concepts and structures. This is the chapter where we set up the environment for the central project of this book that will encompass the many features that the FileMaker API offers when connected to your database.

What Is a Blog?

Throughout this book FileMaker concepts will be demonstrated as they apply to web publishing. The main project that you will develop is a blogging system that will allow you to post updates for your business or personal life, or simply learn FileMaker web publishing. A blog is a web application that allows its writer to keep an online journal for other users to read and comment on. You can use such a journal as a private publication for close family and friends, updating them on your latest road trip or camping trip. You could also use a blog as a business publication that discusses your new products and technologies, and generally keeps your customers updated about your latest offers. A blog could also be used for general public rants and industry commentary; once combined with some ads, it can present a nice extra source of revenue.

A blog generally consists of four sections. The first section your visitor sees is the front page that lists the latest blog posts. Each blog post links to the next section of the site, which is a single blog post page that lists a post and allows a visitor to leave a comment or question for that specific post. The third section is a blog search and archive, which allows the user to search through your entire history of blogging and find relevant information on a subject. The last section is the administrative side of your blog that allows you to make posts from anywhere in the world where a web browser and an Internet connection are available.

Include File Structure of the Blog

In order to efficiently develop a web application, its structure should be developed in advance and be flexible enough to accommodate new pages easily. A very nice way to achieve a flexible site is to develop a template for your application that includes a constant header and footer section with some links, and then a variable body section for the actual information. The big advantage of include files is their independence from other PHP code, allowing you to easily edit them at any time and have the changes instantly propagate throughout the whole application that uses them.

The blog project will include both a header and a footer for its layout, as well as a few extra include files that will appear only on certain parts of the site. It is also a good idea to use a separate style sheet to actually style your objects and text without adding lots of additional style code into your HTML structure. To style the blog with a style sheet, we will be using a cascading style sheet (CSS) file that defines the graphical appearance of many elements and has some nice default settings. The CSS file will be provided as is and can be edited by hand with the knowledge you gained in Chapter 7, "CSS Basics." Don't hesitate to experiment with the design once your blog has been set up.

When using our supplied sample files, the blog should be very similar in appearance to Figure 12-1.

Figure 12-1: Sample page from the Blog FileMaker PHP application

The Header and Footer Files

Each web application that you build will have a similar structure in its header and footer. HTML headers generally contain meta information about the page such as its character encoding, language setting, page titles, and any JavaScript or CSS include files. The footer generally contains copyright information, links to the contact or about page, and other embellishments that go on the bottom of the page. The blog project is no different; its header includes a CSS style sheet and the footer has some elements to make the bottom of the page look nice and rounded.

1. First, we should create the header page. Let's start a new PHP page and name it **blogHeader.php**. This page should have the source code shown in Figure 12-2.

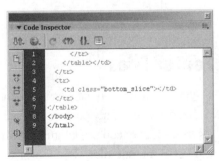

Figure 12-2: Source code of blogHeader.php

2. Once you have the header created, let's create another PHP page named **blogFooter.php**. The page should have the source code shown in Figure 12-3.

Figure 12-3: Source code of blogFooter.php

3. Once both of those pages are created, save and close the files.

They will be used shortly as include files when we build the blog pages throughout the book. Remember that you can edit those pages at any time to give your own blog an exciting custom look and feel.

Cascading Style Sheets

Since the beginning of the web, presenting information that is not plain text has been a challenge with many different solutions. Cascading style sheets (CSS) offer the ability to style fonts, tables, and images by referencing elements on an HTML page using the class and id properties of that element. This allows pinpointed modifications to the way a page would look in a browser using a simple external file. The CSS for this project is used to style the tables and attach background images to the layout, allowing you as the PHP programmer to focus on the logic and the HTML tags.

This separation allows you to leave the site design to a designer, or even yourself when you are wearing the designer hat and not focusing on PHP. From our experience, PHP applications that are built with heavy CSS integration are much more easily modified in the future, and thus it is much cheaper to maintain the image and direction of the client changes. We strongly recommend picking up a book about CSS and graphical design on the web even if you only have the slightest interest in graphical design. The knowledge will make your future PHP work agile and flexible for years to come!

The CSS for the blog is quite lengthy due to the extra effort that went into reducing the HTML code at the expense of adding more graphical definitions into the CSS. For more information about cascading style sheets, see Chapter 7.

1. Create a new CSS file and name it **webstyle.css**.

2. Include the source code from Figures 12-4 and 12-5 into the new page.

This style sheet should be placed alongside your other PHP files and not in a subfolder; otherwise, the image references within it will not properly work without extra modifications.

```
1   .maintext {
2       font-family: Arial, Helvetica, sans-serif;
3       font-size: 14px;
4       font-weight: normal;
5       color: #000000;
6   }
7   .headline {
8       font-family: Arial, Helvetica, sans-serif;
9       font-size: 36px;
10      font-weight: normal;
11      color: #FFFFFF;
12  }
13
14  a {
15      color: blue;
16  }
17
18  p {
19      margin: 5px;
20  }
21
22  a:hover {
23      color: #27539C;
24  }
25
26  body {
27      background-color: #003366;
28      margin: 0px;
29  }
30
31  img {
32      border: 0px;
33  }
34
```

```
35  table{
36      border: 0px;
37      border-collapse: collapse;
38      padding: 0px;
39  }
40
41  table#main td {
42      padding: 0px;
43  }
44
45  table#main {
46      margin-left: auto;
47      margin-right: auto;
48      width: 800px;
49  }
50
51  table#content {
52      margin-left: auto;
53      margin-right: auto;
54      width: 700px;
55  }
56
57  table#blog_about {
58      margin-left: auto;
59      margin-right: auto;
60      width: 202px;
61  }
62
63  table#main td.top {
64      height: 139px;
65      vertical-align: bottom;
66      background-image: url('images/header.jpg');
67      padding-left: 5px;
68  }
```

Figure 12-4: Source code of webstyle.css, part 1

```
69
70  table#main td.top_strip {
71      height: 40px;
72      width: 800px;
73      background-image: url('images/top_strip.jpg');
74  }
75
76  table#main td.middle_slice {
77      background-image: url('images/middle_slice.jpg');
78      background-repeat: repeat-y;
79  }
80
81  table#content p.blog_info {
82      width: 472px;
83      height: 134px;
84      background-image: url('images/blog_orange.jpg');
85  }
86
87  table#content p.contactus_header {
88      width: 702px;
89      height: 42px;
90      background-image: url('images/green_contactus.jpg');
91  }
92
93  table#content p.aboutus_header {
94      width: 702px;
95      height: 42px;
96      background-image: url('images/orange_aboutus.jpg');
97  }
98
99  table#main td.bottom_slice{
100     height: 40px;
101     background-image: url('images/bottom_slice.jpg');
102 }
```

```
103
104  table#content table#blog_about td.top{
105      height: 46px;
106      background-image: url('images/blog_green1.jpg');
107  }
108
109  table#content table#blog_about td.middle{
110      background-image: url('images/blog_green2.jpg');
111      background-repeat: repeat-y;
112  }
113
114  table#content table#blog_about td.bottom{
115      height: 56px;
116      background-image: url('images/blog_green3.jpg');
117  }
```

Figure 12-5: Source code of webstyle.css, part 2

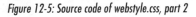

The About Blob Section

Most blogs have a small about section on the right side of the home page, as shown in Figure 12-6. This section should be used to describe what your blog is about, and potentially include your company logo or a photo. This section should also be an easily editable include file that you can include in multiple locations within your application.

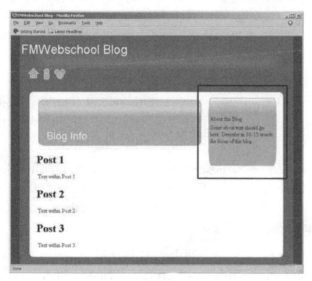

Figure 12-6: Location of the about blob within your blog

1. To create this include file, create a new PHP file named **blogAbout.php** and fill it with the code from Figure 12-7.

```
<td valign="top"><table id="blog_about">
    <tr>
        <td class="top"></td>
    </tr>
    <tr>
        <td class="middle">
            <p>About this Blog</p>
            <p>Some about text should go here.
            Describe in 10-15 words the focus of
            this blog</p>
        </td>
    </tr>
    <tr>
        <td class="bottom"></td>
    </tr>
</table></td>
```

Figure 12-7: Source code for blogAbout.php include file

2. Save and close the file.

This file will be included from your blog home page as well as the blog about page that will be created at a later time.

Preparing the Connection Include Folder

When working with this project, we will be developing a few functions as well as some common PHP files that will be used throughout the entire site. Apart from the HTML layout includes you created earlier, code-based PHP includes should be placed into a directory separate from the rest of your files.

1. Create a folder with the name **include** within your blog project directory. Be sure to use this exact case and spelling; otherwise, further examples will be inconsistent with your setup.

   Now that the folder has been created, it is best to create a local copy of the FileMaker API for PHP. Please refer to "Manually Installing the FileMaker API for PHP" in Chapter 3 for instructions on finding the API.

2. Place all the extracted FileMaker API for PHP files within a FileMaker folder in this newly created include folder.

Once you are done, the following file path should point to a valid file: include/FileMaker/FileMaker.php.

Creating a Connection Include File

When working with a project, it is a very good idea to have a single file that initializes your connection to FileMaker Server. This file would set the host name or IP address of your FileMaker server, the database name you are connecting to, as well as the credentials to use with the connection. This file will also be used to include the FileMaker API files, which will give you access to the actual API functions. Once this is properly set up, all further pages will have access to this connection with one simple line.

1. Create a new PHP file in your include folder, naming it
    db.inc.php, and enter the code from Figure 12-8 into it, making
    sure you remove any other HTML or PHP code from your new
    PHP file.

```
 1  <?php
 2  require_once('FileMaker/FileMaker.php');
 3
 4  $DB_HOST = '127.0.0.1';
 5  $DB_NAME = 'Blog';
 6  $DB_USER = 'webuser';
 7  $DB_PASS = 'webpass';
 8
 9  $blogDB = new FileMaker($DB_NAME, $DB_HOST, $DB_USER, $DB_PASS);
10  ?>
```

Figure 12-8: Source code for db.inc.php

This file includes the FileMaker.php file that initializes the API.
Then four variables are defined:

$DB_HOST = 'the database IP or http address';
$DB_NAME = 'Database Name';
$DB_USER = 'web accessible FileMaker user account';
$DB_PASS = 'web accessible FileMaker password';

These variables might have to be customized by you, especially
the database host and the database name parameters, which can
vary if you are using a hosting company for your database files.

2. Save and close the file.

With the db.inc.php include prepared, you can now include it in any of
your pages with this simple line:

<?php require('include/db.inc.php'); ?>

Constructing the Blog Index Page

With all the include files completed, the first page of the application can now be constructed. Traditionally, the first page of the application is the index page, which is named index.php. This page will serve as the home page for your entire PHP application.

1. Create a new page, naming it **index.php** and be sure to clear any code from it before continuing. This page will include the FileMaker connection file, the standard header, the standard footer, and the about blob on the side.

2. Start by adding the following two lines to the beginning of the file:

   ```
   <?php require('include/db.inc.php'); ?>
   <?php include('blogHeader.php'); ?>
   ```

   The first line includes the database connection and the second line includes the blog header file. Next, we will create a small HTML table cell using the td element with a width setting of 500 pixels. The width setting is used in this case to limit the area of the blog to a portion of the page and allow space for the about blob.

3. Add the following to the end of your file in order to add the table cell:

   ```
   <td width="500" valign="top">
     <p class="blog_info"></p>
   </td>
   ```

   With those lines added, the only remaining thing that we need to do to prepare a page within the application is to add the blog about blob and the standard footer.

4. Append the following two lines to the end of your current block of code:

   ```
   <?php include('blogAbout.php'); ?>
   <?php include('blogFooter.php'); ?>
   ```

With those simple seven lines, you have just created an entire PHP page with a header, footer, and some space for dynamic FileMaker data. The full code listing for this page can be seen in Figure 12-9.

Figure 12-9: Source code for index.php with header and footer includes

Adding a Find All Command to List Posts

Now that the page is ready to accept PHP logic and dynamic data, let's jump straight into using the API for a simple query. The easiest command to use with the FileMaker API is the find all command that simply retrieves all the records from a specific layout. Before the code is actually written, let's take a minute to look at the flow of a FileMaker database command:

- The FileMaker command is initialized with a layout parameter.
- The FileMaker command is executed and returns a result.
- The result has to be checked for errors.

Initializing a FileMaker command requires using a FileMaker object, in this case defined within db.inc.php, to call a new command function on it with a layout name. The generic syntax for this operation is:

```
$command = $fm->newFindAllCommand($layout);
```

1. In the index.php page, move the closing PHP tag from the first line down a few lines to make space for PHP code.

Your first three lines should now contain the following code:

<?php require('include/db.inc.php');

?>

Since within the db.inc.php file we used the blogDB variable to store the FileMaker object, we have to use the same variable to initialize the command. We will use the Posts layout to list all the blog post entries that are currently in the database. We will store the command object inside the postsFind variable. It is good practice to have descriptive names for your commands; in this case, it is clear that the postsFind variable is a find for some posts.

2. Add the following code to the second line of your file to initialize this command:

$postsFind = $blogDB->newFindAllCommand('Posts');

This line completes the first part of our action plan for this page: blogDB was used to initialize the connection with the Posts layout. Since the find all command does not require any further setup, we can move on to the second part of executing the command.

Executing a FileMaker API command involves calling the execute function on it and then assigning the result of it to a variable. Remember that PHP assigns the result from the right side of the equal sign to the left side of it. In this case, we will use the posts variable to hold the results.

3. Assign the execution result of the postsFind command to the posts variable using the following line:

$posts = $postsFind->execute();

This line should go right after the line that initialized the new command. With these two FileMaker API lines in place, you have just created a FileMaker search. Congratulate yourself on this accomplishment and make sure that you understand the main parts of the code up to this point.

The last part of the FileMaker command process is checking the result of the command for errors. Errors within commands are very easy to detect with the FileMaker API since the API returns a special error object instead of a proper result set. To check if the result variable that you have is an error object, the FileMaker:: isError function must be used within an if statement. If the object is indeed an error object, then it will have a getMessage function, which returns a well-formatted error message that is ready for printing. Error handling typically takes three lines of code for the if statement and the error printing. Notice that the error printing in this case uses the die function, which stops execution of the PHP script at the point right after printing out the message. This behavior is desired in most cases since a failed FileMaker command will typically prevent the rest of the page from properly working.

4. Add the following code for the error check after the execute function:

```
if(FileMaker::isError($posts)) {
    die('Database Error: '.$posts->getMessage());
}
```

With these few simple lines you have constructed a proper FileMaker API command that is executed and checked for errors. By following this code, you can use the result object — in this case the posts variable — to output the FileMaker data that was returned from the command. The code up to this point is displayed in Figure 12-10.

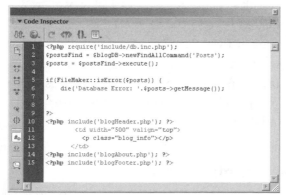

Figure 12-10: Source code of index.php with a FileMaker API command

Displaying a Simple Result Set

The previous section only addressed how to run a FileMaker API command. The next logical step is to actually print out the result set returned from that command. Since this result set contains a list of posts with titles and body content text, we can print those very neatly using a set of HTML header tags and paragraphs. Each entry will have the following structure:

> **<h1>Post Title</h1>**
> **<p>Post content</p>**

1.   Insert the above code as a placeholder after the <p class="blog_info"></p> line.

Now that you have the placeholders in place, PHP code has to be added to print that structure as many times as we have records in the found record set.

Printing repetitive HTML blocks of code is a task for PHP loops. The most appropriate loop in this case is the foreach loop that goes through each value in an array of values and performs a task with it. However, having only the posts result object does not give us access to the array of actual records just yet. The FileMaker API has a special function specifically for this purpose: getRecords. The general syntax for getRecords is:

> **$recordArray = $fmResult->getRecords();**

Since the fmResult in our case is the variable posts, we will adopt the general syntax above to start a foreach loop before the two placeholder lines that you have already inserted into the page. The code below first retrieves the array of records from the posts result and stores it in postsArray, then postsArray is used to start a foreach loop that each time places an element from postsArray into the post PHP variable:

> **<?php**
> **$postsArray = $posts->getRecords();**

```
foreach($postsArray as $post) {
?>
```

2. Add the above code between the placeholders in your page.

   The code above starts the actual loop; however, each loop within PHP must have an ending curly brace in order to confine the looping procedure to a specific part of the script. In this case, we want the loop to end right after the two placeholder lines. Here, ending the loop only requires a closing curly brace within proper PHP opening and closing tags.

3. Add the following line to your code after the placeholders:

   ```
   <?php } ?>
   ```

   Before continuing further, verify that you have placed all the loop start and end tags in the correct location around the post title and post content placeholders by comparing your code to Figure 12-11.

```
Code Inspector
1   <?php require('include/db.inc.php');
2   $postsFind = $blogDB->newFindAllCommand('Posts');
3   $posts = $postsFind->execute();
4
5   if(FileMaker::isError($posts)) {
6       die('Database Error: '.$posts->getMessage());
7   }
8
9   ?>
10  <?php include('blogHeader.php'); ?>
11          <td width="500" valign="top">
12              <p class="blog_info"></p>
13  <?php
14  $postsArray = $posts->getRecords();
15  foreach($postsArray as $post) {
16  ?>
17  <h1>Post Title</h1>
18  <p>Post content</p>
19  <?php } ?>
20          </td>
21  <?php include('blogAbout.php'); ?>
22  <?php include('blogFooter.php'); ?>
```

Figure 12-11: Source code with a record array loop

The last step that has to be performed before you have a fully functioning FileMaker-driven web page is to add the actual printing of data within your FileMaker fields. Each record in the postsArray that is accessible through the post variable in the foreach loop has a function getField, which allows you to retrieve the value of a specific field on your layout. We will be using two instances of getField to print the post title and the post content into the HTML code. The generic syntax for getField resembles other API functions very closely:

$fieldContents = $record->getField('fieldName');

In our case, we are printing into the header and the paragraph tags, and the record object is stored in the post variable.

4. Insert the following code in place of the placeholder code:

    <h1><?php echo $post->getField('title'); ?></h1>
    <p><?php echo $post->getField('body'); ?></p>

Notice that here we are not assigning the result to a variable or using equal signs since echo takes the result of the command to the right of it and prints its results to the user's browser. The final source code for the index.php page can be seen within Figure 12-12, and the output in your browser should closely resemble Figure 12-1.

```
Code Inspector
1   <?php require('include/db.inc.php');
2   $postsFind = $blogDB->newFindAllCommand('Posts');
3   $posts = $postsFind->execute();
4
5   if(FileMaker::isError($posts)) {
6       die('Database Error: '.$posts->getMessage());
7   }
8
9   ?>
10  <?php include('blogHeader.php'); ?>
11          <td width="500" valign="top">
12              <p class="blog_info"></p>
13  <?php
14  $postsArray = $posts->getRecords();
15  foreach($postsArray as $post) {
16  ?>
17          <h1><?php echo $post->getField('title'); ?></h1>
18              <p><?php echo $post->getField('body'); ?></p>
19  <?php } ?>
20          </td>
21  <?php include('blogAbout.php'); ?>
22  <?php include('blogFooter.php'); ?>
```

Figure 12-12: Final source code of index.php

Summary

This chapter contained a lot of condensed information within it, both about include files as well as basic FileMaker queries. Our hope is that you will review any unclear parts in this chapter and keep going back to it as a basic template for future blog application pages or even when setting up your own FileMaker PHP applications. When finished with all the examples in this chapter, make sure that you understand thoroughly how the include files work as well as the purpose of each line that performs the FileMaker find all command on this page. If you feel even more adventurous, do not be afraid to try printing more fields from the post record to see what you can do with the getField function.

Chapter 13

Creating New Records and Sorting

Now that you have a taste of how FileMaker web publishing works, it is time to continue discovering the many other ways to interact with FileMaker from the web. Here, we will discuss creating new records, which will allow you for the first time to have a two-way interaction with the FileMaker database. At the end of this chapter, sorting is also covered in order to help you properly display the records that you create.

Record Creation Process

Creating records within FileMaker using the FileMaker API is a very similar process to the find all command that was covered in the previous chapter. A new step is introduced into the process that involves setting the actual field values within the record before submitting it for execution. Since HTML forms send data first into the PHP script and not directly into the API, this step is necessary to map the form properly into the new record. Before the code is actually written, let's take a minute to look at the flow of an add record FileMaker database command:

- The FileMaker command is initialized with a layout parameter.
- Multiple field parameters are added to the command.

- The FileMaker command is executed and returns a result.
- The result has to be checked for errors.

Once the new record is created, it can be manipulated by PHP and data can be retrieved from it. For example, you can retrieve a confirmation number from the new record that was auto-generated using a FileMaker serial number. You can also use this new record object to add portal rows to the newly created record, an operation that will be covered in Chapter 16.

New Record Command

The new record command is initialized just like most of the other commands, but includes a parameter for the layout name that the operation will be performed on. However, before executing the command a number of fields have to be set; this is done with the setField command, which has the following general syntax:

$fmCommand->setField('fieldName',$value);

The setField command does not return any values and has just two parameters — one for the field name as it appears on your FileMaker layout and the second one for a constant value or a variable to place into that field.

Building the Input Form

Now that you are familiar with how a new record is created, it is time to apply that knowledge to something useful. We shall continue building our blog PHP application by adding a new blog entry section to the blog administration that will create the new record for your post in the database.

Generally, most new record commands are initialized from forms that take in user-supplied data to be placed into a record, and this case is no different. We will start by creating a quick input form that takes in a post title and the contents of the post. Using the usual include files we will create another standard blog page for the form.

1. Create a new page and name it **newEntry.php**.

2. Include the source code in it from Figure 13-1.

Notice that this page is just a simple form that will actually submit its post data to newEntryResponse.php, which we will create later on in this chapter.

```
1  <?php require_once('include/db.inc.php');
2
3  ?>
4  <?php include('blogHeader.php'); ?>
5       <td valign="top">
6          <h1>New Blog Post</h1>
7          <p>Please use this form to post a new blog entry</p>
8          <form method="post" action="newEntryResponse.php">
9             <input type="hidden" name="action" value="newEntry">
10            <table width="300">
11               <tr>
12                  <th>Title</th>
13                  <td><input name="title" type="text" id="title"></td>
14               </tr>
15               <tr>
16                  <th>Content</th>
17                  <td><textarea name="content" cols="70" rows="8"></textarea></td>
18               </tr>
19               <tr>
20                  <th> </th>
21                  <td><input type="submit" name="Submit" value="Submit Post"></td>
22               </tr>
23            </table>
24         </form>
25      </td>
26  <?php include('blogFooter.php'); ?>
```

Figure 13-1: Source code for the newEntry.php input form

Processing Form Data Correctly

You learned in Chapter 9 that post and get form data can be accessed using the $_POST and $_GET variables in the response scripts. However, this form data access method does not properly transmit the data for a few specific characters. Instead, in most PHP configurations, characters such as a double or single quote have slashes added in front of them. For example, the value from an input box that had "It's a PHP script" in it would become "It\'s a PHP script" — recording that extra slash in your database.

This automated manipulation occurs to prevent some security problems with PHP being used with SQL databases, and has no application in FileMaker web publishing except as a distraction for the programmer. In order to get the real value of the variable, you have to use a function that will remove those extra slashes: stripslashes. The functionality of adding slashes automatically is called "Magic Quotes" and is usually enabled on a web server. However, some PHP installations do not add the slashes, and therefore an extra function has to be used in an if statement to check if stripslashes is truly required. That function is get_magic_quotes_gpc, which returns a value of true when slashes are being added. Since this has very little relevance to a FileMaker programmer, you are probably starting to wonder how much it will really take to get data out of a form in your applications. Well, all is not lost — there is a very efficient method to retrieve those values consistently and without dozens of if statements. We will write a few functions to automate this process.

In order to automate the slash character detection, two functions will be defined: POST and GET. Since it is a function, parentheses have to be used for the parameter instead of the square array brackets you would use to retrieve a value from $_POST or $_GET. To contrast the two methods, these lines of code would perform the same function with the exception of the first not stripping the slashes:

```
echo $_POST['variable'];
echo POST('variable');
```

In order to use these two new functions easily throughout the entire site, they should be automatically available to most scripts, and the best way to do that is to place them into an include file. Let's create a new include file for cases like these where you have a function that is extremely helpful and you want to use it throughout your whole project.

1. Create a blank PHP file in your include directory, naming it **commonFunctions.inc.php**.

2. Add the source code for this function as shown in Figure 13-2. This code will be thoroughly explained in the next several sections.

```
 1  <?php
 2  function POST($var=null) {
 3      if($var === null) {
 4          $ret = array();
 5          foreach($_POST as $key=>$value) {
 6              $ret[$key] = POST($key);
 7          }
 8          return $ret;
 9      }
10      if(!isset($_POST[$var])) return false;
11      if(get_magic_quotes_gpc()) {
12          return stripslashes($_POST[$var]);
13      }else{
14          return $_POST[$var];
15      }
16  }
17
18  function GET($var=null) {
19      if($var === null) {
20          $ret = array();
21          foreach($_GET as $key=>$value) {
22              $ret[$key] = GET($key);
23          }
24          return $ret;
25      }
26      if(!isset($_GET[$var])) return false;
27      if(get_magic_quotes_gpc()) {
28          return stripslashes($_GET[$var]);
29      }else{
30          return $_GET[$var];
31      }
32  }
33  ?>
```

Figure 13-2: Source code for commonFunctions.inc.php

3. Save and close the file.

Now that your include file is ready, it is time to integrate it into all your database-driven pages. The easiest way to do this is to include it as part of a connection db.inc.php file.

4.   Add the following line after the "FileMaker.php" include line in db.inc.php:

require_once('commonFunctions.inc.php');

Now whenever we include db.inc.php, we are also including our library of common functions. You can add more functions to the library at a later date to perform tasks that you would like to use on your pages.

Understanding the POST and GET Functions

The POST and GET functions above include a few unusual PHP functions that allow them to effectively return a clean post or get value. Below is the code listing for the POST function (which is practically identical to the GET function), with explanations below each bit of code:

```
function POST($var=null) {
```

This defines a new function with an optional first parameter. If the first parameter is not supplied, then its value will be null.

```
if($var === null) {
```

If the first parameter was not supplied, the code will go into this block, returning an entire array with all the variables in the $_POST array having their slashes stripped.

```
$ret = array();
foreach($_POST as $key=>$value) {
  $ret[$key] = POST($key);
  }
```

```
    return $ret;
  }
```

The six lines above loop through the whole $_POST array and call the POST function with the variable name from the loop. When a function in PHP calls itself, it performs a recursive call, which is very useful functionality to have in very specific cases such as this one. Once it calls the POST function for each key in the $_POST array, the function finishes and returns the $ret array.

```
  if(!isset($_POST[$var])) return false;
```

The above line allows a graceful exit from the function if the POST variable simply does not exist. Attempting to access this variable with the standard method would produce a warning that the variable is not defined, but using isset allows us to return the value of false for undefined variables without producing any warnings.

```
  if(get_magic_quotes_gpc()) {
    return stripslashes($_POST[$var]);
  }else{
    return $_POST[$var];
  }
}
```

The last six lines of the function actually check whether the Magic Quotes functionality is enabled in PHP. If so, it returns a post value stripped of any potential extra slashes; if it is disabled, then a regular non-stripped value is returned.

That is all there is to the POST function, which is nothing more than a few if statements and a loop. It is good practice to write similar functions whenever you have a repetitive task that seems to be using the same statements and error checking routines. Remember that once you write a function for one project, it can just be copied and pasted into another — saving you valuable development time and increasing your profits.

Creating the New Record

The new record has to be created on the page that the new record form submits to. You will recall that the form action attribute was set to newEntryResponse.php.

1. Create a new blank PHP page with the name **newEntryResponse.php**.

   Just like any future pages within the blog application, this one will start with the standard include files.

2. Add the standard include files to the new page.

   ```
   <?php require_once('include/db.inc.php'); ?>
   <?php include('blogHeader.php'); ?>
     <td valign="top">
     </td>
   <?php include('blogFooter.php'); ?>
   ```

   The next step is to initialize a FileMaker API add record command, which is identical to the find all command except the name of the function is newAddCommand instead of newFindAllCommand. The add record command will be placed in a newPostCmd variable, which is named to reflect that it is both a post and a command.

3. Place the following PHP code to initialize the new command after including db.inc.php:

   $newPostCmd = $blogDB->newAddCommand('Posts');

   Once the newPostCmd variable contains the correct FileMaker API command, it is time to go to the second step of adding values into the FileMaker fields on the FileMaker Posts layout. As noted earlier in this chapter, fields are added using the setField function on the command object. In this case we are adding two fields.

4. Place the following code below the initialization of the FileMaker add record command:

$newPostCmd->setField('title',POST('title'));
$newPostCmd->setField('body',POST('content'));

Notice how the POST function was used to bring the title and content post form variables straight into the setField function. Now the command object has those two fields filled in and ready to be submitted with the new record.

The third step in the process of creating a new record is to actually execute the command. Just like the find, we simply call the execute function on the command variable and collect the result into the newPost PHP variable:

$newPost = $newPostCmd->execute();

The last step is to check for and exit the script on any errors using an if statement, which should also be familiar from the find all command. The if statement must go after the execute and have newPost as the variable being checked.

5. Add the following three lines of code to check for any errors.

if(FileMaker::isError($newPost)) {
   die('Database Error: '.$newPost->getMessage());
}

Since this is a simple blog post form, we can now present a nice success message to the author of the blog within the HTML code of the page and offer a link back to the home page. This code should be placed into the table cell between the blog header and footer and can be formatted as you desire.

6. Enter the following simple three lines of code:

<h1>Success</h1>
<p>Your post was made successfully. Please go back to the
   <a href="index.php">home page</a> to see it.</p>

Once you are done inserting all the code, test your page by adding a few new records to your database. If something is not working correctly, verify the code you have with Figure 13-3.

```
1   <?php require_once('include/db.inc.php');
2   $newPostCmd = $blogDB->newAddCommand('Posts');
3   $newPostCmd->setField('title',POST('title'));
4   $newPostCmd->setField('body',POST('content'));
5   $newPost = $newPostCmd->execute();
6
7   if(FileMaker::isError($newPost)) {
8       die('Database Error: '.$newPost->getMessage());
9   }
10
11  ?>
12  <?php include('blogHeader.php'); ?>
13          <td valign="top">
14          <h1>Success</h1>
15          <p>Your post was made successfully.  Please go back to the
16          <a href="index.php">home page</a> to see it.</p>
17          </td>
18  <?php include('blogFooter.php'); ?>
```

Figure 13-3: Source code for the newEntryResponse.php form

Sorting with the FileMaker API

The ability to sort information in your FileMaker result set is an essential feature of many queries. The FileMaker API includes three ways to perform sorting: ascending sort, descending sort, and custom sort based on a value list. The sorting parameters have to be added to the FileMaker command after it is created but before it is executed. The general form of the sorting parameter addition is:

> $fmCommand->addSortRule('fieldName', $precedence, $order);

The first parameter of the addSortRule function is the name of the FileMaker field to sort by. The second parameter has to be a sequential number from 1 to 9, starting with 1 and going up to a maximum of nine parameters — this will determine the order in which the sort rules are applied to the result set. The third parameter is the order of the sort; it can take either one of the two special constant PHP values of FILEMAKER_SORT_ASCEND or FILEMAKER_SORT_DESCEND. These have to be used without any quotes or other characters around them. The other option is to supply a string value that identifies a value list on the layout that will be used as the basis for the sort.

Once the sort rules have been added, it is possible to clear all of them using the clearSortRules function on the FileMaker API command. This function does not have any arguments and will clear all the previously added sort rules.

Adding Sorting to the Home Page

Now that you have a few blog posts within your blog database, you might notice that they appear in chronological order on your home page. Blogs are usually shown in reverse chronological order to allow the latest items to be displayed at the very top. In order to have the same functionality on the web with FileMaker, sorting parameters have to be used before executing a command to specify what field to use for sorting. Let's modify the previously created index.php page to list records in reverse chronological order and see your newest posts at the top of the home page.

To add a sorting parameter we have to isolate the point where the FileMaker command object has been created but execute is not yet called on it. If you have a copy of index.php from Chapter 12, then this point is between the following pair of lines:

```
$postsFind = $blogDB->newFindAllCommand('Posts');
$posts = $postsFind->execute();
```

The sorting parameter that we add will sort the data based on the post timestamp field, which is auto entered during field creation. The field name in this case is timestamp. Since this is the only sort rule, it will have a precedence of 1.

1. Enter the following line between the two lines above:

$postsFind->addSortRule('timestamp', 1, FILEMAKER_ SORT_DESCEND);

The new version of your index.php script should resemble Figure 13-4, and the output in the browser should have the newest posts first just like in Figure 13-5.

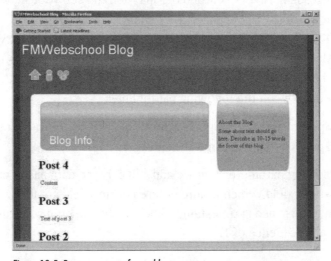

Figure 13-4: Source code for sorting home page

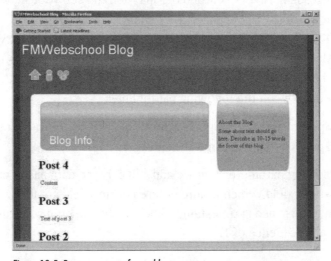

Figure 13-5: Browser output of sorted home page

Summary

Finding and creating records is only the tip of the iceberg when it comes to interacting with FileMaker from the web. With the knowledge you have gained so far, you can already build powerful listing pages of your database information and add simple records. Soon you will be able to edit records and portals, and use value lists all over the site. Take the time to understand the underlying lessons in the previous two chapters and the next few chapters, since they will serve as the foundation for the powerful PHP applications that you will be building for your clients, your office, or yourself!

Chapter 14

Database Searches and Limits

Finding all the records and creating a few new records might not seem like very advanced database functionality within a web site, although it is a very significant achievement in displaying FileMaker data directly to any end user with a browser. Here we will explore the actual detailed finds that power all database-driven systems, allowing you to finally have search forms and create links that point to specific records.

Beyond the Find All

Learning the techniques of using the FileMaker API with the find all command allowed you to see the structure of a FileMaker command without any additional parameters. In this chapter you will use the knowledge from Chapter 13 that includes the setField function along with the structure of a FileMaker command to construct powerful customized queries. This is where interacting with FileMaker from the web becomes exciting and truly dynamic.

There Is Also a Find Any Command

Apart from the usual commands, FileMaker also provides a command that has very limited applications within production systems — the find any command. This command does exactly what its name suggests — finds any random record from the layout specified. While this command is usually not used within most applications, it does have a few interesting uses to the developer during the development process.

One useful application of the find any command is using it in a page that will display search results. Consider the case of building a PHP application with a search page that receives a query from a lengthy form. Let's say, however, you would like to build the results page first and then focus on the forms within your site. In this case, find any provides a good way to get a variety of records that would mimic finding a single record using the search form. Temporarily using find any instead of a regular find in this case shortens your development time and allows you to work with real data immediately. In this case, find any also provides a good variety of data since every time a page is refreshed a different record is displayed.

Within production systems, find any can be used to introduce a random element to a certain location. Some examples of this might be a random page function or a rotating set of advertisements served from a database randomly. The blog application you are building could certainly use the find any command to have a random post functionality that would allow a visitor to your blog to find an interesting random post with a single click of a button. Before implementing this random post functionality, however, let's quickly review how the find any command is called. The find any command is initialized with the newFindAnyCommand that is derived from a FileMaker object and can be immediately executed to receive a result set. To implement this functionality, it is best to create a new page, appropriately named randomPost.php, that will just display a random blog post.

1. The first thing to do to create the random blog post page is to cre-
    ate a quick skeleton page using the blog template. This page
    should have a basic header and footer as well as the connection
    include file. Create a new PHP page, name it **randomPost.php**,
    and insert the code in Figure 14-1 into it.

Figure 14-1: Starting randomPost.php source code

2. Now that you have a blog page ready to go, it is time to initialize
    the find any command and execute it. Since the find any command
    returns a result set, the command and result variables will have
    the prefixes Cmd and Result. Once the command is executed, the
    standard error-handling code is used to trap for any errors. Insert
    the code in Figure 14-2 into the top of your PHP script.

```
1   <?php require_once('include/db.inc.php');
2   $randomPostCmd = $blogDB->newFindAnyCommand('Posts');
3   $randomPostResult = $randomPostCmd->execute();
4
5   if(FileMaker::isError($randomPostResult)) {
6       die('Database Error: '.$randomPostResult->getMessage());
7   }
8
9   ?>
10  <?php include('blogHeader.php'); ?>
11          <td valign="top">
12
13          </td>
14  <?php include('blogFooter.php'); ?>
```

Figure 14-2: Adding the command execution and error handling

3. Now that you have a valid result set returned within the
    randomPostResult variable, it is time to isolate a single record and
    print its contents to the page. Isolating a single record from a
    result set like this one still requires calling the getRecords func-
    tion on the result variable, which will return an array of records.
    However, once the array of records is accessible, we can just
    access the record using the 0 array element. The following code
    would extract the records from the result set and place a record
    into a single variable. Do not insert this into your page since it is
    just to illustrate the 0 array element notation:

    $records = $result->getRecords();
    $record = $records[0];

    Within our example, we will be using the first 0 array element
    notation twice within the echo statements without actually ever
    placing it into a separate record variable. To complete your random
    post PHP page, insert the code from Figure 14-3 into your page.

```php
1   <?php require_once('include/db.inc.php');
2   $randomPostCmd = $blogDB->newFindAnyCommand('Posts');
3   $randomPostResult = $randomPostCmd->execute();
4
5   if(FileMaker::isError($randomPostResult)) {
6       die('Database Error: '.$randomPostResult->getMessage());
7   }
8
9   $randomPost = $randomPostResult->getRecords();
10  ?>
11  <?php include('blogHeader.php'); ?>
12      <td valign="top">
13          <h1><?php echo $randomPost[0]->getField('title'); ?></h1>
14          <p><?php echo $randomPost[0]->getField('body'); ?></p>
15      </td>
16  <?php include('blogFooter.php'); ?>
```

Figure 14-3: Completed randomPost.php script

4. To test this functionality, point your browser to the project folder
    and access randomPost.php. Try refreshing it multiple times; you
    should be able to see random records being accessed and printed,
    as shown in Figure 14-4. Remember that while find any might not

be applicable to most applications, it can add a spice of randomness and dynamic flow to your application when used sparingly.

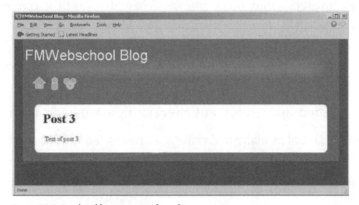

Figure 14-4: Random blog post printed in a browser

Anatomy of a Find

The single find request is one of the core concepts within any database system, and FileMaker is no different. Performing a find command using the FileMaker API involves initializing it with newFindCommand, which as with other commands will expect a layout parameter for your query. Following the command initialization, there are a few different parameters available, such as sorting (which you already know about), database search parameters, and even record range limits. Database search parameters are the core of the advanced search queries since they allow you to isolate blocks of information from within your database. Record ranges, on the other hand, allow you to efficiently traverse large blocks of information using multiple pages of results instead of just a single large result page. We will be taking a look at the search parameters first, followed by record ranges.

About Find Parameters and Logical Operators

Parameters within find commands are added after the command is initialized and before it is executed. Just like adding fields to new records, find parameters have to be added on a field-by-field basis. The function to add find parameters is addFindCriterion, which has the general syntax of:

$findCmd->addFindCriterion('fieldName',$value);

You can add as many find criteria as you would like; however, only one can be specified per field. Attempting to supply the same field name multiple times will result only in the last submitted value affecting the find.

FileMaker offers both OR and AND finds. The OR find will perform logical OR matching, which will return a record if one of the find criteria that you supplied matches the search criteria, while the AND search will only return a specific record in the record set if all the find criteria match within a specific record. The AND query, which is the default FileMaker query, allows exact specific searches. However, we will be using the OR logical search when searching the blog since we want to allow the user to search in both the title and the post body. Overwriting the default AND logical operator is done using the setLogicalOperator function on your command object, which has a single parameter of either FILEMAKER_FIND_AND or FILEMAKER_FIND_OR. The general syntax is:

$findCmd->setLogicalOperator($operator);

Once we review a few important naming limitations, we will use the addFindCriterion function to add a search box to your blog.

Important Field Name Limitations

Before continuing further with learning about the FileMaker API find commands and all the other wonderful functions that the FileMaker API offers to you, it is important to review some limitations of the FileMaker Web Publishing Engine. The FileMaker Web Publishing Engine allows much flexibility in how you name your fields within the layout with one simple exception: Using the period (.) within your field names will render them unusable for FileMaker API commands. The technical reasoning behind this limitation is that the period character is used to specify exact record references; this is never used directly by the user but comes into play when working with portal rows.

Rendering the fields unusable for the specific query only applies to the actual reference to the field in a command. For example, you cannot use such a field name when using setField or addFindCriterion — however, the field is accessible and printable from within the result set. Therefore, if you only need to display a field with a period in its name, then it will be safe to leave it as is. Note, however, that any operations on such a field will produce either the "102 Field is Missing" error or the "401 No Records match the Request" error.

Creating a Blog Search Form

Creating a search form within your blog is just a matter of creating an HTML form that will send data to a search results page. In this case we will name the search results page blogSearch.php, which will expect two variables — a keyword to search and the number of records to skip in the found set. By default, the skipping value will be 0, but as we continue through the chapter the search results page will have paging functionality that will modify this value on every page.

1.   Adding a search form to the blog should be done using an include
     file since you will want to have the search box appear within multi-
     ple pages on your blog. Therefore, let's create a new PHP page to
     store the form HTML as an include file. Create a blank PHP page
     now, placing it next to your other blog files and naming it
     blogSearchForm.php.

2.   Next we will add the actual form to this fresh include file. In this
     case the form will not be a post form but will use the get form
     method; this will place the search parameters into the URL of the
     results page, which is essential for bookmarking search result
     pages. You should always use the get method in pages that search
     data, and the post method on pages that actually modify data. This
     simple get search form should now be inserted into your
     blogSearchForm.php file by adding the code in Figure 14-5.

Figure 14-5: Search form include file source code

3.   The last step in this process is to include this search form as part
     of an existing blog page. index.php is a perfect candidate to have
     this search form. Open up your copy of index.php now and add the
     following line after the blog_info empty paragraph bit:

     <?php include('blogSearchForm.php'); ?>

     The final source code of index.php at this stage should match Fig-
     ure 14-6. The browser output of our simple search form is
     displayed in Figure 14-7.

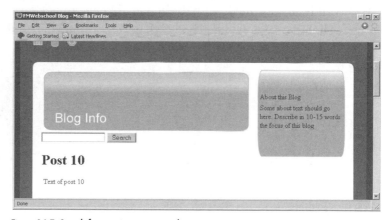

```php
<?php require('include/db.inc.php');
$postsFind = $blogDB->newFindAllCommand('Posts');
$postsFind->addSortRule('timestamp', 1, FILEMAKER_SORT_DESCEND);
$posts = $postsFind->execute();

if(FileMaker::isError($posts)) {
    die('Database Error: '.$posts->getMessage());
}

?>
<?php include('blogHeader.php'); ?>
        <td width="500" valign="top">
            <p class="blog_info"></p>
<?php include('blogSearchForm.php'); ?>
<?php
$postsArray = $posts->getRecords();
foreach($postsArray as $post) {
?>
            <h1><?php echo $post->getField('title'); ?></h1>
            <p><?php echo $post->getField('body'); ?></p>
<?php } ?>
        </td>
<?php include('blogAbout.php'); ?>
<?php include('blogFooter.php'); ?>
```

Figure 14-6: Source code of index.php with the search form

Figure 14-7: Search form as it appears in a browser

Creating the Results Page

Now that everything else is ready, it is finally time to create the search results page and add a powerful search query to it.

1. First, let's create the search results page. Recall that in the search form we referenced blogSearch.php, which appropriately will become the search results page. Create a new blog PHP page and save it as **blogSearch.php**. Since this page will be almost identical to the home page, it makes sense to start with the source code of index.php as the basis of this page. Copy and paste your index.php source code into blogSearch.php now.

2. The next step is to modify the command from a find all to a simple find, leaving the sorting parameter in place; after all, the search results should also be sorted in reverse chronological order. Next we will use addFindCriterion for the first time to set both the title and the body fields with the supplied keyword get variable from the user. The modified find with both criteria will resemble Figure 14-8.

```
1  <?php require('include/db.inc.php');
2  $postsFind = $blogDB->newFindCommand('Posts');
3  $postsFind->addSortRule('timestamp', 1, FILEMAKER_SORT_DESCEND);
4
5  $postsFind->addFindCriterion('title', GET('keyword'));
6  $postsFind->addFindCriterion('body', GET('keyword'));
7
8  $posts = $postsFind->execute();
9
10 if(FileMaker::isError($posts)) {
11     die('Database Error: '.$posts->getMessage());
12 }
13
14 ?>
15 <?php include('blogHeader.php'); ?>
```

Figure 14-8: Find command with two find criteria

3. Now that the find parameters have been added to the search, we have to make this search an OR search. This is done by adding the following simple line somewhere between the command initialization and the command execution:

$postsFind->setLogicalOperator(FILEMAKER_FIND_OR);

Figure 14-9 displays the final source code for the top of this modified index.php page, which is now ready to receive a search query from a search form.

```php
<?php require('include/db.inc.php');
$postsFind = $blogDB->newFindCommand('Posts');
$postsFind->addSortRule('timestamp', 1, FILEMAKER_SORT_DESCEND);

$postsFind->addFindCriterion('title', GET('keyword'));
$postsFind->addFindCriterion('body', GET('keyword'));

$postsFind->setLogicalOperator(FILEMAKER_FIND_OR);

$posts = $postsFind->execute();

if(FileMaker::isError($posts)) {
    die('Database Error: '.$posts->getMessage());
}
```

Figure 14-9: Completed PHP script for blogSearch.php

4. Since we started out with a page that already lists a number of records from the database, the slight modifications to the command above were the only modifications needed for this page. Try this page out now by going to your home page and searching for text within one of your blog posts.

Adding Limits to the Search Results

Now that you have used parameters within your search results, it is
time to look at further find command modifiers.

Using Skip Record Parameters

Skipping records within a find or a find all command has to be specified
using the setRange function before the command is executed. The
setRange function accepts two parameters. The first one is the number of records to skip and the second one is the number of records to
return. The function has the following general syntax:

$command->setRange($skip, $max);

The skip parameter should be a number starting from 0 and specifying
the number of records to skip. For example, using 5 here will place the
sixth record in a found set as the starting record of the result set. The
second parameter is an optional parameter for the number of pages to
return. It should be set to a low number such as 10 or 20 in order to
keep your queries fast and efficient. Please note that the number of
records to return is counted from the skip value; therefore, specifying
a skip of 5 and the maximum number of records as 10 would return
records 6 through 16.

Integrating Limits and Skip to Achieve Paging

Using skipping to limit records is vital in PHP database applications for
both speed optimization purposes and user interface purposes. First of
all, returning smaller result sets will always result in a speed improvement within your application. This improvement is even more
noticeable if the resultant layout has fields that are unstored calculations, which greatly slow down FileMaker API commands. The second
reason to limit records is a bit more obvious. Doing so allows you to
present the user with a manageable list of records and convenient Previous and Next links to browse a larger result set. We will be adding

those links on our search results page in order to browse through the found set.

1.   The first step in implementing a paging system within your application is to specify the actual limit in the find command. Recall that when we were building the search form, we included a hidden variable named skip with a value of 0. This allows us to always have a skip value set even on the first result page. Since now we have this variable within our get form data, we can always access the skip value using GET('skip'). Combining this with the setRange function produces the following line:

$postsFind->setRange(GET('skip'), 3);

As you can see, the maximum value here was set to 3, showing only three records on each result page. You should add the line above right after the setLogicalOperator function to complete the modifications required to the top of blogSearch.php. All the other code will be building the actual Previous and Next links. Figure 14-10 shows the relevant section of blogSearch.php that your code should closely resemble.

```php
<?php require('include/db.inc.php');
$postsFind = $blogDB->newFindCommand('Posts');
$postsFind->addSortRule('timestamp', 1, FILEMAKER_SORT_DESCEND);

$postsFind->addFindCriterion('title', GET('keyword'));
$postsFind->addFindCriterion('body', GET('keyword'));

$postsFind->setLogicalOperator(FILEMAKER_FIND_OR);
$postsFind->setRange(GET('skip'), 3);

$posts = $postsFind->execute();

if(FileMaker::isError($posts)) {
    die('Database Error: '.$posts->getMessage());
}
```

Figure 14-10: Skip limit added to blogSearch.php

2.   Now that we have the skip limit in place and ready to accept requests with a variety of skip get variables, it is time to build the Previous and Next links that will actually provide the user with the properly shifting skip values. The links should go right below the

blogSearchForm.php include, so find that point in your code and start a new PHP code block in that location. First, you have to calculate the appropriate previous and next skip values. Since three records are displayed on each page, the previous skip value will be three less than the current one, and the next skip value will be three more than the current one.

The skip value calculation is performed with a few very simple PHP calculations. If you have trouble understanding the code from this section, please review Chapter 8 for an overview of the PHP comparison operators. We define the prev and next PHP variables that will hold the two values, placing the result of the subtraction and the addition into them:

$prev = GET('skip') – 3;
$next = GET('skip') + 3;

However, on the first page, skip is set to 0; therefore, prev would contain the value 3, which is not a valid point within our result set. A small if statement must be used to bring any negative prev values back to 0:

if($prev < 0) $prev = 0;

This new block of PHP code should be identical to what is shown in Figure 14-11.

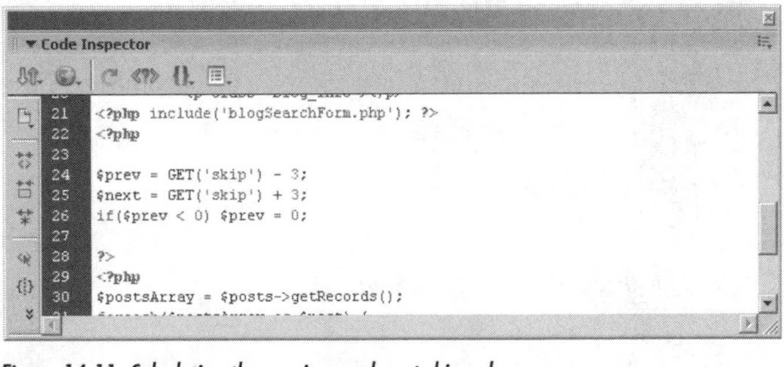

Figure 14-11: Calculating the previous and next skip values

3. Next we have to print the actual links to the page for the user to use. Since the search has a keyword within it as well as the skip value, both of those have to be part of the link as get parameters. Get parameters are variable key/value pairs that appear in a URL after the page name and a question mark, in the following format:

   pageName.php?var1=value1&var2=value2

   In this case, the links will be in the following format:

   blogSearch.php?keyword=searchKeyword&skip=integer

   Printing a link in the following format from within PHP is very simple and takes only three lines per link. This code should be placed below the calculation of the prev and next PHP variables, and will start with printing the opening link <a> tag:

   echo '<a href="blogSearch.php?keyword=';

   Next, the actual keyword value is printed from the current get form data. Notice the use of the urlencode function. This function makes any user-supplied values safe to use within links such as quote characters or spaces that are converted to "%20" with this function:

   echo urlencode(GET('keyword'));

   Then we just print the second get variable for the skip value, followed by the actual link text and a closing <a> tag:

   echo '&skip=' . $prev . '">Previous Page</a>';

4. With that code in place, we also add an extra echo to print some separator characters between the two links and then repeat the three lines above with the next skip value instead. The final result for both links and the separator should closely resemble Figure 14-12.

Figure 14-12: Source code for printing Previous and Next links

5. The last improvement that we will make to these Previous and Next links will be hiding them when there are no more previous or next records. To check if a previous record is possible, we simply check if the current skip value is 0. When it is not 0, the Previous link should be printed. This check is accomplished with the following if statement:

if(GET('skip') != 0) {

As for the Next link, it should not be printed if the next variable value will be more than the number of records within this found set. To find the number of records within the current found set, the FileMaker API provides the getFoundSetCount function. It has to be called on the result variable that was returned from the execute function of the command object. The if statement to compare the next value and the total number of records in the found set is:

if($next < $posts->getFoundSetCount()) {

Both of these if statements should wrap the echo statements for their respective link printing blocks of code. The final source code for this result page should closely resemble Figure 14-13.

```
▼ Code Inspector
21   <?php include('blogSearchForm.php'); ?>
22   <?php
23
24   $next = GET('skip') + 3;
25   $prev = GET('skip') - 3;
26   if($prev < 0) $prev = 0;
27
28   if(GET('skip') != 0) {
29       echo '<a href="blogSearch.php?keyword=';
30       echo urlencode( GET('keyword') );
31       echo '&skip=' . $prev . '">Previous Page</a>';
32
33   }
34
35   echo ' | ';
36
37   if($next < $posts->getFoundSetCount() ) {
38       echo '<a href="blogSearch.php?keyword=';
39       echo urlencode( GET('keyword') );
40       echo '&skip=' . $next . '">Next Page</a>';
41   }
42   ?>
43   <?php
44   $postsArray = $posts->getRecords();
```

Figure 14-13: Source code for search result page navigation links

Exact Searches and Other Modifiers

While knowing how to perform regular searches for FileMaker data is a very valuable skill to have, at times it is necessary to perform much more exact searches for data. For example, if you wanted to look up a specific confirmation number or a primary key from within your FileMaker table, you would want an exact match to be made only if a record were found. This functionality can be very easily achieved on the web using the same operators you would use in FileMaker Pro desktop client software to achieve an exact match, in this case using the "==" prefix before the search term. There are also other prefixes that you can use before a find such as ">," "<," or even the ".." between two parameters for searching ranges of data.

Using prefixes from within PHP with a search query requires the use of PHP string concatenation operators such as "=="to combine a variable with a constant value. For example, adding a find criterion that takes an id variable from the get form data and adding the "==" prefix to it would have the general syntax of:

$command->addFindCriterion('fieldName','==' . GET('id'));

This exact method will be used to create a blog post detail page by adding a Read More link to each blog post on the home page.

Adding a View Blog Post Link

Now that you have a home page with the latest blog posts as well as a searchable archive of your blog content, it is time to expand the functionality of the actual blog post. Currently you are listing the blog posts on the home page as a list; however, we will be adding functions such as commenting for specific blog posts as well as categories that the blog post belongs to. Therefore we need a way to isolate a specific blog post with a link and display only that post with some extra features in its own page. This page will have the name viewPost.php and will be created in the next section. Here, we will create the link to viewPost.php.

1. Open your current copy of index.php and find the location where the output of each post title and post body is being made. The link will be placed between those two lines; for now we will place a quick placeholder link in there:

    **<a href="viewPost.php">Read More</a>
**

2. Now using the placeholder link, we will add an id get variable to it and echo the postId primary key from our Posts layout into the get variable. The full code for this link is:

    **<a href="viewPost.php?id=<?php echo $post->getField('postId'); ?>">Read More</a>
**

The final source code for this link on your index.php page should resemble Figure 14-14.

Figure 14-14: Single blog post link on index.php

Viewing a Single Blog Post Record

With a link pointing to viewPost.php in place, it is time to actually construct the view single post page. This page will be using the passed id variable in the URL to retrieve the specific post record with a matching postId FileMaker field.

1. Create a new blog skeleton page and save the file as **viewPost.php**. Enter the source code shown in Figure 14-15.

Figure 14-15: Initial code for the viewPost.php page

2. Next, we add the find command initialization, placing the command into the findPostCmd PHP variable. Right after the command is initialized, we use the addFindCriterion function to add the search parameter for the postId FileMaker field. Be sure to note that the syntax discussed above is used to prefix the value from the get id variable with "==" for a more exact database search. Right after adding the find criterion, we can execute the command and place the result in a result variable. Add the following code to your page:

```
$findPostCmd = $blogDB->newFindCommand('Posts');
$findPostCmd->addFindCriterion('postId', '==' . GET('id') );
$findPostResult = $findPostCmd->execute();
```

3. The standard error checking is then performed to make sure the search was successful. In this case, the search if statement should be:

```
if(FileMaker::isError($findPostResult)) {
    die('Database Error: '.$findPostResult->getMessage());
}
```

4. Now that we know the result variable does not contain an error object, it is time to retrieve the actual record. Remember that this is a two-step operation of first using getRecords to retrieve all the records and then retrieving the first and only record from the set using the 0 array element. This is done with the following PHP lines that place the single record into the post variable:

```
$posts = $findPostResult->getRecords();
$post = $posts[0];
```

5. Once all of this code has been added to your page above the blogHeader.php include, it is time to print the actual blog contents. This is very similar to any of the other pages we have printed; simply call the getField function on the record that is stored in the post PHP variable. The code to print these lines is:

```
<h1><?php echo $post->getField('title'); ?></h1>
<p><?php echo $post->getField('body'); ?></p>
```

6. Now that all of the code is in place, make sure it is in the correct locations by comparing your source code to Figure 14-16, and then test this functionality in a browser by navigating into a single record.

```
1  <?php require_once('include/db.inc.php');
2  $findPostCmd = $blogDB->newFindCommand('Posts');
3  $findPostCmd->addFindCriterion('postId', '==' . GET('id') );
4  $findPostResult = $findPostCmd->execute();
5
6  if(FileMaker::isError($findPostResult)) {
7      die('Database Error: '.$findPostResult->getMessage());
8  }
9
10  $posts = $findPostResult->getRecords();
11  $post = $posts[0];
12  ?>
13  <?php include('blogHeader.php'); ?>
14      <td valign="top">
15          <h1><?php echo $post->getField('title'); ?></h1>
16          <p><?php echo $post->getField('body'); ?></p>
17      </td>
18  <?php include('blogFooter.php'); ?>
```

Figure 14-16: Full source code for viewing a single post

Summary

This chapter has introduced plenty of new concepts about the different FileMaker find commands. The instructions in this chapter will serve as the basis for future chapters that discuss manipulating record sets or specific parts of records; after all, you must be able to find a record before you can edit or delete it. However, now that you do know how to find records, it is time to learn how to work with them.

Editing and Deleting Records

Editing and deleting records is the next logical step in working with
FileMaker data. Editing or deleting records generally involves a
two-step process of finding the record first and then performing
actions on it.

Overview of the Record Object

The FileMaker API allows you to access data within the database using
a variety of find methods that all return a set of records to the PHP
application. As you already know, the returned record set allows access
to the records within it using the getRecords function, which returns
an array of records. This array of records is a special FileMaker API
object that allows you to perform a variety of functions on it. One such
function that you are already familiar with is the getField command,
which allows you to retrieve the value of a specific field within that
record.

The record object contains functions to modify the field values
within it, setting them to new values ready to be saved back into the
FileMaker database. The record object also has a function to delete
itself or retrieve related portal records that are associated with it. This
chapter will explore the modification, saving, and deleting of records
using the FileMaker record object.

Linking to a Single Editable Record

Before a record can be edited, we need a way to effectively find it and prepare it for modification. This step is usually accomplished by having an Edit Record link that links a specific edit page with the record primary key value, with the link itself appearing on a page that lists the records. Within the blog application, it is best to create a special list of blog posts with links to edit pages. This page will be password protected later when we get to Chapter 19, but for now simply naming it editPosts.php should be enough to keep it private. This page is based on a simplified version of the index.php page and simply prints a list of links to an editPost.php page. Let's create this page now.

1. The first step in creating a page with links is to set up a quick skeleton page with our blog template. Create a new PHP page, naming it **editPosts.php**. This page should have the standard starting code of the blog as it appears in Figure 15-1.

Figure 15-1: Starting source code for editPosts.php

2. Next, add some header text to the page, as well as a dummy link to the editPost.php page that we will be linking to for each post in our blog. Simply add the following code within the <td> tag:

```
<h1>Edit Posts - Select a Post</h1>
<a href="editPost.php?id=">Post Title</a><br>
```

3. With the code above in place, it is time to add a find all command that will find all the posts within the blog. The find all should be sorted in reverse chronological order as usual and include the standard error checking code. The code to add is shown in Figure 15-2.

```
▼ Code Inspector

1   <?php require('include/db.inc.php');
2   $postsFind = $blogDB->newFindAllCommand('Posts');
3   $postsFind->addSortRule('timestamp', 1, FILEMAKER_SORT_DESCEND);
4   $posts = $postsFind->execute();
5
6   if(FileMaker::isError($posts)) {
7       die('Database Error: '.$posts->getMessage());
8   }
9
10  ?>
11  <?php include('blogHeader.php'); ?>
12      <td valign="top">
13          <h1>Edit Posts - Select a Post</h1>
14              <a href="editPost.php?id=">Post Title</a><br>
15      </td>
16  <?php include('blogFooter.php'); ?>
```

Figure 15-2: Source code for find all command and placeholder links

4. The last step of building the list of links is to actually loop through the record set and print links to the page with the get id variable containing the postId of the post in question. The code here has a very similar structure to the other pages that list blog posts with the exception that in this case we are printing two FileMaker fields on the same line — postId is printed into the link's href attribute and the post title is printed as the link text. The completed code should match Figure 15-3, and the output of this page in a browser should resemble Figure 15-4.

```php
<?php require('include/db.inc.php');
$postsFind = $blogDB->newFindAllCommand('Posts');
$postsFind->addSortRule('timestamp', 1, FILEMAKER_SORT_DESCEND);
$posts = $postsFind->execute();

if(FileMaker::isError($posts)) {
    die('Database Error: '.$posts->getMessage());
}

?>
<?php include('blogHeader.php'); ?>
        <td valign="top">
            <h1>Edit Posts - Select a Post</h1>
<?php
$postsArray = $posts->getRecords();
foreach($postsArray as $post) {
?>
            <a href="editPost.php?id=<?php echo $post->getField('postId'); ?>">
            <?php echo $post->getField('title'); ?>
            </a><br>
<?php } ?>
        </td>
<?php include('blogFooter.php'); ?>
```

Figure 15-3: Source code for editPosts.php

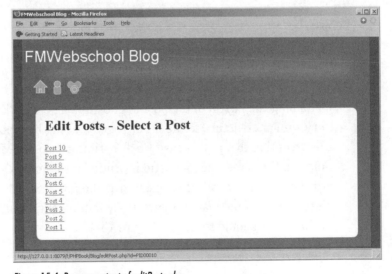

Figure 15-4: Browser output of editPosts.php

Building Editable Forms

Before you can modify a record and save changes, you have to be able to display this record to the user for modification. To display the record to the user, regular form inputs are used with their starting values set dynamically to the current value of the field within the record. Once the form is submitted, the record is found again and isolated for editing. At this stage, the submitted values are placed into the updated FileMaker fields and the entire record is saved back to the database.

Whenever you are faced with building an editable form, it is best to perform the following steps:

- Build the HTML form, including PHP echo statements where input element values should be.

- Build the record retrieval code that isolates the specific record in question.

- Test the form to make sure that all values are filled in properly.

- Add post data detection to the form, saving changes to the record whenever data is submitted to it.

The first step usually takes some time with your favorite HTML editor in order to get the look and feel that you desire for your form. The PHP echo statements should be added with an appropriate variable name and a getField function for this form. This requires a bit of fore-thought, but you can generally do this step before writing the record retrieval code itself. For example, an input with a PHP code with a post variable that would hold the record object would be:

```
<input name="title" type="text" value="<?php echo
$post->getField('title'); ?>">
```

It is also very important to include a record identifier into the form's action attribute since the page that will be processing this form must know which record you are browsing. For example, in the case of the editPost.php page that we will create shortly, the action attribute will be the same page with the postId passed in as part of the URL:

<form method="post" action="editPost.php?id=<?php echo $post->getField('postId'); ?>">

Next you would add the FileMaker API find command to the top of this page to isolate the actual FileMaker record and place it into the post object, which is then used throughout the form to fill it in. This is a good time to test your form since it can be filled in with real database data. Once you have tested the form and made sure that all the values are being properly filled in, it is time to add code that will accept a submitted form and use the record object to edit the record. Editing a record with a FileMaker API record object involves calling a number of setField functions for each field that you are modifying and then calling the commit command that will use the supplied data to update the record. Note that now the record object contains the new data and will print it accordingly in the rest of your script.

Editable forms usually use the same edit and response page, which means that the form's action attribute would be pointing at the current form's edit page. This method allows you to build the form once and just use a little bit of conditional logic to update the record if a form has been submitted. The updated record object will then reflect the newly submitted values when printing the filled-in form. At this stage, a variable is added to hold a message such as "Your changes have been saved." This variable is conditionally displayed to users so they know that even though it is still the same page, the record has actually been saved. With all this theory out of the way, let's try applying this to the editing of a single post; within a few minutes you should have a form that both displays and saves FileMaker data!

Building the Edit Post Script

As outlined in the previous section, building a filled-in form starts with building the HTML and then adding the relevant PHP code to retrieve the data that will be filled in on the form.

1. The first step in building this form is to create the PHP page. Since this page has links to it already on editPosts.php, it should be named **editPost.php**. Note that the form's action attribute should be pointing to this same page with the same ID value. Create this page now, using the source code in Figure 15-5 to create the actual filled-in form.

```
1   <?php require_once('include/db.inc.php');
2
3   ?>
4   <?php include('blogHeader.php'); ?>
5       <td valign="top">
6           <h1>Editing a Post</h1>
7           <p>Please use this form to post a new blog entry</p>
8           <form method="post" action="editPost.php?id=<?php echo $post->getField('postId'); ?>">
9               <input type="hidden" name="action" value="editEntry">
10              <table width="300">
11                  <tr>
12                      <th>Title</th>
13                      <td><input name="title" type="text" id="title" value="<?php echo $post->getField('title'); ?>"></td>
14                  </tr>
15                  <tr>
16                      <th>Content</th>
17                      <td><textarea name="content" cols="70" rows="8"><?php echo $post->getField('body'); ?></textarea></td>
18                  </tr>
19                  <tr>
20                      <th> </th>
21                      <td><input type="submit" name="Submit" value="Save Changes"></td>
22                  </tr>
23              </table>
24          </form>
25      </td>
26  <?php include('blogFooter.php'); ?>
```

Figure 15-5: Basic HTML form with minimal PHP

2. Now that this form is built, it is time to access the FileMaker database and place a record into the post variable. Since we are passing in postId through the link, it will be contained in the id get form variable and will be set as an exact search within the find. Once the find is executed and checked for any errors, we isolate its result into the post variable, which is then used within the form to

fill in the values. The source code for this find, error checking, and record isolation is found in Figure 15-6.

```
<?php require_once('include/db.inc.php');
$findPostCmd = $blogDB->newFindCommand('Posts');
$findPostCmd->addFindCriterion('postId', '==' . GET('id') );
$findPostResult = $findPostCmd->execute();

if(FileMaker::isError($findPostResult)) {
    die('Database Error: '.$findPostResult->getMessage());
}

$posts = $findPostResult->getRecords();
$post = $posts[0];
?>
<?php include('blogHeader.php'); ?>
        <td valign="top">
          <h1>Editing a Post</h1>
          <p>Please use this form to post a new blog entry</p>
          <form method="post" action="editPost.php?id=<?php echo $post->getField('postId'); ?>">
            <input type="hidden" name="action" value="editEntry">
            <table width="300">
```

Figure 15-6: FileMaker API find for a single post

3. Since this form is pointing to the same script in its action attribute, if statements have to be used in order to distinguish whether this is a display of a filled-in form or a display with a save action. Note that the filled-in form submits a hidden variable called action with the text of editEntry; this will be used in the if statement as the trigger for the save, since it will only appear as a post variable when the form has been saved. Let's add that if statement right now on the line right after assigning the FileMaker record object to the post variable:

    if(POST('action') == 'editEntry') {
    }

4. With the if statement in place we are ready to add code that will modify the record in the if block. The code that we are using will first perform a number of setField commands, which you might remember from creating a new record, on the record object to update the fields. Following the setField calls, the commit function will be called; it will return either a value of true or a FileMaker error object. The following three lines should be added to the if statement above:

```
$post->setField('title', POST('title'));
$post->setField('body',POST('content'));
$result = $post->commit();
```

5. Now that this code is in place, the result variable will contain the result of this operation. It is very important to conduct error checking at this point and report any problems back to the users; otherwise, they will be under the impression that everything has worked perfectly and their modifications are saved. Before performing error checking, however, we should set up a system that allows us to easily show an error message to the user using a PHP variable. The first thing to do to set this up is to define the variable as blank for cases when there are no messages. This line should be placed before the if statement above to do just that:

```
$message = '';
```

With this message variable in place, we should then place a conditional if statement into the printable part of your HTML code to display it to the user. The following line to print an error message should be placed right before the opening tag of your HTML form:

```
<?php if($message != '') echo '<p><span
style="color:red;">'.$message.'</span></p>'; ?>
```

The if statement makes sure that nothing is printed there when the message remains empty.

6. Now that the message collection and printing functionality is in place, the last step in the form editing process is to add error checking code and set the message variable to either a success message or the error description. Find the if statement that edits the record and captures the result into a variable, and add the following code, staying within the if statement:

```
if(FileMaker::isError($result)) {
    $message = 'Error saving your record: '.$result->
                getMessage();
}else{
```

$message = 'Thank you, the changes have been saved';
   }

7. Now that all the code is in place, it should be very similar to Figure
    15-7. Take a minute to verify the location of both the if statement
    and the message printing code.

```
▼ Code Inspector
10   $posts = $findPostResult->getRecords();
11   $post = $posts[0];
12
13   $message = '';
14   if(POST('action') == 'editEntry') {
15       $post->setField('title', POST('title'));
16       $post->setField('body',POST('content'));
17       $result = $post->commit();
18       if(FileMaker::isError($result)) {
19           $message = 'Error saving your record: '.$result->getMessage();
20       }else{
21           $message = 'Thank You, the changes have been saved';
22       }
23   }
24
25   ?>
26   <?php include('blogHeader.php'); ?>
27           <td valign="top">
28             <h1>Editing a Post</h1>
29             <p>Please use this form to post a new blog entry</p>
30   <?php if($message != '') echo '<p><span style="color:red;">'.$message.'</span></p>'; ?>
31             <form method="post" action="editPost.php?id=<?php echo $post->getField('postId'); ?>">
32               <input type="hidden" name="action" value="editEntry">
33               <table width="300">
34                 <tr>
35                   <th>Title</th>
```

Figure 15-7: Final source code for editPost.php

   This is a good time to try running this form and editing a record. The
   first time you access the form, a filled form should be displayed. When
   that form is submitted, you should receive a success message within
   your form with the option of further editing this record. Figure 15-8
   displays a record that was just edited and a success message.

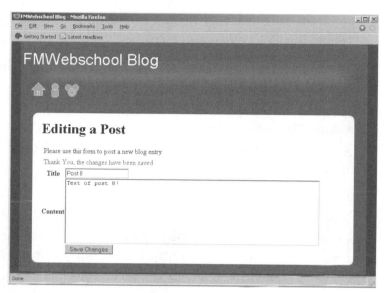

Figure 15-8: Browser output of an edited record

Deleting Records

Deleting records using the FileMaker API is even simpler than editing them. All it requires is a single function and a redirect to a success page. We will now add a Delete button to the edit post page to allow you to remove an unwanted blog post. Deleting a record requires you to have the record object in a variable and then call the delete function on that record.

1. The delete functionality will be implemented as another form that will have a Delete Record button and will send a deleteEntry action variable. This form should once again submit to its own page; in this case, editPost.php with the id get variable as part of the action form attribute. This form should have a Submit button with the text that the user will see and press, as well as a hidden field for an action post variable that will be used to send the actual

action to PHP. Add this code now after the other form block at the bottom of your page to create this form:

```
<form method="post" action="editPost.php?id=<?php
echo $post->getField('postId'); ?>">
<input type="hidden" name="action"
value="deleteEntry">
<input type="submit" name="button" value="Delete
Record">
</form>
```

2. Now that the form is in place, it is time to add another if statement to the top of your page that will perform an action when the action post variable contains deleteEntry. Place this if statement block after the if statement block that checks for editEntry:

```
if(POST('action') == 'deleteEntry') {
}
```

3. Within this if statement, the record can now be deleted and its result checked with the usual error checking code. If the delete was unsuccessful, then the filled form is shown once again with the appropriate error message; however, if the record was deleted successfully, then there is no filled form to show and a redirect should be made. The following code implements this delete and redirects the user back to the list of posts for editing. This should be placed within the if statement you created above:

```
$result = $post->delete();
if(FileMaker::isError($result)) {
   $message = 'Error deleting your record: '.$result->
              getMessage();
}else{
   header('Location: editPosts.php');
}
```

Both of the if statements for editing and deleting can be verified with
Figure 15-9.

```
▼ Code Inspector
10   $posts = $findPostResult->getRecords();
11   $post = $posts[0];
12
13   $message = '';
14   if(POST('action') == 'editEntry') {
15       $post->setField('title', POST('title'));
16       $post->setField('body',POST('content'));
17       $result = $post->commit();
18       if(FileMaker::isError($result)) {
19           $message = 'Error saving your record: '.$result->getMessage();
20       }else{
21           $message = 'Thank You, the changes have been saved';
22       }
23   }
24
25   if(POST('action') == 'deleteEntry') {
26       $result = $post->delete();
27       if(FileMaker::isError($result)) {
28           $message = 'Error deleting your record: '.$result->getMessage();
29       }else{
30           header('Location: editPosts.php');
31       }
32   }
33
34   ?>
```

Figure 15-9: Source code for editing and deleting records

Summary

This chapter completes the overview of the basic functionality offered
by a database system. With the knowledge you've gained by this point,
you should be able to construct a full database application that
searches, creates, edits, and deletes records. FileMaker, however,
offers a few other interesting capabilities to developers. The two most
significant capabilities that are unique to FileMaker and the FileMaker
PHP API are portals for accessing related records and value lists for
storing lists of data within the database. The rest of this book will
focus on those functions as well as other more advanced PHP-specific
chapters.

Working with Data Portals

Data portals provide FileMaker with extremely rapid relational database capabilities. They are an essential feature of FileMaker and have been a major selling point of the product for years. Portals are tables within a FileMaker layout containing a list of related records, commonly from a one-to-many relationship, that can be created, edited, and deleted without any additional scripting for connecting the foreign keys of the two records together. The FileMaker API for the first time allows portal records to be created, edited, and deleted; previously only reading and creating records was supported. This chapter begins with an overview of the structure that the FileMaker API uses to power portals on the web and provides a practical example of adding, deleting, and editing portal records when working with categories for a blog post.

Reviewing Related Records and Portals

Using portals in FileMaker Pro clients requires first creating a portal object on the FileMaker layout that includes the name of the related table from which the records should be populated as well as some editable fields on each row of the portal object for that record. These editable fields within the record object allow transparent editing of related records through a FileMaker relationship that is specified in the relationship graph. Be sure to review the next section for the proper setup of your portals for the web.

Related Record Portal Web Requirements

Just like any other FileMaker fields on the web, portals must be on the requested layout in order to be accessible from the web. Furthermore, portals must also have the fields that you intend to read or edit set as the actual field object. Using merge fields or text within the portal object, or any other merge fields for that matter, will make them invisible on the web. The web user also must have the permissions to access the related records and the layout that you are using. If you ever have trouble using a specific portal, try to log in to your database using a FileMaker Pro desktop client with the web user account and see if the portal is working properly.

Using global fields within your portal relationships can introduce unpredictable and hard to debug behavior with the Web Publishing Engine. Generally, global fields cannot be saved in between FileMaker API calls and have to be set to their proper value with each call. Thus, using global fields within relationship definitions can produce lists of records that are highly different from the lists you would expect with a relationship that works perfectly within the FileMaker Pro desktop client software.

Notable Limitations

Portals have a few limitations that are notable on the web for their effect on system performance. Portals that are used on standard FileMaker layouts will often display data five to 10 records at a time, allowing a list with potentially thousands of related records to be easily scrolled through and manipulated. This list is fetched by FileMaker Pro client software on demand as the scrolling and navigation through it is initiated. On the web, however, the story becomes a bit different: Once a record is fetched, all the related records for that record will be returned, with a significant performance penalty in both data transfer and result set XML parsing that is performed within the FileMaker API.

Consequently, paging of related records is not natively supported but can be implemented within PHP using a combination of get variables and loops that start in the middle of the related set result array. However, this method of paging is inefficient since on each page data from all the related record pages has to be loaded into PHP before paging is implemented. In these cases, it is best to use a separate find command with the appropriate foreign key inside the page that searches in a layout containing the related records themselves, allowing you to page through that result set properly.

Portal Workflow within PHP

Despite all these warnings, limitations, and prerequisites, portals allow very powerful record editing schemes that would take hours to implement as manual relationships between FileMaker tables. Now that you know the prerequisites and assumptions about portals, it is time to review how we would access portal records from within PHP. The portal workflow can be broken down into a number of logical steps that are taken to isolate a specific portal row and manipulate it.

1. First of all, the parent record that contains the portal rows you want to edit has to be found using a FileMaker API find command and isolated into a record variable. Once this record is found, related records can be added to it, read from it, and then edited or deleted.

2. With the parent FileMaker API record object isolated, you can now add a portal row by calling the newRelatedRecord command on it with the first parameter being the name of the related table occurrence that the portal is using. This function returns a record object that is ready to have its fields filled in with values and then committed into the database. The general syntax for this operation is:

    $relatedRecord = $record->newRelatedRecord ('relatedSetName');
    $relatedRecord->setField('relatedSetName::fieldName');
    $relatedRecord->commit();

3. All portal operations other than creating new related records require you to access the portal related record collection first and retrieve specific portal records. This is accomplished using the getRelatedSet function on the record object with the first parameter being the name of the related table occurrence that the portal is using. This function returns an array of FileMaker record objects, each representing a row within the portal.

4. The array of record objects can now be used as an array of records to print them out to the user, or edit or delete records.

5. When the related set is modified, such as deleting or adding records, it is a good idea to reload the result page or refresh the parent record object by fetching it again from the database.

Generally, once you have a clear understanding of each step in the process above, working with related records becomes quite easy and natural. The hardest part of the process is isolating specific records from within an array of related records, which just involves a quick loop and comparison of record IDs.

Accessing a Related Set of Data

Before creating, editing, or deleting related records, it is best to create a script that can list those records. Implementing this example as part of the blog is very simple. We will be using it to add a system that can add, remove, and edit categories for a single post. Categories within a blog allow your posts to be organized better within your database, and some advanced blogging systems allow browsing through the posts using the tags. Using tags as related records is a perfect example of their power since you can have multiple tags per blog post and want to be able to manipulate them effortlessly. We will start this example by editing the editPost.php page from the previous chapter since it already finds a record for us and we can jump straight into related records.

Make sure before continuing that you have a few records with some categories listed in them. If you are unsure about which records have related portal records, open the FileMaker database now and add some categories to a few records. Then it is best to go to editPosts.php and select the record that has the categories; with that record open you will be able to follow the example below and occasionally refresh it to see real progress.

1. Let's start learning about related records by opening up a previous
    copy of editPost.php, which you created in Chapter 15, or by copy-
    ing it from the sample files package under Chapter 15. Once the
    file is open, we will begin by adding an empty list to the end of it
    that will house the dynamic list of related records associated with
    this record. We will create a second-level header for this area of
    the page and then use the unsorted list <ul> tag and the list item
    <li> tags to list the actual categories. Add the code in Figure 16-1
    to editPost.php, making sure to place it between the </form> and
    </td> tags.

Figure 16-1: Source code for skeleton category list

2. The next step is to retrieve the list of records from the current
    post. This operation will be done before printing the list items
    but after the starting <ul> tag. The first step is using the
    getRelatedSet function to retrieve an array of categories, so add
    the following line into a new PHP code block between the <ul>
    and the <li> tags:

    $categories = $post->getRelatedSet('Categories');

    Once this line is executed, it will return an array of records. If
    there are no related records, however, a FileMaker API error will
    be returned. At this stage it is safe to assume that an error means

no records were found. The best way to compensate for that with PHP is to set the variable back to an empty array. This error checking should be placed right after assigning the related set to the categories variable, and should have the following code:

if(FileMaker::isError($categories)) {

  $categories = array();

}

3. Next, we create a loop around the area that will be repeated for each related record. This is as simple as adding a foreach before the <li> tag and then a closing <?php } ?> line after the <li> tag:

foreach($categories as $category) {

?>

<li>Post Category</li>

<?php } ?>

Once all this code is combined and placed in the correct location, it should closely resemble Figure 16-2. Notice that if you try loading the page now it will print the correct number of categories, but for each line in the list only "Post Category" will be displayed. Adding the dynamic getField action is our next step.

```
▼ Code Inspector
63              <h2>Post Categories</h2>
64              <ul>
65  <?php
66  $categories = $post->getRelatedSet('Categories');
67  if(FileMaker::isError($categories)) {
68      $categories = array();
69  }
70
71  foreach($categories as $category) {
72  ?>
73              <li>Post Category</li>
74  <?php } ?>
75              </ul>
76
77          </td>
78  <?php include('blogFooter.php'); ?>
```

Figure 16-2: Code to retrieve a list of related records

4. Once the loop is in place, it is time to print real category names into this list. Working with related record objects is identical to working with regular record objects. (This is one of the advantages of the FileMaker PHP API — its attempt to maintain consistency throughout all its functions.) However, there is a slight difference in naming conventions here that you might have seen within your FileMaker layout already: The field name in a related record includes both the related set name and the field name. This means that in our example the name of the related category field will be "Categories::category," which is identical to the way it appears on your FileMaker layout. Add this to the PHP page with the following line, which should replace the previous <li> block tag:

<li><?php echo $category->getField('Categories::category'); ?></li>

5. At this stage the page is now ready to display related records. Verify your code with Figure 16-3 now to make sure everything appears in the correct order and then test a page out in your browser; the output should closely resemble Figure 16-4.

```
▼ Code Inspector
63              <h2>Post Categories</h2>
64              <ul>
65  <?php
66  $categories = $post->getRelatedSet('Categories');
67  if(FileMaker::isError($categories)) {
68      $categories = array();
69  }
70
71  foreach($categories as $category) {
72  ?>
73              <li><?php echo $category->getField('Categories::category'); ?></li>
74  <?php } ?>
75          </ul>
76
77      </td>
78  <?php include('blogFooter.php'); ?>
```

Figure 16-3: Final source code of printing a related set

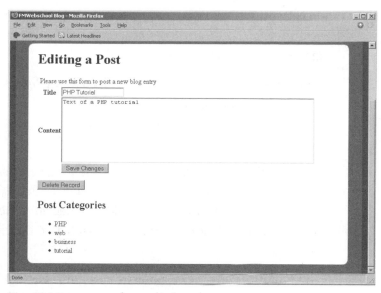

Figure 16-4: Browser output of some related records

Adding a New Related Record

The next logical step after listing some related records is adding a new one to the list. This is the easiest related record action to perform after displaying the records themselves. In this example, a new category will be added using an empty input box under the list of categories. Once the new record is added, the page will be refreshed to reflect the changed record.

1. In this example we are continuing to develop the editPost.php page, which now lists all the categories associated with a blog post. The next step is to add the input form for a new category. Just like the other input forms on this page, its action will be pointing to editPost.php with the postId variable of the current blog post. The form will also have a hidden action variable that will contain addCategory, easily allowing us to detect this action with an if statement and perform the related record addition. This form

should start before the opening <ul> tag in your list of categories, right after the Post Categories header. Insert the following two lines at that location now:

**<form method="post" action="editPost.php?id=<?php echo $post->getField('postId'); ?>">
<input type="hidden" name="action" value="addCategory">**

Next we will add the actual form inputs. It is a good idea to make these form inputs part of the list to make it clear that this will add a new item. This input li block should be added after the closing foreach loop PHP block of <?php } ?> but before the closing <ul> tag:

<li><input type="text" name="category"> <input type="submit" name="button" value="Add"></li>

At last we add the closing <form> tag right after the </ul> tag and before the </td> tag. The completed code for this section is reflected in Figure 16-5.

```
▼ Code Inspector
68. ⊙.  C  ⟨?⟩ {}, ▤,
63          <h2>Post Categories</h2>
64          <form method="post" action="editPost.php?id=<?php echo $post->getField('postId'); ?>">
65              <input type="hidden" name="action" value="addCategory">
66          <ul>
67  <?php
68  $categories = $post->getRelatedSet('Categories');
69  if(FileMaker::isError($categories)) {
70      $categories = array();
71  }
72
73  foreach($categories as $category) {
74  ?>
75              <li><?php echo $category->getField('Categories::category'); ?></li>
76  <?php } ?>
77  <li><input type="text" name="category"> <input type="submit" name="button" value="Add"></li>
78          </ul>
79
80          </form>
81      </td>
82  <?php include('blogFooter.php'); ?>
```

Figure 16-5: HTML form to add a new category

Trying to use this page in a browser would now display the input box and the Add button as part of your list, as shown in Figure 16-6.

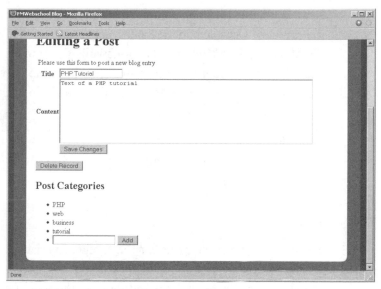

Figure 16-6: Browser view of the input box as part of the list

2. The next step is to create the actual code that detects the addCategory action and executes the appropriate FileMaker API function to add the portal record. Start by finding the if statement block that checks if the post action variable is deleteEntry, and place your cursor after this block. Now it's time to add the if statement for the addCategory value of the post action variable:

```
if(POST('action') = = 'addCategory') {
}
```

3. With the if statement in place, the rest of the code will be going into the if statement block. We start by calling the FileMaker API function that creates the new related record, newRelatedRecord. This function takes the name of the related table as its first parameter:

```
$category = $post->newRelatedRecord('Categories');
```

4. Next we should be doing some error checking to make sure that the category variable contains an actual record and not a FileMaker API error object. The following if statement will accomplish this. Remember that this still goes within the previous if statement since if statements can be nested within each other and are often structured that way:

    if(FileMaker::isError($category)) {
    $message = 'Error adding category: '.$result->
    getMessage();
    }else{
    }

5. Now that the error checking for the category variable is in place, it is time to work within the else block of that if statement to add the actual field modification code. In this case, the else statement will contain all the code that should be executed when the category has been successfully created. The code to execute on the new related record object is the setField operation, followed by the commit operation, which saves data into the new related record. An important note here is that just like with getField, the related field name has to have both the related table name and the field name; in our case, Categories::category. The following two lines perform the setField and commit. Place them within the else block of the if statement:

    $category->setField('Categories::category',POST
    ('category'));
    $result = $category->commit();

6. The last thing to do is check if the result is an error. If it is not, then we will refresh this page to reflect the modifications to the record. This error checking code is similar to all the other blocks:

    if(FileMaker::isError($result)) {
    $message = 'Error saving category: '.$result->
    getMessage();

```
}else{
  header('Location: editPost.php?id='.GET('id'));
}
```

7. The code for this operation is now complete and ready for testing. Open up your web browser and point it to editPosts.php, selecting a post with some categories within it. Then add a new category and watch it appear under the categories list. If you were to check FileMaker Pro now, you would see that the new data is reflected within the portal.

```
34  if(POST('action') == 'addCategory') {
35      $category = $post->newRelatedRecord('Categories');
36      if(FileMaker::isError($category)) {
37          $message = 'Error adding category: '.$result->getMessage();
38      }else{
39          $category->setField('Categories::category',POST('category'));
40          $result = $category->commit();
41          if(FileMaker::isError($result)) {
42              $message = 'Error saving category: '.$result->getMessage();
43          }else{
44              header('Location: editPost.php?id='.GET('id'));
45          }
46      }
47  }
48
```

Figure 16-7: Completed source code to add a related record

Creating related records is a very big step in making your database applications dynamic and truly relational. Once you have mastered this record creation skill — along with the rest of the editing and deleting topics in this chapter — you will be able to create complex forms and multiline systems such as shopping carts, and perform much more advanced data manipulation.

Isolating a Related Record

Before a record can be edited or deleted, it has to be found and placed into a PHP variable. You already know this from the previous chapter, as it applies to records found using a FileMaker API find command. Related records within the FileMaker API are no different; they certainly have to be found first and then edited or deleted. However, there is no easy mechanism to find a specific related record with a parent record; you have to find the parent record using the standard FileMaker API methods and then isolate the specific related record using its record ID. This is accomplished by looping through the related records array, just as you do to print the related records, and using an if statement combined with the FileMaker API getRecordId function to isolate the specific record object. Here, we will be creating a link to a separate page that edits categories as they are linked from the editPost.php page.

Creating a Related Record Edit Link

Creating a related record link is a simple process with two very important requirements. The first requirement is that just like any other record link, it has to refer somehow to the parent record just like the id get variable in the URL of the editPost.php page. The second requirement is that along with the parent ID, the link also has to identify the actual related record. The FileMaker API record getRecordId function is very convenient to use for this identifier. For the Edit Category link, we will first build the link URL in a variable and then print it as part of the HTML list that lists the categories.

1. The first step is to isolate the correct location to build the link URL within the editPost.php script. The best location for this step is right after the beginning of the categories loop, since each time the loop starts we want to generate a fresh link URL for that specific category. Therefore, place the following two lines within the PHP block right after the beginning of the foreach loop. Note how the postId of the current post now goes into the postId get variable and the record ID goes into the id get variable:

   $link = 'editCategory.php?postId='.$post->getField ('postId');
   $link.= '&id='.$category->getRecordId();

2. Next we have to print the actual linking HTML code; in this case, it's a simple <a> tag. The link will be in the following format, where categoryText is the name of the current category:

   categoryText [Edit Category]

   In order to create such a link, move the closing <li> tag that is part of the getField line two lines below. Then add the following line before the closing <li> tag on the empty line that you have just created:

   [<a href="<?php echo $link; ?>">Edit Category</a>]

3. The editPost.php page is now complete. It links to a page that will find and isolate the related record and present it to the user for editing. The completed code for this page is reflected in Figure 16-8, and the browser output of the Edit Category links can be seen in Figure 16-9.

```
▼ Code Inspector
87
88   foreach($categories as $category) {
89   $link = 'editCategory.php?postId='.$post->getField('postId');
90   $link.= '&id='.$category->getRecordId();
91   ?>
92                  <li><?php echo $category->getField('Categories::category'); ?>
93   [<a href="<?php echo $link; ?>">Edit Category</a>]
94                  </li>
95   <?php } ?>
96   <li><input type="text" name="category"> <input type="submit" name="button" value="Add">
```

Figure 16-8: Source code of a related record link

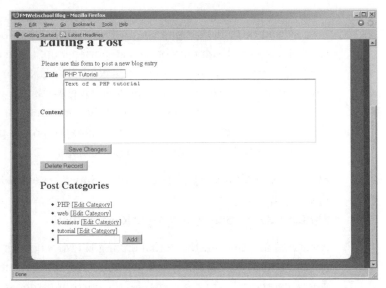

Figure 16-9: Browser output of related record links

The related linking process is now almost complete. With the link in place, the only remaining thing to do is create the editCategory.php page that will show the current value within the category and allow it to be saved.

Isolating the Linked Related Record

The link we just created points to editCategory.php, a page that up to this point does not exist but is assumed to be supplying the category editing services to the user. In this section we will build this page to both edit the related record and be able to delete it.

1. Create a new blank PHP page, naming it **editCategory.php**. This page will have the usual blog template skeleton code, as well as the if statement from the previous editPost.php page for any messages that we might want to display to the user. Be sure to enter the source code shown in Figure 16-10 before continuing further.

```
▼ Code Inspector
1   <?php require_once('include/db.inc.php');
2   $message = '';
3   ?>
4   <?php include('blogHeader.php'); ?>
5           <td valign="top">
6               <h1>Editing a Category</h1>
7               <p>Please use this form to edit a category</p>
8   <?php if($message != '') echo '<p><span style="color:red;">'.$message.'</span></p>'; ?>
9
10          </td>
11  <?php include('blogFooter.php'); ?>
```

Figure 16-10: Starting source code for editCategory.php

2.   Next we add the code to find the parent record. This code block is almost identical to the beginning of editPost.php with a slight modification. Since this time the link uses the get variable postId to pass in the postId, we will have to adjust it accordingly. This block of code, combined with the appropriate error checking, is shown in Figure 16-11.

```
▼ Code Inspector
1   <?php require_once('include/db.inc.php');
2
3   $findPostCmd = $blogDB->newFindCommand('Posts');
4   $findPostCmd->addFindCriterion('postId', '==' . GET('postId') );
5   $findPostResult = $findPostCmd->execute();
6
7   if(FileMaker::isError($findPostResult)) {
8       die('Database Error: '.$findPostResult->getMessage());
9   }
10
11  $posts = $findPostResult->getRecords();
12  $post = $posts[0];
13
14  $message = '';
15  ?>
16  <?php include('blogHeader.php'); ?>
```

Figure 16-11: Standard find of parent record

3.   Now we need to retrieve the related record array from the found parent record. This retrieval is very similar to the foreach loop used within the editPost.php page, except that this time nothing is printed during the foreach loop. We will start this block right after the post PHP variable is isolated using the $post = $posts[0]; statement, first defining a variable to hold our found category record:

$foundCategory = false;

Notice that foundCategory is set to false by default. This allows us to detect whether the selected category was not found, since in that case it will just remain false. Next, we retrieve the related set and check it for errors, setting the categories array to an empty array in case of an error:

```
$categories = $post->getRelatedSet('Categories');
if(FileMaker::isError($categories)) {
    $categories = array();
}
```

Once we have the categories related set in an array, it is time to loop through each category and check if it is the currently selected record. Let's create just the foreach loop itself at this time into which we will insert further code:

```
foreach($categories as $category) {
}
```

That completes the step of retrieving the entire categories related set. Verify your code with that shown in Figure 16-12.

```
▼ Code Inspector

    15
    16    $foundCategory = false;
    17    $categories = $post->getRelatedSet('Categories');
    18    if(FileMaker::isError($categories)) {
    19        $categories = array();
    20    }
    21    foreach($categories as $category) {
    22
    23    }
    24
```

Figure 16-12: Retrieval of the related record set

4. Once the categories foreach loop has been set up to loop through all records, it is time to add the if statement to it. This if statement will compare the record ID of the current category and the id get variable that was passed into the page. The record ID of the current category is accessed by calling the getRecordId function on the category variable, while the id get variable is accessed with

the standard GET function. The following is the if statement to place into the foreach loop:

```
if($category->getRecordId() == GET('id')) {
    $foundCategory = $category;
}
```

5. Once the if statement has been added to the foreach loop, we should check that a category was actually found. This is very simple to do by comparing the value of foundCategory after the loop and seeing if it's still false or now set to something else. The code to perform this error check is:

```
if($foundCategory == false) {
    die('Category not found');
}
```

The completed block of code for both finding the related record and checking if it was found during the loop is reflected in Figure 16-13.

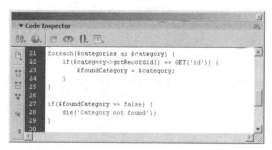

Figure 16-13: Isolating a specific related record using a record ID

6. Now that the related record is isolated within the foundCategory variable, it can be printed back to the user. In this case, the related record values will be used to fill in the form elements and then edit the related record. The form should be created right after the conditional printing of the message variable, and must include both the postId and the related record ID as part of its action attribute. The following code starts this form:

```
<form method="post" action="editCategory.php?postId=
<?php echo $post->getField('postId'); ?>&id=<?php echo
$foundCategory->getRecordId(); ?>">
</form>
```

7. Next, we need to add a hidden action variable to this form and the appropriate text input area for the category. First, we add the following code into the form to create the editCategory action post variable:

```
<input type="hidden" name="action"
value="saveCategory">
```

Then we place both a text input and a Submit button into the form. The text input starting value is dynamically printed using the getField function on the foundCategory variable:

```
<p>
<input type="text" name="category" value="<?php echo
$foundCategory->getField('Categories::category'); ?>">
<input type="submit" value="Save">
</p>
```

The completed source code for this form is reflected in Figure 16-14.

Figure 16-14: HTML form display a single related record

This is a good time to try loading this page in a browser by following a link to any category from the editPost.php page. The form should be filled in with the name of the category, and the browser should resemble Figure 16-15.

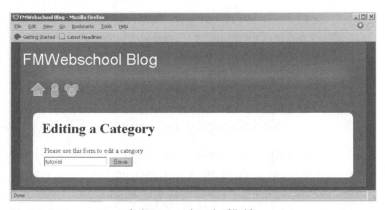

Figure 16-15: Browser output of editCategory.php with a filled form

Now that the single related record is isolated and entered into a form, it can be submitted back to the page for saving. This is a step that you should always strive for first whenever you are building an application that contains editable records: First get it all into a form that is filled in with the correct data, and the rest of the process usually becomes quite simple.

Editing a Related Record

Editing a related record is an operation that is extremely similar to editing a regular record. We first trap the condition — in this case the saveCategory action post variable — into an if statement. Then the record variable, foundCategory in this case, is modified with the updated fields. Finally, it is committed back into the database and checked for errors.

1. Start by finding the location where the message variable is defined. Right after this variable we will place the if statement that detects whether the post action contains saveCategory:

   **if(POST('action') == 'saveCategory') {
   }**

2. Next we edit the foundCategory record object by using a setField
    and a commit. The result is placed in the result variable for error
    checking purposes:

    **$foundCategory->setField('Categories::category',
    POST('category'));
    $result = $foundCategory->commit();**

3. The last step is to add error checking. In this case, if there is an
    error the message variable is set and the error is printed back to
    the user. However, if a save was successful, then there is no point
    keeping the user on this page; therefore, the user is redirected
    back to the editPost.php page for this specific post and a list of
    related records that should have the new updated value.

    **if(FileMaker::isError($result)) {
      $message = 'Error saving your record: '.$result->
      getMessage();
    }else{
      header('Location: editPost.php?id='.$post->getField
      ('postId'));
    }**

    This entire if statement block should be verified with Figure
    16-16, which contains the complete source code for this related
    record edit operation.

```
Code Inspector
30
31   if(POST('action') == 'saveCategory') {
32       $foundCategory->setField('Categories::category', POST('category'));
33       $result = $foundCategory->commit();
34       if(FileMaker::isError($result)) {
35           $message = 'Error saving your record: '.$result->getMessage();
36       }else{
37           header('Location: editPost.php?id='.$post->getField('postId'));
38       }
39
40   }
41
```

Figure 16-16: Editing a related record

Deleting a Related Record

The last action that needs to be covered with portals is deleting the related records. As you might already imagine, deleting a related record involves trapping for the correct HTML form submit and executing a delete instead of a commit on the related record variable.

1.   In order to provide an option to the user to delete this related category, we should create a new form just below the save category form. The code in Figure 16-17 must be placed after the closing <form> tag of the edit form and before the closing <td> tag of the page.

```
▼ Code Inspector
                                                                        ⌘
       </p>
  55   </form>
  56
  57   <form method="post" action="editCategory.php?postId=<?php echo $post->getField('postId'); ?>&id=<?php
       echo $foundCategory->getRecordId(); ?>">
  58       <input type="hidden" name="action" value="deleteCategory">
  59       <p>
  60           <input type="submit" value="Delete Category">
  61       </p>
  62   </form>
  63               </td>
  64   <?php include('blogFooter.php'); ?>
```

Figure 16-17: HTML delete category form

2.   Once this form is submitted, the action variable contains deleteCategory, which can be easily trapped with an if statement and the record deleted. Add the following if statement below the if statement that checks for saveCategory:

if(POST('action') == 'deleteCategory') {
}

3.   Within this if statement we do not have to modify the record object and can immediately call the delete function on the foundCategory FileMaker API related record object. The result should be placed within a variable for error checking purposes:

$result = $foundCategory->delete();

4. The last step is to add error checking, which just like the save will redirect the user back to editing the blog post if the delete was successful. The if statement to use for error checking is:

    if(FileMaker::isError($result)) {
    $message = 'Error deleting your record: '.$result->
    getMessage();
    }else{
    header('Location: editPost.php?id='.$post->getField
    ('postId'));
    }

5. Now that it is complete, verify that the last section of your code matches Figure 16-18.

```
▼ Code Inspector                                                    ⊞
 ⅄.  ⊛.  c  <?>  ⅃.  ▤.
41
42   if(POST('action') == 'deleteCategory') {
43       $result = $foundCategory->delete();
44       if(FileMaker::isError($result)) {
45           $message = 'Error deleting your record: '.$result->getMessage();
46       }else{
47           header('Location: editPost.php?id='.$post->getField('postId'));
48       }
49   }
50
51
```

Figure 16-18: Source code for deleting a related record

Now go back to the editPost.php page and add a new category to one of your posts. Once this category is added, click the Edit link and try saving changes to the postId field. Once the changes are saved, edit it again and choose Delete this time. The category should now be gone, but the feeling of success should remain within you for some time.

Summary

You have now created a number of chained pages, starting with a list of regular records that point to a single record, and then using that single record as a base from which you manipulate a number of related records. Using this structure you should now be able to create very complex database relationships on the web. We hope that this chapter demonstrated the power of the FileMaker API, specifically its consistency in manipulating specific records, which allows you to focus on the task of isolating the record and then being certain that the FileMaker API will take care of the rest in a very uniform and predictable manner. This completes the discussion on database record access methods. The rest of the book will focus on a few other features of the FileMaker API as well as PHP topics that are relevant to a database-driven web application.

FileMaker Value Lists

Now that you are familiar with searching, creating, and editing records in a FileMakcr database, it is time to use value lists, an excellent feature of FileMaker. Value lists are relatively unusual within relational databases at this time, and thus this feature is not readily integratcd into PHP although it is easily usable with a bit of PHP and HTML.

What Are FileMaker Value Lists?

Value lists within a FileMaker database are used to populate a drop-down menu, a radio button set, or a check box set with values. Often the values are constant, such as a yes/no selection for a radio button set, which allows FileMaker to construct nice input elements for those values. At other times, those values are dynamic, such as all the unique values already entered into this field or values from a related table that contains a collection of values.

Value lists themselves are not actual data stored within database records. Rather, they are treated as extended layout information from the database that can be accessed on demand by an application. Thus, we have to use a separate set of functions to retrieve the values within a value list and display them on the web. This is not hard to do and can easily produce the familiar behavior of value lists within FileMaker layouts.

Why Use FileMaker Value Lists on the Web?

Using FileMaker value lists on the web provides a number of very important advantages to both the user and the programmer of the system. From the database perspective, value lists can be easily replaced with a table that contains a set of records and a single field; however, such tables add complexity and extra maintenance to the database system. On the web, the value lists can be used for the same elements as within FileMaker layouts — drop-down lists, radio button sets, and check box arrays. However, there are other possibilities that are useful for some systems such as using value lists for lists of category links or even sorted lists such as the top 10 commenters on the blog.

The users of your FileMaker system can easily manipulate value lists from within a familiar FileMaker interface instead of having to tweak PHP configuration files or add and delete records from a value list table. This provides the advantage of manipulating the web system from within FileMaker and eliminating potential points of failure and tech support nightmares.

The programmer can benefit from value lists as well when working within PHP. The first advantage is eliminating an extra find all command on a table and the code associated with that, as well as allowing your user to change the way the web system works painlessly. There is also a speed advantage that you receive from value lists; generally, fetching a value list with some sorted values that could contain 100 to 150 values is much faster than attempting a find on a table and retrieving 150 records. This speed difference can be very significant, especially for complex databases or if that list is used throughout the entire site. This can be used to display a list of categories in your web site menu bar that persists throughout all your pages or any other frequently accessed list.

Requirements for Value Lists

Before you can use value lists on the web, a few very important requirements have to be met within the FileMaker database. The first and most important thing is to make sure your value list is on the FileMaker layout that you are going to be using with the form. Also, you have to make sure that the value list itself is tied to the actual field you will be using it with. That will allow you to change value list names in the database while keeping the code on the web the same, as long as the value list is still attached to the field.

HTML Drop-downs, Radio Buttons, and Check Boxes

At this stage in the book you should already be very familiar with the HTML form tags, as well as basic input and textarea elements. Those elements are very simple to use for text entry and allow you to create a very functional site; however, adding more advanced elements can bring your form to a new level of professionalism and ease of use. We will explore three types of input controls that will allow your user to select values from a list, make an exclusive choice, and check multiple choices.

Drop-downs give the user a choice from a long list of values such as a country, state, or other lengthy list of preselected values. Creating drop-down lists within HTML is relatively simple: You open a named <select> tag, add an <option> tag for each value in the list, and close the <select> tag. The <select> tag should be in the format of "<select name="inputName">," where the name specifies the variable name that PHP will receive when the form is submitted. Within the <select> tag you will have a number of <option> tags, which have the format of "<option value="optionValue">Display Value</option>." While the <option> tag does allow a different option value to be sent while the user only selects the display value, FileMaker value lists only have a single value; therefore, both the option value and the display value will be set to the same value list item.

Figure 17-1 shows the source code for a drop-down, and Figure 17-2 displays the code's output.

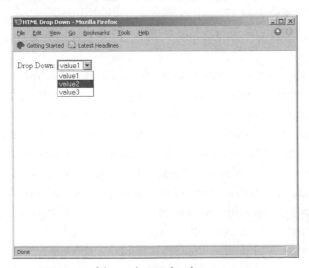

Figure 17-1: Sample HTML drop-down

Figure 17-2: Output of the sample HTML drop-down

Radio buttons give the user an exclusive choice with all the options visible at once. That is, only one of the options can be selected at a time just like the drop-down, but in this case all choices are always visible to the user. Radio buttons are best used for lists of 10 or fewer values; otherwise, drop-downs might be a better option to hide all the values until the drop-down is clicked. Radio buttons are very easy to build with HTML; all you need is a regular <input> tag with its type attribute set to radio. In order to group radio buttons into exclusive groups, all of the <input type="radio"> tags must have the same name attribute. When the form is submitted, only the currently selected radio button value will be sent.

Figure 17-3 shows the source code for a radio button set, and Figure 17-4 displays the output.

```
▼ Code Inspector

1   <!DOCTYPE HTML PUBLIC "-//W3C//DTD HTML 4.01 Transitional//EN"
    "http://www.w3.org/TR/html4/loose.dtd">
2   <html>
3   <head>
4   <meta http-equiv="Content-Type" content="text/html; charset=utf-8">
5   <title>HTML Radio Buttons</title>
6   </head>
7
8   <body>
9   <form name="form1" method="post" action="">
10      <p>
11
12      Radio Buttons:
13      <input type="radio" name="radioButtonSet" value="value1">value1
14      <input type="radio" name="radioButtonSet" value="value2">value2
15      <input type="radio" name="radioButtonSet" value="value3">value3
16
17      </p>
18  </form>
19  </body>
20  </html>
21
```

Figure 17-3: Sample HTML radio button set

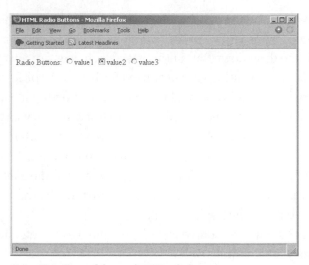

Figure 17-4: Output of the sample HTML radio button set

Check boxes are slightly different from the other input controls that
HTML offers. Check boxes allow the user to select multiple values
from a list of choices, a single value, or no value at all. Check boxes are
used when you would expect the user to have more than one option
that they would want to select. Generally, you should not have more
than 10 to 20 check boxes in a single set; otherwise, the choices may
become overwhelming for the user. Constructing a set of check boxes
is very similar to building a radio button set with one very important
difference: The name for each check box element must have empty
square brackets after it and the type attribute must be set to "check
box." Using the empty square brackets in the check box name allows
PHP to process the input as an array and store all the checked values
in an array variable that can be easily looped through and the values
added to a FileMaker database. Notice how Figure 17-5 includes the
empty square brackets in the name element of the <input> tag.

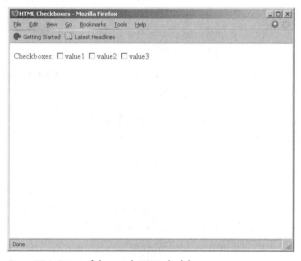

Figure 17-5: Sample HTML check box set

Figure 17-6 displays the output of the source code.

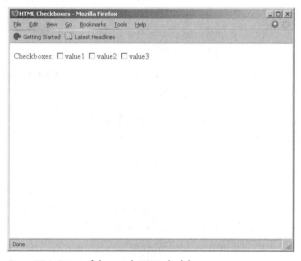

Figure 17-6: Output of the sample HTML check box set

Retrieving a Value List from the Database

The FileMaker API for PHP makes it very easy for a PHP developer to get a value list from a FileMaker layout. It is a two-step process that first involves getting the layout object and then getting a value list from a field on that layout. This is best demonstrated with a very small example file that will fetch the Commenters layout from the blog database and then fetch the value list for the operating system option.

We will start by getting the FileMaker layout object using the getLayout($layoutName) function of the FileMaker PHP API:

```
<?php
require_once('../../include/db.inc.php');
$layout = $blogDB->getLayout('Commenters');
if(FileMaker::isError($layout)) die('Error fetching layout');
```

Once we have the $layout object in PHP and it is free of errors, we can use it to fetch a value list associated with a field on the layout. To do this, we will use the getField($fieldName) function of the layout object and then the getValueList() function on the result. We can actually combine both of those into a single line:

```
$operatingSystems = $layout->getField
('operatingSystem')->getValueList();
```

The technique used above is extremely useful for retrieving value lists based on the field on the layout and not the value list name, since if the value list on that field changes, the getValueList() function will retrieve the new value list tied to that specific field.

Now we will just put all the bits above together into an example that uses print_r to output the value list to the browser, as shown in Figures 17-7 and 17-8. If you are having trouble understanding how to retrieve value lists from the database, it might be a good idea to try getting a value list from a different field name by modifying our sample code. Once you feel comfortable with this method and syntax for value lists, then you are ready to start inserting those lists into actual HTML forms.

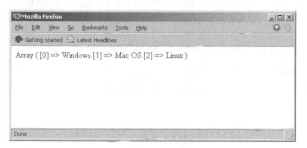

Figure 17-7: PHP code to output a value list

Array ([0] => Windows [1] => Mac OS [2] => Linux)

Figure 17-8: Browser view of PHP code that outputs a value list

We will start working with value lists in this chapter by first building the three types of lists within simple sample pages, and then we will bring it all together at the end of the chapter to create a commenter profile form that will use all the types of value lists.

Building a Dynamic Value List Drop-down

Dynamic drop-down value lists are relatively easy to build with PHP. First the <select> HTML tags are created; they will hold the printout of the value list. Then a PHP foreach loop is added that will retrieve the value list and print the values into the <select> tag.

We will start by creating the HTML <select> tags in an HTML form. For drop-down elements, you just need to supply a field name that will be submitted with the value of the selected list. Let's create a pair of <select> tags for the country field on the layout:

```
<select name="country">
</select>
```

Once the <select> tags have been added with space between them for the <option> tags, we move on to the loop that will print those <option> tags.

PHP includes many different types of loops for traversing arrays of data, and in this case we will be using the foreach loop that simply loops through all the values within an array. This array will be the result of the getValueList() function on the country field on our layout. Place your cursor between the opening and closing <select> tags and add the following code for the loop:

```
<?php foreach($layout->getField('country')->
getValueList() as $country) {
$country = htmlspecialchars($country);
?>


<?php } ?>
```

Notice that right after the start of the loop we have added a function that takes each country and passes it through the htmlspecialchars function, which will make the FileMaker value safe for printing in a browser. Without this function, values that have characters such as quotes will interfere with the HTML and likely break your drop-down or submit only partial values that come before the quote. Also, right before the closing <select> tag, a closing curly brace was added in order to complete the foreach loop.

Next we will add the actual output for the <option> tag each time the code loops through a value in our value list. Adding the <option> tag in a loop is as simple as just printing it with a few PHP bits to echo the value itself. The <option> tag should have the following code in your loop:

<option value="<?php echo $country ?>"><?php echo $country; ?></option>

The $country variable that contains the current value from the value list is printed as both the value of the <option> tag as well as the display value of the <option> tag that comes right before the closing <option> tag.

Let's review the final output of this example in Figures 17-9 and 17-10. Please do not hesitate to try adding another drop-down list to this page in order to practice your skill with this concept.

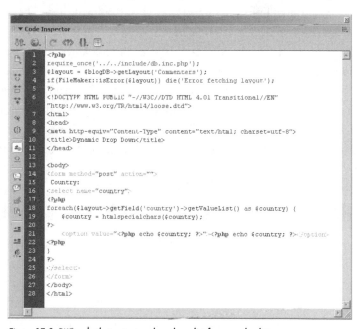

Figure 17-9: PHP code that outputs a drop-down list from a value list

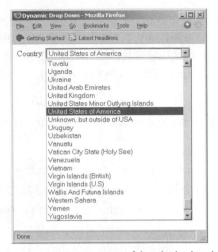

Figure 17-10: Browser output of the value list drop-down

Once a drop-down list is built and is part of the form, it will be submitted as a single variable to PHP. The variable will contain the value attribute of the currently selected item in the list and can be processed just like a standard text input box. While there is no special treatment required for the drop-downs when the form is submitted, it is a slightly more complex procedure when displaying the drop-down in an edit form with a value preselected. This subject will be thoroughly covered later in this chapter when we build the editable profile form for the blog.

Building a Dynamic Value List Radio Button Set

Radio buttons are similar to drop-down lists, especially when used within PHP. Since radio buttons are individual <input type="radio"> elements, printing a radio button set from a value list will just require a loop that outputs multiple input elements. Make sure that the name of the input element contains the field name that you want submitted with your form.

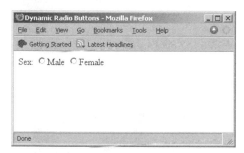

```
1   <?php
2   require_once('../../include/db.inc.php');
3   $layout = $blogDB->getLayout('Commenters');
4   if(FileMaker::isError($layout)) die('Error fetching layout');
5   ?>
6   <!DOCTYPE HTML PUBLIC "-//W3C//DTD HTML 4.01 Transitional//EN"
    "http://www.w3.org/TR/html4/loose.dtd">
7   <html>
8   <head>
9   <meta http-equiv="Content-Type" content="text/html; charset=utf-8">
10  <title>Dynamic Radio Buttons</title>
11  </head>
12
13  <body>
14  <form method="post" action="">
15    Sex:
16  <?php
17  foreach($layout->getField('sex')->getValueList() as $sex) {
18      $sex = htmlspecialchars($sex);
19  ?>
20      <input type="radio" name="sex" value="<?php echo $sex; ?>"><?php echo $sex;
    ?>
21  <?php
22  }
23  ?>
24  </form>
25  </body>
26  </html>
```

Figure 17-11: PHP code that outputs radio buttons from a value list

Figure 17-12: Browser output of the value list radio
buttons

Once a radio button set is built and is part of the form, it will be submitted as a single variable to PHP. The variable will contain the value
attribute of the currently selected radio button in the list and can be
processed just like a standard text input box. Just as with the drop-
down, selecting which radio buttons are selected when the form loads
will be covered later in this chapter when we build the editable profile
section of the blog.

Building a Dynamic Value List Check Box Set

Check box sets are extremely similar to radio button sets. Check boxes are represented as individual <input type="check box"> elements, and therefore printing a check box set from a value list will just require a loop that outputs multiple input elements. Make sure that the name of the input element contains the field name that you want submitted with your form. Most importantly, be sure to assign a name to the check box with empty square brackets at the end. For example, the operatingSystem field should become "<input type="check box" name="operatingSystem[]">" since multiple values will be submitted, making PHP interpret the square brackets as a variable that will contain multiple entries (also known as an array).

Figure 17-13: PHP code that outputs check boxes from a value list

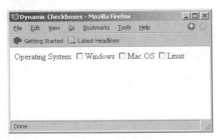

Figure 17-14: Browser output of the value list check boxes

Once a check box set is built and is part of the form, it will be submitted as an array variable to PHP. Check boxes require a few special functions in order to get the results back into a FileMaker database. Generally, array variables from PHP cannot be directly submitted into a FileMaker field. In the case of check boxes, the entire array has to be converted into a string where every array element is separated by a carriage return character. The array to string conversion will be covered in depth in the "Processing Form Results for Check Boxes" section later in this chapter. Just as with the drop-down, selecting which check boxes are checked when the form loads will also be covered later in the chapter.

Adding Empty Default Values

Most FileMaker users are familiar with the option of being able to erase a drop-down selection even if an empty value is not part of the usual value list. The easiest way to have this functionality on the web is to hard-code the blank values into the form before printing the value list. This process is required for drop-downs and radio buttons, while check boxes can simply all be unchecked.

Adding a blank option to a drop-down menu involves adding an <option> tag with an empty value attribute and an optional empty display value. The code for such an option would look like this:

```
<option value=""></option>
```

In order to combine such an option with dynamic options, we can simply modify the code from the previous example and add this option before the foreach loop begins. Make sure that the option is inserted before the loop begins; otherwise, you will have a blank option before every value in the list. Notice in the example below that the empty option appears right after the opening <select> tag:

```
<select name="country">
<option value=""></option>
<?php
```

```php
foreach($layout->getField('country')->getValueList() as
$country) {
  $country = htmlspecialchars($country);
?>
  <option value="<?php echo $country; ?>"><?php echo
$country; ?></option>
<?php
}
?>
</select>
```

Another alternative to the hard-coded empty drop-down item is to add a blank value to your value list within the database. This blank value, which can be added by inserting a new line for one of the lines, will show up in the drop-down as an empty choice and can be added at the top, bottom, or middle of the list.

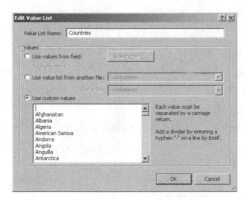

Figure 17-15: Empty value at the top of a FileMaker list

Adding a blank radio button option is very similar to adding one for the drop-down list. The value attribute of the radio button input has to be set to an empty set of double quotes, and a label should be provided to indicate that this option is a "no choice" option. The following line can be used to make this easy for your users:

```html
<input type="radio" name="fieldName" value="">
Undecided
```

Notice the Undecided label; otherwise, it will look just like any other radio button in the set and could confuse the user.

Creating a Value List Driven Form

Integrating value lists into an actual form is the next step in learning to use value lists properly. The most logical place to start is expanding the blog web application by adding a registration form for blog commenters. This form will collect personal information by using all three types of value list selections.

1. The first step is to create an empty form that has some of the standard non-value list fields on it. This form will be based on the standard blog template and will include the standard text fields for some of the information as well as the Submit button. Create a blank PHP page now, naming it **newCommenter.php**. The starting source code for this form should be copied from Figures 17-16 and 17-17. When you test this form in your browser, it should look similar to Figure 17-18.

```
<?php require_once('include/db.inc.php');

?>
<?php include('blogHeader.php'); ?>
    <td valign="top">
        <h1>New Commenter Registration</h1>
        <form method="post" action="newCommenterResponse.php">
            <input type="hidden" name="action" value="newCommenter">
            <table width="300">
                <tr>
                    <th>First Name</th>
                    <td><input name="nameFirst" type="text"></td>
                </tr>
                <tr>
                    <th>Last Name</th>
                    <td><input name="nameLast" type="text"></td>
                </tr>
                <tr>
                    <th>Email</th>
                    <td><input name="email" type="text"></td>
                </tr>
                <tr>
                    <th>Country</th>
                    <td></td>
                </tr>
```

Figure 17-16: Starting source code for newCommenter.php, part 1

Figure 17-17: Starting source code for newCommenter.php, part 2

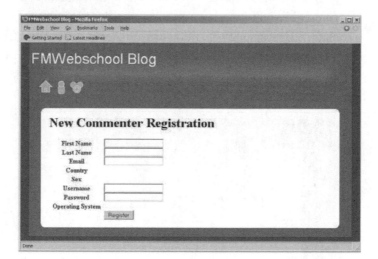

Figure 17-18: Initial commenter registration form viewed in a browser

2. At this stage we have left blank all the areas where the value lists
    will be, since currently this page does not have the value lists
    loaded from the database. We will change that now by accessing
    the FileMaker database and retrieving the three value lists. Place
    the cursor within your first PHP code block after including the
    database file; this is where we retrieve all the value lists that will

be used on this page. First we retrieve the FileMaker API layout object:

$layout = $blogDB->getLayout('Commenters');
if(FileMaker::isError($layout)) die('Error fetching layout');

3. Next, the value lists themselves have to be retrieved from the layout object and placed into their own variables. The code to retrieve a value list and place it into a variable is identical to the examples earlier in this chapter, except in this case we are retrieving all three of the lists at the beginning of the script. Add the following code to your page to retrieve the value lists:

$countries = $layout->getField('country')->getValueList();
$sexes = $layout->getField('sex')->getValueList();
$operatingSystems = $layout->getField('operatingSystem')
->getValueList();

Figure 17-19 lists the completed source code for the top of this page. Once that is synchronized with the code, we write the code that actually prints these value lists as part of the form.

Figure 17-19: Value lists retrieved in the beginning of the script

4. The first value list that was retrieved is the countries value list, which should be printed as a simple drop-down. Based on the previous examples, we will be using the same code that depends on a foreach loop to print each value and the htmlspecialchars function to make the values safe for printing within HTML code. Figure 17-20 has the source code for this section, which should be placed into the empty <td> tag within the Country row of the form:

```
▼ Code Inspector
28              <tr>
29                  <th>Country</th>
30                  <td>
31      <select name="country">
32      <?php
33      foreach($countries as $country) {
34          $country = htmlspecialchars($country);
35      ?>
36          <option value="<?php echo $country; ?>"><?php echo $country; ?></option>
37      <?php
38      }
39      ?>
40      </select>
41                  </td>
42              </tr>
```

Figure 17-20: Source code for Country drop-down

5.   Next, it is time to print the radio button input elements for the sex
     selection. While this is certainly a trivial radio button due to the
     constant nature of this value list, it is nonetheless a good example
     of an "either/or" choice, where the selection is restricted to being
     only one of the two values. The code for this value list is very sim-
     ilar to the drop-down code, and simply prints a number of input
     elements. The code for this section is in Figure 17-21 and should
     be placed in the empty <td> tag within the Sex row of the form.

```
▼ Code Inspector
43              <tr>
44                  <th>Sex</th>
45                  <td>
46      <?php
47      foreach($sexes as $sex) {
48          $sex = htmlspecialchars($sex);
49      ?>
50          <input type="radio" name="sex" value="<?php echo $sex; ?>"><?php echo $sex;
        ?>
51      <?php
52      }
53      ?>
54                  </td>
55              </tr>
```

Figure 17-21: Source code for the Sex radio button group

6.   The last value list to add is the check boxes value list. For this list
     we decided to use an operating system example since many devel-
     opers use multiple operating systems, making it an appropriate
     question to ask on a FileMaker blog. The source code for this sec-
     tion, shown in Figure 17-22, is also similar to the other sections

with the typical foreach loop and the htmlspecialchars encoding of the value. The only minor difference between this and the other value lists, which was discussed earlier in this chapter, is the use of the empty square brackets in the name of the input element. The empty square brackets allow the values to be submitted and processed as a PHP array, which will be discussed in depth in the next section.

```
Code Inspector
64                    <tr>
65                        <th>Operating System</th>
66                        <td>
67    <?php
68    foreach($operatingSystems as $operatingSystem) {
69        $operatingSystem = htmlspecialchars($operatingSystem);
70    ?>
71        <input type="checkbox" name="operatingSystem[]" value="<?php echo $operatingSystem; ?>">
72        <?php echo $operatingSystem; ?><br>
73    <?php
74    }
75    ?>
76                        </td>
77                    </tr>
```

Figure 17-22: Source code for the Operating System check box set

This form is now complete and ready to accept user input. The text fields and value lists submitted from this form will be processed with newCommenterResponse.php, which will be built in the next section. The final visual appearance of this form should resemble Figure 17-23.

New Commenter Registration

First Name
Last Name
Email
Country   USA
Sex   Male   Female
Username
Password
                   Windows
Operating System   Mac OS
                   Linux
                   Register

Figure 17-23: Final rendering of the form in a web browser

Processing Form Results for Drop-downs and Radio Buttons

Processing the form from the previous section is just a matter of creating an add record FileMaker API command that will take in all the submitted fields and add them to the record. Radio buttons and drop-down lists are accessed in the same way as regular text fields and text areas. Check boxes, however, are processed differently and will be covered in the next section.

1. The new record page at this time will simply create a new record and then print an acknowledgment message to the user. Once the edit commenter profile page is complete, this page will redirect users to their profile page. Start this page right now by creating a new PHP file named **newCommenterResponse.php**, with the following source code:

   <?php require_once('include/db.inc.php');

   ?>
   Thank you for registering.

2. Next, we initialize the FileMaker API command that will create a new record in the Commenters layout. This is done through the regular newAddCommand function on the FileMaker API object defined in our database include file. The code below should be added starting on the second line after the inclusion of db.inc.php:

   $newCommenterCmd =
   $blogDB->newAddCommand('Commenters');

3. Then, we add all the fields through the repetitive use of the setField command. Notice that the last field, operatingSystem, is not added at this stage:

   $newCommenterCmd->setField('nameFirst',POST
   ('nameFirst'));
   $newCommenterCmd->setField('nameLast',POST
   ('nameLast'));

```
$newCommenterCmd->setField('email',POST('email'));
$newCommenterCmd->setField('country',POST('country'));
$newCommenterCmd->setField('sex',POST('sex'));
$newCommenterCmd->setField('username',POST
('username'));
$newCommenterCmd->setField('password',POST
('password'));
```

4. The last step to this process is using the execute command on the
   newCommenterCmd PHP object to execute the actual addition to
   the database. Following the execute we add the standard error
   checking code to make sure that the record was actually successfully created:

```
$newCommenter = $newCommenterCmd->execute();
if(FileMaker::isError($newCommenter)) {
   die('Database Error: '.$newCommenter->getMessage());
}
```

As you have seen up to this point, the drop-down and radio button
value lists did not make any difference in the FileMaker API command
creation and execution stage. The final code for this segment can be
verified with Figure 17-24. Next we will address the usage of check
boxes. They are not hard to use but do require a bit of extra error
handling.

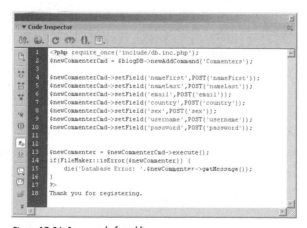

Figure 17-24: Source code for adding a new commenter

Processing Form Results for Check Boxes

Check boxes behave quite differently within PHP when compared to
the rest of the form objects. The first difference is their name attribute, which should be in the form of "fieldName[]" instead of the usual
"fieldName." This naming convention creates an array automatically
within PHP, allowing each individual check box choice to be looped
through. However, there is a catch with check boxes: When no value is
selected, the PHP variable is not initialized at all. This is because a
browser does not send any data at all about check boxes that were not
selected, which means that you cannot rely on the post variable always
being there when using check boxes. There are, however, a few very
simple methods to get past that hurdle.

The easiest way to handle check boxes is to use the following if
statement, which will make sure you have a usable variable — even if
it is an empty array when no check boxes were selected:

```
$fieldValues = array();
if(isset($_POST['fieldName'])) {
   $fieldValues = $_POST['fieldName'];
}
```

As you can see, the value is retrieved only when fieldName is set; otherwise, fieldValues remains a blank array.

The second hurdle with check boxes is that FileMaker expects
check box lists to be submitted as a list of values separated by carriage
return characters. This character is known within PHP as "\r" and
within FileMaker as "¶"; however, an array in PHP is an array. This
means that the array has to be converted into a carriage return delimited string. Luckily there is a function within PHP that does just that.
This function is the implode function, which takes a string as its first
argument for the "glue" to use in order to put the array pieces
together, and the array itself as the second argument. The following
code would be needed to use it with a FileMaker check box set:

```
$fieldValues = implode("\r", $fieldValues);
```

1. We will now combine all of the above into code that adds the operatingSystem check box set to the FileMaker database. Let's start with the if statement that checks whether a check box was submitted and retrieves the array. The following code should be placed after the last setField statement but before the execute statement:

```
$operatingSystem = array();
if(isset($_POST['operatingSystem'])) {
    $operatingSystem = $_POST['operatingSystem'];
}
```

2. Next, we add the implode function to create the carriage return delimited list:

```
$operatingSystem = implode("\r", $operatingSystem);
```

3. The last step in this process is to add a standard setField function call to set the actual field value. In this case, the operatingSystem PHP variable will already contain this list:

```
$newCommenterCmd->setField('operatingSystem', $operatingSystem);
```

That is all there is to processing check boxes within PHP and the FileMaker API. Figure 17-25 shows the final source code for the block of code that was just created. Next, we will be creating the PHP page that lets you edit a commenter profile, allowing you to learn how to use FileMaker data when prefilling a form with value lists within it.

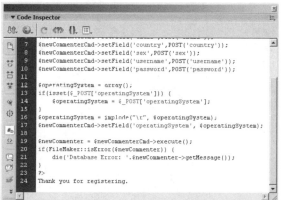

Figure 17-25: Final source code for newCommenterResponse.php

Taking It to the Next Level — Selecting Values with PHP

The next step is to create a filled-in form that has value lists within it. At this stage, we assume that you are familiar with filled-in forms, since the code for the filled-in text values will be briefly explained and then presented for copying. Once this page is created, we will move on to creating the value lists that have values preselected based on the current value within the record.

First we will quickly create an editCommenters.php page that allows the administrator to quickly access a list of registered commenters on the blog and edit their individual records. This page is modeled after the editPosts.php page, which lists links to individual edit pages. Create this page now by using the source code from Figure 17-26.

```php
1  <?php require('include/db.inc.php');
2  $commentersFind = $blogDB->newFindAllCommand('Commenters');
3  $commenters = $commentersFind->execute();
4
5  if(FileMaker::isError($commenters)) {
6      die('Database Error: '.$commenters->getMessage());
7  }
8
9  ?>
10 <?php include('blogHeader.php'); ?>
11         <td valign="top">
12             <h1>Edit Commenters - Select a Commenter</h1>
13 <?php
14 foreach($commenters->getRecords() as $commenter) {
15 ?>
16             <a href="editCommenter.php?id=<?php echo $commenter->getField('commenterId'); ?>">
17             <?php echo $commenter->getField('username'); ?>
18             </a><br>
19 <?php } ?>
20         </td>
21 <?php include('blogFooter.php'); ?>
```

Figure 17-26: Source code for editCommenters.php

Creating the Commenter Find Request and Basic Form

Now that you have the editCommenters.php page ready to navigate to the individual editCommenter.php pages, it is time to actually build that page. We will start by adding the basic search query to it, which will find the commenter record. Then we will build the form that fills in the standard text values from the record. In the following sections, we will build the value list driven filled-in form elements.

1. The first step is to create editCommenter.php. Start by creating this PHP page and place the source code from newCommenter.php into editCommenter.php. This provides a nice form that already has the plain value lists within it as well as all the properly named text fields.

2. Next we will create the FileMaker API find command to find the record using the commenterId value passed into this form using the id get variable. This code should be placed after the retrieval of the three value lists at the beginning of the PHP page. The code for this find command is:

```
$commenterFind = $blogDB->newFindCommand
('Commenters');
$commenterFind->addFindCriterion('commenterId',
'=='.GET('id'));
$commenters = $commenterFind->execute();
```

3. Then we add the standard error reporting to this request, by adding the following code right after the execute statement:

```
if(FileMaker::isError($commenters)) {
   die('Database Error: '.$commenters->getMessage());
}
```

4.   The last step within this find is isolating the single commenter record, which is done through a combination of getRecords and accessing the 0 array element:

$commenterRecords = $commenters->getRecords();
$commenter = $commenterRecords[0];

The completed block of code at the top of the page is shown in Figure 17-27.

```
▼ Code Inspector
1   <?php require_once('include/db.inc.php');
2   $layout = $blogDB->getLayout('Commenters');
3   if(FileMaker::isError($layout)) die('Error fetching layout');
4
5   $countries = $layout->getField('country')->getValueList();
6   $sexes = $layout->getField('sex')->getValueList();
7   $operatingSystems = $layout->getField('operatingSystem')->getValueList();
8
9   $commenterFind = $blogDB->newFindCommand('Commenters');
10  $commenterFind->addFindCriterion('commenterId','=='.GET['id']);
11  $commenters = $commenterFind->execute();
12
13  if(FileMaker::isError($commenters)) {
14      die('Database Error: '.$commenters->getMessage());
15  }
16
17  $commenterRecords = $commenters->getRecords();
18  $commenter = $commenterRecords[0];
19
20
21  ?>
22  <?php include('blogHeader.php'); ?>
```

Figure 17-27: Find request for a single commenter

5.   Now that the commenter record is isolated in the commenter PHP variable, we can edit the form to prefill those values into the standard text fields. However, before doing that we should modify the form element to point to editCommenter.php instead of the previous newCommenterResponse.php. Remember that since we are using the get id variable to identify the record that we want to edit, this has to be kept within the HTML form action URL. Figure 17-28 shows this change to the form action attribute, as well as a slight change to the <h1> page header tag.

```
22   <?php include('blogHeader.php'); ?>
23          <td valign="top">
24             <h1>Edit Commenter</h1>
25   <form method="post" action="editCommenter.php?id=<?php echo $commenter->getField('commenterId'); ?>">
26             <input type="hidden" name="action" value="newCommenter">
27             <table width="300">
28                <tr>
29                   <th>First Name</th>
30                   <td><input name="nameFirst" type="text"></td>
```

Figure 17-28: The form element modified with the commenter ID

6. It is time to add the filled-in text elements. As you may recall, add-
    ing values to elements is just a matter of using the value attribute
    of the <input> HTML element, combined with a PHP echo state-
    ment that echoes the field value for that specific field. Figures
    17-29 and 17-30 display those additions to the HTML.

```
27                  <table width="300">
28                   <tr>
29                      <th>First Name</th>
30                      <td>
31   <input name="nameFirst" type="text" value="<?php echo $commenter->getField('nameFirst'); ?>">
32                      </td>
33                   </tr>
34                   <tr>
35                      <th>Last Name</th>
36                      <td>
37   <input name="nameLast" type="text" value="<?php echo $commenter->getField('nameLast'); ?>">
38                      </td>
39                   </tr>
40                   <tr>
41                      <th>Email</th>
42                      <td>
43   <input name="email" type="text" value="<?php echo $commenter->getField('email'); ?>">
44                      </td>
```

Figure 17-29: Prefilled values for the top portion of the HTML form

```
74                      <tr>
75                         <th>Username</th>
76                         <td>
77   <input name="username" type="text" value="<?php echo $commenter->getField('username'); ?>">
78                         </td>
79                      </tr>
80                      <tr>
81                         <th>Password</th>
82                         <td>
83   <input name="password" type="password" value="<?php echo $commenter->getField('password'); ?>
     ">
84                         </td>
85                      </tr>
86                      <tr>
87                         <th>Operating System</th>
88                         <td>
89   <?php
90   foreach($OperatingSystems as $OperatingSystem) {
```

Figure 17-30: Prefilled values for the bottom portion of the HTML form

Now that the form has the PHP code to find the record and display the text portions of the commenter record, it is ready for the additional value list code to select those values properly when it loads. At this time you might want to try loading this form by first accessing editCommenters.php and then clicking one of the links. If you've done everything right so far, you should see the text fields with the appropriate values from within the currently browsed record.

Selecting Drop-down Values

Drop-down values are one of the easier value list types to prefill when editing a record. Drop-downs, more specifically HTML <select> elements, have a special property that allows one of the options to be selected. This property is the selected attribute of the <option> tag, which should be set if that option element is to be selected. That means that a standard drop-down list option such as "<option value= " testValue">test</option>" would become "<option value= " testValue" selected>test</option>" if it should be selected when the form loads.

The main task when working with drop-downs is isolating when the "selected" string should be printed into the <option> element. Within PHP, this functionality can be achieved through an if statement and the default printing of a non-selected value. Follow the steps below to construct this small PHP block and get a drop-down that has a selected value only if it matches the stored value in the database.

1.   First, find where the Countries drop-down is constructed using the foreach statement. Then find the line that calls htmlspecialchars on the current country PHP variable:

     $country = htmlspecialchars($country);

2.   Following that statement, create a new PHP string variable containing a blank string. This string should be added before the statement above since we want to compare the country variables before they are encoded with htmlspecialchars. Add the following code before the line above:

$selected = "";

3. Next, we add an if statement that checks whether the current country variable matches the country field from the commenter record. The if statement compares the two values; if they match, it sets the selected PHP variable to " selected". Notice that the value " selected" has a leading space; this is done intentionally to properly print it within the <input> element. The following code shows the if statement:

if($country == $commenter->getField('country')){
$selected = " selected";
}

4. Now that the selected PHP variable will either be blank or contain the string " selected" with a leading space, we have to integrate this variable into the <input> element. This is done by adding a PHP echo statement into the printing of the <option> element:

<option value="<?php echo $country; ?>"<?php echo $selected; ?>><?php echo $country; ?></option>

This is all there is to selecting drop-down values. If you test the page now, the correct drop-down value should be selected. If you already have the page loaded, you might want to restart your browser since some browsers cache form values and will not display the updated selected element with a simple refresh. Figure 17-31 shows the source code for this. Double-check it if your drop-down does not seem to properly select the correct value.

```
48                  <td>
49  <select name="country">
50  <?php
51  foreach($countries as $country) {
52      $selected = "";
53      if( $country == $commenter->getField('country') ){
54          $selected = " selected";
55      }
56      $country = htmlspecialchars($country);
57  ?>
58      <option value="<?php echo $country; ?>"<?php echo $selected; ?>><?php echo $country; ?></option>
59  <?php
60  }
61  ?>
62  </select>
```

Figure 17-31: Source code for a selected drop-down menu

Selecting Radio Button Values

Radio buttons are quite similar to drop-down lists when it comes to selecting their values based on a FileMaker field value. Instead of the selected attribute, radio buttons use the checked attribute with the value of checked. Therefore, a checked radio button would have the following code:

```
<input type="radio" checked="checked">
```

Follow the steps below to add this functionality to your commenter profile page now.

1. To implement this within our profile page, we would use the same selected variable with a different value set to it within the if statement. Start by placing your cursor above the htmlspecialchars statement of the Sex radio button group, then add the following code:

```
$selected = "";
if( $sex == $commenter->getField('sex') ){
    $selected = " checked=\"checked\"";
}
```

2. Notice that in the code above, the quote characters within the string have back slashes before them; this is needed to include actual quote characters as part of the selected PHP variable. The last remaining thing to do here is to integrate the printing of selected into the printing of the <input> HTML element. The code to do this is:

```
<input type="radio" name="sex" value="<?php echo $sex;
?>"<?php echo $selected; ?>><?php echo $sex; ?>
```

With those few simple statements, you now have a radio button group that has an item automatically selected based on the field value within the database. Try this out by browsing to the page within your browser. Figure 17-32 lists the source code for this section of the code; inspect it carefully if the radio buttons do not work for you.

```
      66              <th>Sex</th>
      67              <td>
      68  <?php
      69  foreach($sexes as $sex) {
      70      $selected = "";
      71      if( $sex == $commenter->getField('sex') ){
      72          $selected = " checked=\"checked\"";
      73      }
      74      $sex = htmlspecialchars($sex);
      75  ?>
      76      <input type="radio" name="sex" value="<?php echo $sex; ?>"<?php echo $selected; ?>><?php echo $sex; ?>
      77  <?php
      78  }
      79  ?>
      80              </td>
```

Figure 17-32: Source code for a radio button group with a selected radio button

Selecting Checked Check Boxes

Check box selection is slightly different from drop-downs and radio buttons. The main difference is that check boxes can have multiple selected values in the database. This means that as you are printing each check box, you have to compare it against each value in the database. PHP provides a few convenient functions to make it easy to decide if a specific check box should receive the selected value.

1. Since you can have multiple values within the database, the easiest way to work with those values is by converting them into an array. When values are retrieved from the database, they are separated by new line characters, which are represented within PHP as "\n". To convert this list of values into an array, we use the explode PHP function. This function takes a string as its first parameter, which it uses to break up a larger string into array chunks. The larger string is the second parameter to this function. We will now use it with our value from the database by adding the following code right before the foreach statement that prints the operating systems list:

    $checkedValues = $commenter->getField
    ('operatingSystem');
    $checkedValues = explode("\n", $checkedValues);

2. As you can see, the checkedValues PHP variable first contains the
    new line delimited field contents, and then is broken apart into an
    array. Next, we have to construct the if statement within the
    foreach loop that checks whether the current operatingSystem
    PHP variable is part of the checkedValues array; if it is, then that
    check box should be selected within the form. To accomplish this
    feat, we use the built-in PHP in_array function that takes a search
    string as its first parameter and an array as its second parameter.
    The function returns true if the search string matches any of the
    array elements. Place the following code after the start of the
    foreach loop and before the htmlspecialchars statement:

    $selected = "";
    if(in_array($operatingSystem, $checkedValues)){
    ** $selected = " checked=\"checked\"";**
    }

3. The last step in this process is adding the printing of the selected
    PHP variable into the check box <input> element. This is done
    just like in the previous two examples with the following code:

    <input type="check box" name="operatingSystem[]"
    value="<?php echo $operatingSystem; ?>"<?php echo
    $selected;?>>

With all the code in place, we have completed the form portion of this
exercise. The source code of the check boxes can be found in Figure
17-33, which can be referenced if your version is not properly working.
The next section of this chapter will implement the actual edit command to accept those values back into the database.

```
       95              <th>Operating System</th>
       96              <td>
       97    <?php
       98    $checkedValues = $commenter->getField('operatingSystem');
       99    $checkedValues = explode("\n", $checkedValues);
      100
      101    foreach($operatingSystems as $operatingSystem) {
      102        $selected = "";
      103        if( in_array($operatingSystem, $checkedValues) ){
      104            $selected = " checked=\"checked\"";
      105        }
      106        $operatingSystem = htmlspecialchars($operatingSystem);
      107    ?>
      108        <input type="checkbox" name="operatingSystem[]" value="<?php echo $operatingSystem; ?>"<?php echo $selected;?>
      109        <?php echo $operatingSystem; ?><br>
      110    <?php
      111    }
      112    ?>
      113              </td>
```

Figure 17-33: Source code for a check box group with selected check boxes

Implementing the Edit Command

Now that the filled-in form is complete and properly working, it is time to make it do something useful. In this case, we will just perform a standard edit operation when the form is submitted.

1. Before jumping into editing the commenter FileMaker API record object, we should prepare this form for both sending the correct action and having the ability to display a message to the user. Please refer to Figure 17-34 for the changes to make around your opening <form> tag.

```
       22    <?php include('blogHeader.php'); ?>
       23              <td valign="top">
       24                  <h1>Edit Commenter</h1>
       25    <?php if($message != '') echo '<p><span style="color:red;">'.$message.'</span></p>'; ?>
       26    <form method="post" action="editCommenter.php?id=<?php echo $commenter->getField('commenterId'); ?>">
       27                  <input type="hidden" name="action" value="editCommenter">
       28                  <table width="300">
```

Figure 17-34: PHP message printing and setting of the action form variable

2. Next, we will define the message variable and create the if state-
    ment that will be executed when the editCommenter value is
    within the action post variable. This code should be placed toward
    the top of the page right after the commenter variable is assigned
    the record object:

    $message = '';
    if(POST('action') == 'editCommenter') {
    }

3. Then we add the setField functions that will be used on the
    commenter record object before using the commit function on it.
    Figure 17-35 displays this code along with the commit function
    that assigns its result to the result PHP variable.

Figure 17-35: Editing the commenter record object

4. The last step is to add the error detection code to the if statement,
    and you are done. The following code checks the edit operation for
    errors and assigns the appropriate value to the message PHP
    variable:

    if(FileMaker::isError($result)) {
    ** $message = 'Error saving your record: '.$result->**
    ** getMessage();**

```
}else{
    $message = 'Thank You, the changes have been saved';
}
```

Please test out the whole process right now: You should have a fully editable, value list powered PHP form. We hope that by using the knowledge in this chapter you will be able to make your applications dynamic and easily customizable from within the FileMaker database, while using PHP to create forms that are easy to use.

Limitations of FileMaker Value Lists on the Web

While value lists are extremely powerful on the web, there are a few very important limitations to keep in mind so you can avoid common pitfalls and hours of tedious debugging. The first very important pitfall is the fact that value lists that are populated based on a related value are not supported at this time within FileMaker web publishing. This is due to the fact that when value lists are retrieved they are not tied to any specific result set or records; therefore, the context in which to evaluate that relationship is simply missing.

The second important limitation is the inability for value lists to return display values. This means that if you are using one table for the value list values and another for the actual list items, only the actual value list values will be returned and the display values will be missing. There is no easy way around this except to write code that retrieves both the value list and the list of display values and then combine them. This is rarely done and is outside the scope of this book, but it is certainly possible using a combination of a value list retrieval and a find.

Summary

Possessing the knowledge of using value lists on the web allows you to exploit one of the most powerful features of FileMaker. Using value lists to construct dynamic forms allows you to build flexible web applications that can be controlled from within FileMaker. For example, keeping all lists of big registration forms in the database allows you to instantly make changes to the form without having to do any modifications on the web. Do not hesitate to use value lists when you think the end user of the solution will often change the contents of a list or a series of choices.

PHP Sessions

Sessions are an invaluable tool to any web programmer who builds an application that is slightly more complicated than a search page. Communication on the web is stateless: As each page is called by the browser, the application starts fresh and does not keep the variables from the previous page visited by the user. Cookies were initially devised as a way to keep some variables persistent throughout the site. Cookies are small bits of text with expiration dates placed by a web site within your browser settings, and are accessible to the web server and your browser at any time. However, cookies are easily modifiable by the user and very limiting in the amount of data they can store. Therefore, sessions were invented that still use cookies to identify themselves, but do so securely while keeping all the information that needs to be shared between pages easily accessible to the running script.

What Are Sessions?

Sessions are small temporary files on the server hard drive that are identified by a cookie on the user's computer. They are a set of variables stored on the server and retrieved as needed by your application. A good analogy would be a trip to the bank: You provide the account number (the cookie) and the banker looks up the account (opens a file on disk) and sees information about you (variables), but you never get to see what is on the banker's screen.

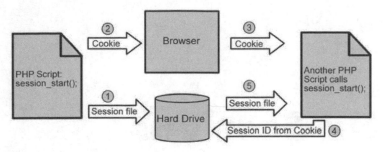

Figure 18-1: Flow of session data between two PHP scripts

Each time a page that uses sessions is accessed, the cookie from the browser is sent to the server, and the session file is looked up and opened by the PHP script. PHP makes this process very simple and completely automated: Just call session_start(); and your session is ready to use.

Why Use Sessions?

Sessions provide a safe way to store sensitive data temporarily while the user browses your site. Usually you would store a user's account details, login credentials, and temporary data such as the contents of a shopping cart. Since all the user has is a cookie with a number, your application can safely manipulate the internal application state on multiple pages in the site.

Using Sessions

To use sessions, first the session is initialized using the session_start() command. This step creates a new session on the server hard drive or opens an existing session and reads it into memory. If a new session has been started, a cookie is sent back to the user with the session identifier in order to access the same session when the user goes to another page. A script that simply initializes or opens an existing session would look like this:

```php
<?php session_start(); ?>
```

Once a session has been initialized, data should be written into it for storage. PHP makes this process very transparent. Simply read the special $_SESSION array to retrieve session variables or set new array keys inside of the $_SESSION array to store session variables. Saving data into a session would look similar to the code below:

```php
<?php $_SESSION['testVariable'] = 'This is a test'; ?>
```

Retrieving data is just as simple:

```php
<?php $test = $_SESSION['testVariable']; ?>
```

The last thing that you need to know to work with sessions effectively is how to erase data from them. You can selectively erase data using the unset command on a specific session variable or destroy the entire session with the session_destroy(); command. You would use a complete session destroy for logouts, while the partial removal of variables would be useful for clearing a single item from a shopping cart that is stored in a session. Both of those actions would resemble the code below:

```php
<?php
unset($_SESSION['testVariable']); // Remove a single variable
session_destroy(); // Destroy all session variables within the $_SESSION array
?>
```

Now that you know a bit more about how sessions work, it's time to use them for something useful. We will create a very simple example first with just a basic form, and tie it all together into a login system for commenters on the blog in Chapter 19. The session data within this login system will be used to store the user details of the logged-in user.

Session Example — Remembering Form Data

The simplest example to demonstrate the power of sessions would be a form that takes in some data and repeatedly displays it, even when coming back to the page at a later time. In this case we will just be submitting a form with a single text field for a name and then using the same PHP page to output the results.

1. Let's start this example by creating a new PHP file named **sessionForm.php**.

2. Next, we should make a quick HTML form, setting the form action to the same sessionForm.php page. The form method should be set to post, and the form elements should be just a text input box and a Submit button. The final form should resemble this simple code:

    ```
    <form method="post" action="sessionForm.php">
      Your Name:
      <input name="name" type="text">
      <input name="submitForm" type="submit">
    </form>
    ```

3. Next, we will add a bit of informational code under the form, which will allow us to view information about the session. In this area we will first print the session ID, which is the number stored in the cookie, and then a printout of the whole $_SESSION array. The code to do this is relatively simple, with the <pre> tags used here

in order to give a well-formatted look to the output of the variable printout. We are using the session_id function to get the session ID; this is purely for informational purposes and generally does not serve any purpose in a PHP application. Add the following code below your HTML form:

```
<p>
Your current session ID is: <?php echo session_id();
?><br>
Your current $_SESSION contents are: <pre><?php
print_r($_SESSION); ?></pre>
</p>
```

4. The last thing to do is to create the code to start the session and check whether the form was submitted. The form submission check will allow us to capture new values into the session whenever the form has data entered into it. A conditional isset is used to determine if a name variable was posted from the web form. All of this should go at the very top of your page before any of the form code. The code below starts the session, and then conditionally assigns the name to the session variable:

```
<?php
session_start();
if(isset($_POST['name'])) {
   $_SESSION['name'] = $_POST['name'];
}
?>
```

Here is the entire source code listing for sessionForm.php:

```
<?php
session_start();
if(isset($_POST['name'])) {
   $_SESSION['name'] = $_POST['name'];
}
?>
```

```
<!DOCTYPE HTML PUBLIC "-//W3C//DTD HTML 4.01
Transitional//EN" "http://www.w3.org/TR/html4/loose.dtd">
<html>
<head>
<meta http-equiv="Content-Type" content="text/html;
charset=utf-8">
<title>Simple Session Example</title>
</head>

<body>
<form method="post" action="sessionForm.php">
  Your Name:
  <input name="name" type="text">
  <input name="submitForm" type="submit">
</form>
<hr>
<p>
Your current session ID is: <?php echo session_id();
?><br>
Your current $_SESSION contents are: <pre><?php
print_r($_SESSION); ?></pre>
</p>
<hr>
<a href="sessionForm.php">Click Here to Refresh This
Page
</a>
</body>
</html>
```

Testing the Session Form Flow

To test and understand how sessions work in this example, we can simply submit the data from sessionForm.php and immediately see the data. Follow these steps:

1. Point your browser to sessionForm.php.

2. Enter your name into the form and submit it. The page will refresh, and you should now see your name on the bottom of the screen.

3. Now open a new window and access the page; notice that your name is still on that page.

Since the data was stored in a session variable and not a form variable like GET or POST, it will still be on that page even if you left it and came back or simply opened another instance of it. This is the exact behavior you would expect when signing into a site — being able to navigate from page to page without being asked repeatedly for information on each page.

Figure 18-2: Output of the sample sessionForm.php file after a form submission

Summary

With your knowledge of sessions, you can now construct many systems that store data between pages. Sessions are invaluable to projects that involve user authentication, shopping carts, wish lists, and multipage entry forms.

Creating Login Authentication Schemes

Now that you have worked with the FileMaker API and have seen how PHP interacts with databases, it is time to bring security and authentication into the picture. Authentication schemes have to go beyond the regular hard-coded user name and password inside your connection include file and request additional information from the user of the site before accessing your FileMaker PHP application. Once the information has been acquired from the user, it has to be tested for validity. If it passes the test, then it is stored in a session variable and reused for the rest of the browsing session as the credential for database operations.

Authentication Methods

When working with FileMaker databases, there are two main methods of authentication that are available for use with PHP. The first method uses a FileMaker database table to store user names and passwords. When a login is attempted, it is just a matter of finding the record successfully in the user's table to validate the supplied information. The second method is a bit more complicated, and involves using a real FileMaker account with the fmphp extended privilege enabled for it to make the connection and perform actions on the database.

Both of those methods have their time and place, and selecting which one to use usually depends on the number of users in the system as well as the frequency of adding and modifying users.

Table-based Authentication

Using a FileMaker table for authentication is best suited for systems that already have a list of users within a table or have a list that is intended to be changed often from many different locations. For example, an online registration form on your site that adds a user to the system and then allows the user to log in would be best suited for the table authentication model. The main advantage with this model is being able to add, remove, or modify user information from the web without requiring any outside intervention.

However, as with anything, table-based authentication has its disadvantages. The most serious disadvantage is the lack of native control over data and the permissions the user would have. For example, limiting write access to the data would require extra logic on the PHP side of the application. However, developing a more complex authentication model using lists of permissions within the table for each user can be a desirable outcome in a larger system that demands very flexible security controls.

Account-based Authentication

FileMaker accounts are the user names and passwords that are used to log in to the database. Up to this point in the book we have had a hard-coded user name and password within the connection file that was used to access and modify data in the database. The permissions specified within the FileMaker database for this hard-coded account as well as the fmphp extended privilege are what allowed us to access the database in the first place. With account-based authentication, there is no default user name used within the system. That information is requested from the user before the FileMaker object is created, allowing only real FileMaker accounts with the fmphp extended privilege to access the system.

Account-based authentication offers the advantage of enforcing database restrictions seamlessly within the application. For example, only specific ranges of records can be displayed to the user based on a calculation specified in the FileMaker Accounts management screens within your database; this provides enormous security advantages to the web application. However, you cannot obtain information on the web about the permissions that a specific user has. Therefore, if you need to make distinctions between the areas a read-only user and a read-write user can access, the table-based authentication method can be used to store much more information about the user itself.

The disadvantages of account-based authentication include the lack of ability to add or modify accounts from the web within the FileMaker database. Modifying accounts requires opening a FileMaker Pro client application as a user who has the rights to make the modifications and then using the built-in account management tools to add or remove accounts. This system works well on intranet PHP applications with a small set of users who can be controlled from within the office with little effort. The other advantage here is the ability of the user to use a single user name and password both on the PHP application side and when using a local copy of FileMaker Pro to access certain database functions that are not natively available from within your PHP system.

Table-based Authentication — Building the Login Form

Table-based and account-based authentication schemes generally use the same login HTML form. The form has a text field for the user name, a password field for the user password, and a hidden field for the action the form performs. We will be demonstrating the login form using the blog template to allow a commenter from the blog system to access the control menu with a list of links to the user profile or other future features that a commenter would be able to use.

1. Integrating this form into the blog template is very straightforward; we just add a nice header and a <form> tag to submit the form onto its own page. PHP logic will be added at the top of this page to check whether the data was submitted. If so, attempt the login; otherwise, an error can be returned. The completed form should contain the code in Figure 19-1, and the appearance in the browser should resemble Figure 19-2. This page should be named **commenterLogin.php**:

```
1   <?php require_once('include/db.inc.php'); ?>
2   <?php include('blogHeader.php'); ?>
3       <td valign="top">
4           <h1>Commenter Login</h1>
5           <p>Please Login with your Commenter Account information</p>
6           <form method="post" action="commenterLogin.php">
7               <input type="hidden" name="action" value="login">
8               <table width="300">
9                   <tr>
10                      <th>Username</th>
11                      <td><input name="username" type="text" id="username"></td>
12                  </tr>
13                  <tr>
14                      <th>Password</th>
15                      <td><input name="password" type="password" id="password" value=""></td>
16                  </tr>
17                  <tr>
18                      <th> </th>
19                      <td><input type="submit" name="Submit" value="Login"></td>
20                  </tr>
21              </table>
22          </form>
23      </td>
24  <?php include('blogFooter.php'); ?>
```

Figure 19-1: Source code of commenter login form

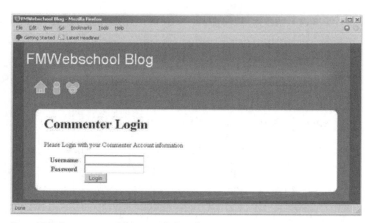

Figure 19-2: Browser output of commenter login form

2. Now that the form has been completed, it is time to add the login procedure code and session initialization code in case of a successful login. We will start by checking whether there is a post action variable submitted and if it contains the keyword login; if so, the Commenters table will be searched for the combination of the user name and the password. Let's start by detecting the login form submission by adding this simple if statement as well as a blank error variable after the inclusion of the database connection file:

```php
<?php require_once('include/db.inc.php');
$error = '';

if(POST('action') == 'login') {
}
?>
```

3. Now whenever the form is submitted with a proper action variable, it will go into the if block and perform the FileMaker search actions. Next we add the actual search into that block. We will be using a standard two-field search here. The following code should be added right after the beginning of the if statement:

```
$userFind = $blogDB->newFindCommand('Commenters');
$userFind->addFindCriterion('username','=='.POST
('username'));
$userFind->addFindCriterion('password','=='.POST
('password'));
$userResult = $userFind->execute();
```

4. The userResult variable should now be either an error or the user record that is logged in. In order to check whether the login failed, we use the standard FileMaker isError function and assign an error message to the error variable if there is an error. However, if the login is successful we will initialize the session, place the post username and password variables into the session, and redirect the user to the successful login page, which is commenter.php. The following code, which accomplishes all that, should be placed below the find execution line:

```
if(FileMaker::isError($userResult)) {
    $error = 'Incorrect username or password';
}else{
    if(!session_id()) session_start();
    $_SESSION['login_user'] = POST('username');
    $_SESSION['login_pass'] = POST('password');
    header('Location: commenter.php');
    exit();
}
```

5. The next step on this page is displaying the error message. Error messages can be easily constructed using a <span> tag with its color style set to red. The following PHP code can be used on any page that defines an error variable:

```
<?php if($error != '') echo '<span
style="color:red;">'.$error.'</span>'; ?>
```

Add the code above right before the <form> tag on the login page. It will display output similar to Figure 19-3 if the login was incorrect.

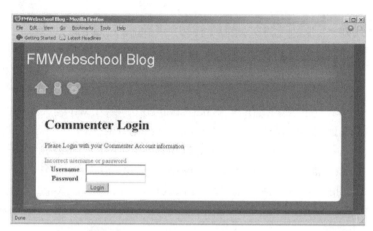

Figure 19-3: Incorrect login browser output

6. The last step for this page is to add a logout option for a logged-in user. Logout is usually performed using a get link with a logout action. In this case, the login will be defined as a link that points to the login page with the get action set to logout. The link would have the following URL:

commenterLogin.php?action=logout

Integrating this condition into our page is very simple: Just add the following new if statement after the if statement that checks for the post action of login:

```
if(GET('action') == 'logout') {
    if(!session_id()) session_start();
    unset($_SESSION['login_user']);
    unset($_SESSION['login_pass']);
    $error = 'You have been logged out';
}
```

Notice that we once again start the session if it hasn't been started and then unset the login variables. It is also a good idea to set the error message to let the user know that the logout action has been successful.

Table-based Authentication — Building a Protected Page

Now that the login page has been completed, we have to build a page that will be protected from unauthorized access. This page will have to check whether the session variables have been set for the logged-in user as well as provide a way to log out and destroy those session variables. Since the login page redirects a successful login to commenter.php, it is logical to have that as our first protected page.

1. Start by creating a simple **commenter.php** page with a link to the commenter profile as well as the logout link. The commenter.php commenter code should contain the minimal page listed in Figure 19-4. When viewed in a browser, it should look like Figure 19-5.

Figure 19-4: Source code for minimal commenter menu page

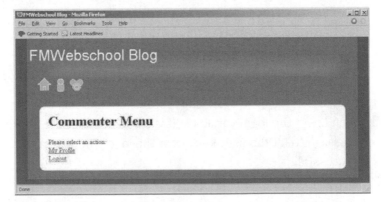

Figure 19-5: Browser output of commenter menu page

2. Now that we have the basic commenter menu page, it is time to check if the user is logged in at the top of the page. If the user is not logged in, then a redirect to commenterLogin.php is performed. The code to perform this check should be placed after including the database connection file but before the header of the page since a redirect must happen before any HTML is sent to the user. The final page source code should resemble Figure 19-6. Once it is complete, try using the logout link by opening it in a new window and then refreshing the previous window. You should notice that you have been redirected to the login page since the logout happened and erased the session information.

```
1  <?php require_once('include/db.inc.php');
2  if(!session_id()) session_start();
3  if(!isset($_SESSION['login_user']) || $_SESSION['login_user'] == '') {
4      header('Location: commenterLogin.php');
5      exit();
6  }
7  ?>
8  <?php include('blogHeader.php'); ?>
9          <td valign="top">
10             <h1>Commenter Menu</h1>
11             <p>Please select an action:<br>
12             <a href="commenterProfile.php">My Profile</a><br>
13             <a href="commenterLogin.php?action=logout">Logout</a><br>
14             </p>
15          </td>
16  <?php include('blogFooter.php'); ?>
```

Figure 19-6: Protected commenter menu page with login page redirect

Account-based Authentication — Implementation

Implementing account-based authentication involves a slightly more complex procedure than table-based authentication. To simplify the process for you, we have created a function that can be used for account-based authentication on any protected pages. This procedure has a few simple requirements:

■ The login form action has to point to a protected page.

- Each protected page must call the accountLogin function.
- The logout link has to point to a protected page.

The function itself is in the form of:

accountLogin($fmConnection, $loginPage)

This function should be called on each protected page with both parameters set to valid values. The first parameter is the actual connection object from your connection file; in our case this is $blogDB. The second parameter is the name of the login page; in our case it is adminLogin.php.

The following accountLogin PHP function should be defined within your include/FMWebschool.inc.php file. Either copy the source code from Figure 19-7 or use the downloadable companion files to get a copy of FMWebschool.inc.php that includes the accountLogin function.

```php
<?php

function accountLogin($fmConnection, $loginPage) {
    if(session_id()) session_start();
    if(POST('action') == 'login') {
        $fmConnection->setProperty('username',POST('username'));
        $fmConnection->setProperty('password',POST('password'));
        $layouts = $fmConnection->listLayouts();
        if(FileMaker::isError($layouts)) {
            header('Location: '.$loginPage.'?error='.urlencode('Authentication Failed'));
            exit();
        }else{
            $_SESSION['account_user'] = POST('username');
            $_SESSION['account_password'] = POST('password');
        }

    }
    if(GET('action') == 'logout') {
        unset($_SESSION['account_user']);
        unset($_SESSION['account_password']);
        header('Location: '.$loginPage);
        exit();
    }
    if(!isset($_SESSION['account_user'])) {
        header('Location: '.$loginPage);
        exit();
    }
    $fmConnection->setProperty('username',$_SESSION['account_user']);
    $fmConnection->setProperty('password',$_SESSION['account_password']);
}
```

Figure 19-7: accountLogin PHP function

With the accountLogin PHP function defined, we should construct the adminLogin.php page, as shown in Figure 19-8. Notice that the form action attribute points to admin.php. The login page also takes its error variable from the get error variable; this is because the accountLogin function transmits its error messages using get variables within the header redirect.

```php
<?php require_once('include/db.inc.php');
$error = GET('error');
?>
<?php include('blogHeader.php'); ?>
        <td valign="top">
            <h1>Account Login</h1>
            <p>Please Login with your FileMaker Account information</p>
<?php if($error != '') echo '<span style="color:red;">'.$error.'</span>'; ?>
            <form method="post" action="admin.php">
                <input type="hidden" name="action" value="login">
                <table width="300">
                    <tr>
                        <th>Username</th>
                        <td><input name="username" type="text" id="username"></td>
                    </tr>
                    <tr>
                        <th>Password</th>
                        <td><input name="password" type="password" id="password" value=""></td>
                    </tr>
                    <tr>
                        <th> </th>
                        <td><input type="submit" name="Submit" value="Login"></td>
                    </tr>
                </table>
            </form>
        </td>
<?php include('blogFooter.php'); ?>
```

Figure 19-8: adminLogin.php page source code

Now that the account login form is built, it is time to build the admin.php page and implement the accountLogin function on it. The admin.php page should include the connection file and then call accountLogin with the connection variable and the login page name. Notice that within the source code in Figure 19-9 the logout link points to admin.php and not adminLogin.php. This is because the logout code is within the accountLogin function, which is called from admin.php and not adminLogin.php.

```php
<?php require_once('include/db.inc.php');
accountLogin($blogDB, 'adminLogin.php');
?>
<?php include('blogHeader.php'); ?>
        <td valign="top">
            <h1>Admin Menu</h1>
            <p>Please select an action:<br>
            <a href="newEntry.php">New Blog Entry</a><br>
            <a href="listEntries.php">Manage Blog Entries</a><br>
            <a href="admin.php?action=logout">Logout</a><br>
            </p>
        </td>
<?php include('blogFooter.php'); ?>
```

Figure 19-9: Source code of a protected account login page

This is all it takes to perform an account-based login using the accountLogin function. If you are interested in knowing how the accountLogin function works, then see the next section for a thorough explanation.

Detailed Overview of accountLogin Function

In this section we will be working with the source code of the accountLogin function to understand how it works to create an account-based login procedure. This section is a full code listing for the function with appropriate explanations inserted after relevant blocks of code:

```
function accountLogin($fmConnection, $loginPage) {
    if(session_id()) session_start();
```

The code above defines the function with two parameters and initializes the session if it has not yet been initialized.

```
if(POST('action') == 'login') {
    $fmConnection->setProperty('username',POST
    ('username'));
    $fmConnection->setProperty('password',POST
    ('password'));
    $layouts = $fmConnection->listLayouts();
```

If a login post action is present, the setProperty function of the FileMaker object is used to set a user name and password to the FileMaker object. Once that is set, the listLayouts function is used to try to get a list of layouts using the current user name and password; an incorrect user name and password at this stage would not allow a successful listing of the layouts.

```
if(FileMaker::isError($layouts)) {
  header('Location: '.$loginPage.'?error='.urlencode
  ('Authentication Failed'));
  exit();
```

If a FileMaker error object is returned, then we assume that the authentication credentials provided were incorrect. The loginPage function parameter is then used to redirect the user with an error get variable set to "Authentication Failed".

```
}else{
  $_SESSION['account_user'] = POST('username');
  $_SESSION['account_password'] = POST('password');
}
}
```

In the case of a successful listing of layouts, we assume that the user name and password are correct and set them to the session variables for later use within the function. The second curly brace is used to end the if statement that detected the login post action.

```
if(GET('action') == 'logout') {
  unset($_SESSION['account_user']);
  unset($_SESSION['account_password']);
  header('Location: '.$loginPage);
  exit();
}
```

The if statement above detects whether a logout action was passed using a get variable. If so, the session variables are unset and the user is redirected to the loginPage function parameter. Optionally at this stage you could add an error message to the redirect line to let the user know that the logout has been performed.

```
if(!isset($_SESSION['account_user'])) {
  header('Location: '.$loginPage);
  exit();
}
```

```
$fmConnection->setProperty('username',$_SESSION
['account_user']);
$fmConnection->setProperty('password',$_SESSION
['account_password']);
}
```

The last part of this function checks whether a session variable is set at all. If not, then it means no attempted login was performed and the user should simply be redirected to the login page. However, if the user is not redirected to the login page, then the end of the function is reached where the setProperty functions are used to set the user name and password of the FileMaker connection object for usage throughout the rest of the PHP script. Any calls to the FileMaker connection object once it exits the function will use the new user name and password with all the appropriate permissions and restrictions as they are defined within your FileMaker database.

Other Authentication Methods — Active Directory

Active directory authentication is possible to achieve from within PHP using the LDAP PHP extension. The LDAP extension allows access from within PHP to servers running an active directory service, such as a Microsoft Active Directory server. Using this extension you can query the information within a directory service and use the results in your PHP scripts. This system is not covered in this book since the architecture of directories can vary greatly between organizations, and would require a programmer within your organization who is familiar with both PHP and the local directory service architecture. We recommend using http://php.net/ldap as a starting point in your directory services authentication implementations.

Troubleshooting Authentication Schemes

Authentication schemes can be tricky to troubleshoot from within PHP, especially the account-based methods. For table-based methods, an incorrect login would usually produce error "401 Record Not Found," which is easy to catch and display to the user as an incorrect user name or password. However, if an incorrect account is used, you could either get error "802 Unable to Open File" or an HTTP authentication failed error. Generally it is safe to assume that if an error object is returned, the user name is to blame, unless the database has been closed on the server or the address has changed.

We recommend having a page on your site that uses a hard-coded user name and password with the same credentials to access the database in cases when you are unsure if it is a real database problem or just a failed user name authentication. This file could be as simple as:

```php
<?php
require_once('FileMaker/FileMaker.php');
$DB = new
FileMaker('dbName','127.0.0.1','webuser','webpass');
print_r($DB->listLayouts());
?>
```

With the file above you would be able to have a user name and password that would always work, and if something were to happen to the database itself, such as it being unavailable or the server being down, using print_r would print a FileMaker_Error object that can be visually inspected in your browser for clues regarding the malfunction. However, a successful test with the file above would produce a list of your database layouts. In that case, the failing authentication can likely be blamed on the user entering incorrect details or badly configured PHP sessions that are documented below.

Another common problem with any authentication scheme is the database login information not being carried through from page to page. The general symptom is the login working for the first page but any subsequent page forces the user back to the login page. Generally this behavior is caused by incorrect configuration of the session storage on the PHP server, which should leave some errors in the error log or even print out a warning to the user about not being able to access the session file. In this case, we recommend reinstalling PHP and doing a few simple examples from Chapter 18 to make sure that your sessions work correctly.

Another issue that can affect sessions is an incorrect system time on your server. This would send cookies to the user with expiration dates that have already passed, forcing the browser to discard the cookies after the page has loaded. The incorrect system time issue should not cause problems unless it is grossly off by days or even months. Session creation can also fail if you use session_start after some output has been sent to the browser, including any output from previously included files. This would not allow PHP to set a cookie, and the session information would certainly be lost at this stage.

Summary

Authentication schemes within PHP can greatly vary, both within FileMaker systems and other PHP systems that you might write in the future. Generally, authentication requires knowledge of forms and sessions. Once you build one authentication system, all of them will seem identical with the exception of the validation step that is specific for each method.

Chapter 20

File Uploads with PHP and FileMaker

Uploading files has long been a mysterious subject to many web developers. Some programming environments force the programmer to write lengthy blocks of code to correctly parse file uploads, while others make it cumbersome and unintuitive. PHP, however, allows very easy handling of file uploads. Uploading files is the operation of selecting a file on your hard drive from within a web form.

How Do File Uploads Work?

The structure of the web dictates that file uploads be initiated by the user through direct interaction with a form within a web browser. All web browsers have a special form element that allows cross-platform file selection capability, which allows a user to click a button and select a file on his or her hard drive. Next, the user fills out the rest of the web form, such as text fields that describe the files being uploaded, and eventually clicks Submit. Once the form is submitted, the browser starts sending a stream of data to the web server that contains the file. The web server receives the file and writes it to a temporary location. Once the file has been fully received by the server, your PHP script that was the action of the form is called.

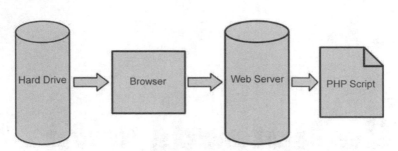

Figure 20-1: Uploading files from your hard drive to the PHP script

At this stage the control over the upload passes to your script, which receives a variable with the information about the uploaded file. It now becomes your responsibility to acknowledge the file upload, record information about it in your database, and move it to a permanent location. A file upload that has not been moved to a permanent location will be erased from the server automatically once your script has finished.

Preparing a Form for a File Upload

Forms in HTML documents need to be specifically designed for file uploads by making a few small modifications to their code. The form first needs to have the correct encoding type set to allow PHP to see the form as an uploaded file and not another text field. Next, the form will need a special named input element to select a file; this is the element that places the Browse… button in the browser. Take a look at the sample file browse form input in Figure 20-2.

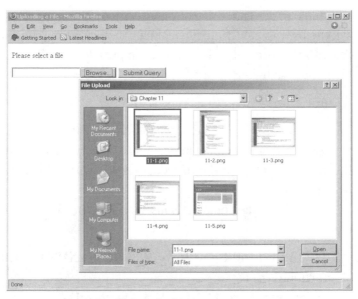

Figure 20-2: Browsing for a file on the hard drive

1. Setting the correct encoding for your form is a very simple process. Start by finding your opening <form> tag, which should resemble the following line:

    <form action="fileUpload.php" method="post">

    To make the form within this tag capable of uploading files along with its other elements, we need to add the enctype attribute with the value "multipart/form-data". The following line shows a form that is ready for file uploads:

    <form enctype="multipart/form-data" action="fileUpload.php" method="post">

    Once the form has been set up properly, we will be adding the actual file selector element to this form.

2. We then need to create the actual form input element that will allow the selection of a file. This element is an <input> tag with its type set to "file". Please note that this element will not be modifiable or readable with most JavaScript implementations due to the security considerations that must be taken when interacting

with files on the hard drive of the user; therefore, you must always ask the user to select the file manually before attempting to interact with the form using JavaScript. Simply add the following form element within your <form> tag:

```
<input name="userFile" type="file">
```

In this case we will name the variable that the file should be placed in userFile. It is extremely important to specify a proper name for the input element in order to access the file with PHP once it has been uploaded.

Following is the complete source code listing for uploading a file:

```
<!DOCTYPE html PUBLIC "-//W3C//DTD XHTML 1.0
Transitional//EN"
"http://www.w3.org/TR/xhtml1/DTD/xhtml1-
transitional.dtd">
<html xmlns="http://www.w3.org/1999/xhtml">
<head>
<meta http-equiv="Content-Type" content="text/html;
charset=utf-8" />
<title>Uploading a File</title>
</head>

<body>
<p>Please select a file</p>
<form enctype="multipart/form-data" action=
"fileUpload.php" method="post">
  <input name="userFile" type="file" />
  <input type="submit" />
</form>
</body>
</html>
```

Accessing the File Upload with PHP

Once the file has been selected by the user and the form is submitted, the server will start receiving the file. Once the file is received, your PHP script is called, allowing you to take control of the uploaded file and manipulate the data as you wish.

All uploaded files are registered within the $_FILES array when your script starts. The array includes entries for all the element names from the previous form that had a file selected for uploading. The array contains a simple structure for each file input:

```
$_FILES array(
  [userFile] => Array (
    [name] => Original filename
    [type] => MIME Type of the file
    [tmp_name] => Full path to temporary uploaded file
    [error] => Error code; will be 0 for successful upload
    [size] => File size of the uploaded file in bytes
  )
)
```

When handling uploads, there are two important things to check for before processing the upload. The first is to make sure a file has been selected, and the second is to check for any errors with the upload.

1. We will start the script with a line that checks that the userFile file input is in the $_FILES array with a simple isset statement:

    ```
    if(!isset($_FILES['userFile'])) die('No file was selected for uploading');
    ```

2. Next we will check that the error code is 0, which signifies a successful file upload:

    ```
    if($_FILES['userFile']['error'] != 0) die('File upload error '.$_FILES['userFile']['error']);
    ```

Once the file upload has been verified, we can move on to permanently storing the uploaded data to the hard drive of the web server.

3. Storing the file upload on the server permanently is quite simple: Just select a destination and use the move_uploaded_file($source, $destination) PHP function. The source file for this function should always be the tmp_name attribute from the uploaded $_FILES array, and the destination should be a location of your choice. In this example, create a directory named **uploads** next to the PHP files and use the following line to move the uploaded file into it:

```
$file = $_FILES['userFile'];
move_uploaded_file( $file['tmp_name'],
'uploads/'.$file['name']);
```

Once the file has been moved into the uploads directory, you can link to it in the future using a simple link such as:

```
<a href="uploads/fileName.jpg">See the file</a>
```

Following is the entire source code listing for accessing a file:

```
<?php
if(!isset($_FILES['userFile'])) die('No file was selected for
uploading');
if($_FILES['userFile']['error'] != 0) die('File upload error
'.$_FILES['userFile']['error']);
$file = $_FILES['userFile'];
move_uploaded_file( $file['tmp_name'],
'uploads/'.$file['name']);
?>
<!DOCTYPE html PUBLIC "-//W3C//DTD XHTML 1.0
Transitional//EN"
"http://www.w3.org/TR/xhtml1/DTD/xhtml1-
transitional.dtd">
<html xmlns="http://www.w3.org/1999/xhtml">
<head>
```

```
<meta http-equiv="Content-Type" content="text/html;
charset=iso-8859-1" />
<title>Uploading a File</title>
</head>

<body>
<p>Thank you for uploading your file, <a href=
"uploads/<?php echo $file['name']; ?>">See the
file</a></p>
</body>
</html>
```

Debugging File Uploads — Error Codes Explained

Generally, once an upload form has been set up, the only error that you will usually receive is "error 4" when the user chooses not to select a file when submitting the form. However, there are many other situations that can initially affect the upload form, especially during the setup process of the system and the initial testing. The following list of PHP error codes is specific to the file upload process.

Error 0: This is a success value that indicates no error was detected.

Error 1: The file that the user was trying to upload exceeded the upload_max_filesize directive in php.ini. Either change the directive or instruct the user to choose smaller files.

Error 2: When you attempt to limit the upload file size using the MAX_FILE_SIZE hidden form variable, then this error code will be used for a file that exceeded the specified variable.

Error 3: Due to network problems or other unexpected causes, only part of the file was uploaded. Ask the user to try uploading the file again.

Error 4: The user did not select a file when submitting the form. This behavior should be handled properly in forms where the upload portion of the form is optional.

Error 6: The selected temporary folder in which to store the upload is missing. Check your php.ini settings and set a proper path. This error was introduced in PHP 5.0.3.

Error 7: Writing the temporary file to disk has failed. Check php.ini for the file upload save path and make sure it is writable by the web user. When all else fails, just select a simple path such as "C:/Temp/upload." This error was first introduced in PHP 5.1.0.

Error 8: The extension of the file upload has been blocked. This error was introduced in PHP 5.2.0.

Connecting Uploaded Files to FileMaker Data

Once a file has been uploaded and stored on the server, you would normally want to record it into your database and associate it with a record. Since we are storing the file on the server hard drive, the best thing to do is to record a URL to the file or just the file name itself. Recording just the file name itself into the database record allows you to dynamically construct the URLs later and use them in a web viewer window within your FileMaker solution or a dynamic PHP page.

To store the file name into your record, use a standard add record command, which should look similar to:

```
$newFile = $filesDb->newAddCommand('Files');
$newFile->setField('fileName',$_FILES['userFile']['name']);
$newFile->execute();
```

The lines of code above should be part of a larger script that stores more information about the file than just the name.

Important Limitations

Just like any system, PHP has its own limitations with file uploading. PHP provides a perfect way to quickly upload files to your server as long as they meet the following criteria:

- The file size needs to be less than 2MB.

  - This is generally enough for photos and documents, but will not suffice for music or video.

  - This limit can be changed in php.ini by modifying upload_max_filesize.

- The permanent destination of the file must be in a folder that is writable by the web server user.

- File uploads cannot be stored in FileMaker container fields but can be viewed through the web viewer.

Summary

With your knowledge of file uploads you can now manipulate much more than just form data. Some of the possibilities include image manipulation, spreadsheet imports, or simple attachments for your database records.

Sending Emails with PHP

Email has been at the core of Internet communication for the last 20 years. Despite innovations in instant messaging technologies and other competitive forces, it remains the main method of sending notifications and confirmations online. This chapter explores the technologies and techniques of using email from within PHP as well as integrating and formatting FileMaker data into an email.

Anatomy of an Email

Most people have used email in the workplace, at home, and anywhere in between, but likely have no idea of how email actually works. An email is a long message delivered between two servers with a set of informational headers and the message body itself. The header section consists of individual header lines separated by new line characters. Each header line serves a special purpose for either the web server or your email client. For example, there are address headers such as to, from, cc, and bcc. These headers allow the delivery of the message to the proper inbox. The subject of the message has its own header line as well, conveniently named subject.

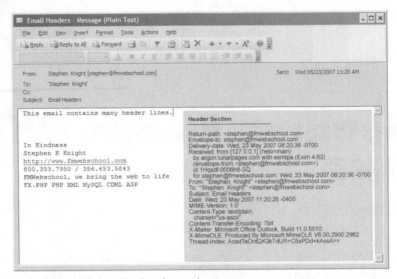

Figure 21-1: Email body and headers of a typical message

The body section of the email contains the actual content of the message. Usually this is just a plain text area with line breaks used for ending lines and no special formatting allowed, although at times HTML is used in the body for advanced formatting.

Requirements for Sending Email from PHP

Sending email requires the proper setup of a mail server as well as configuration within your php.ini file. If you are using a hosting company for your PHP hosting, it will have PHP already set up for the local mail servers and you can safely skip this section. If you are setting up a test server for emails at home or in a small office, you need to be aware of a few limitations that exist with this scenario.

In order to send emails, you will need the correct mail server software, such as sendmail on the Mac or Microsoft Exchange on Windows. However, we strongly discourage using mail servers in testing environments due to both the complexity of the setup and the security risks that they introduce. Generally, mail servers are hard to configure, do not work well with firewalls and routers unless special settings are activated, and are not easily trusted by other mail servers. Security is another issue since many automated scans are constantly performed by spammers to detect mail servers and exploit them for sending spam, which could cause you to lose connectivity to the Internet for an extended period of time. Lastly, many Internet service providers, especially for small businesses and homes, block connections on the standard port 25 for any mail servers but their own, limiting your ability to send email on behalf of your own domain name.

However, once you have a functioning SMTP-compatible mail server setup, you will need to configure PHP to use that mail server as its primary mail server. The following options can be found in php.ini that are relevant to mail server setup:

- SMTP — The hostname of your SMTP server; default is localhost

- smtp_port — The port for your SMTP server; default is 25

- sendmail_from — The name and email to set for the from header

- sendmail_path — Path to sendmail or a sendmail-capable utility

Once a mail server has been set up and working, you should be able to connect to it with both your email client, such as Outlook, and PHP to send and receive email.

Basic Email from PHP

Sending email from PHP requires the use of the mail PHP function and some string manipulation to properly construct the email message. Before continuing with this chapter, make sure that you are comfortable with string concatenation as well as special characters in double quoted strings such as "\n" and "\r".

1. First let's try creating and sending a very simple email message to become familiar with the mail function. The mail function has the following function prototype:

   bool mail (string $to, string $subject, string $message [, string $additional_headers [, string $additional_parameters]])

   This function is used by supplying a to email address for the first parameter, a subject in the second parameter, and a message in the third. The fourth parameter is used to add extra headers to the message; we'll use it to add extra headers for advanced functions. Let's create a small message right now and send it out with the following two-line PHP script:

   ```php
   <?php
   $result = mail('you@domain.com','Test Email','Email
   body');
   var_dump($result);
   ?>
   ```

2. In the script above, enter your own email address and then load the page in a browser. If the output within your browser displays "true," then the email was sent successfully and should be arriving in your inbox within a few minutes. Most likely the from address will have a strange or generic name such as "admin" or your hosting account user name; we will learn in the following section how to modify the from address to display a correct value for you.

Adding a Proper From Address

Since you can now send a simple email message from PHP, it is time to properly format it with the correct return name and address. This is accomplished with the from header, which has the following syntax:

From: "Display Name" <example@domain.com>

This from header is all we need to add to the code on our previous page. We will do so by creating a new $header string that includes the correct header, and then we supply that string as the fourth argument to the mail function. Your code should resemble the following three lines, with your own email addresses and names substituted in the correct locations:

```php
<?php
$headers = 'From: "Your Name" <you@domain.com>';
$result = mail('you@domain.com', 'Test Email', 'Email body', $headers);
var_dump($result);
?>
```

Once again, use your browser to access the page; in a few minutes an email will be in your inbox with a proper return name set.

CC and BCC Address Headers

When sending an email to a single recipient is not enough, you will often use carbon copies and blind carbon copies in your email client. PHP is no different and can send you copies of emails with very little effort. This functionality is often used to send a blind carbon copy of confirmation emails on your site or supply multiple recipients within your office support or feedback forms. Adding an extra carbon copy header can be done by adding a new line after the from header and then using the following syntax:

CC: "Name" <email@domain>, "Name2" <email2@domain>

We will now modify the email script from the previous section to have a cc header as well as a proper from header. The new script should be similar to the code below:

```php
<?php
  $headers = 'From: "Your Name" <you@domain.com>';
  $headers.= 'CC: "Sally" <sally@domain.com>';
  $result = mail('you@domain.com', 'Test Email', 'Email body', $headers);
  var_dump($result);
?>
```

With these few little bits of headers within emails, you can now send varied email messages directly from your PHP script — no FileMaker scripting or external plug-ins are needed! If anything is unclear at this stage, do not hesitate to change a few variables within the above scripts and watch your inbox as it receives automated emails.

Reply-To Address Headers

When an email is received, pressing the Reply button will usually result in the response being sent to the address specified in the from header of the email. However, at times it is desirable to have a reply address that is different from the from address, such as when the email is sent by a PHP application on behalf of another user. In this case, it will be addressed from the setting in the PHP application that includes the name of your site, but replying to the email allows the reply to be sent directly to the user of your site. The reply-to header should have the following syntax:

Reply-to: "Your Name" <you@domain.com>

Be sure to use the hyphen in the header name; otherwise, the mail server will reject the header and cause unpredictable behavior on both the server and your email client.

Sending HTML Emails

Once you have mastered basic email formatting and email headers, you might want to include links or other HTML code within your emails. In order to use HTML inside PHP emails, you will need to add an extra header and send HTML code within the body argument of the mail function. The header to add in this case is a modified content-type header that would set the content type from its default setting of text/plain to text/html. This alerts email clients that the email body should be shown in an HTML window instead of as just a plain text area. This header has the following syntax:

> **Content-Type: text/html**

In this example, we will create a simple email with a link within it that should be rendered as HTML with a clickable link. We will add the usual from header to the email and then add the content type. Then a simple HTML body section is constructed and passed in as the third argument to the mail function. The code for this example is:

```php
<?php
$headers = 'From: "Your Name" <you@domain.com>';
$headers .= "\n".'Content-Type: text/html';
$html = 'Check out this <a href=
"http://fmwebschool.com">link</a>!';
$result = mail('you@domain.com', 'Test Email', $html,
$headers);
var_dump($result);
?>
```

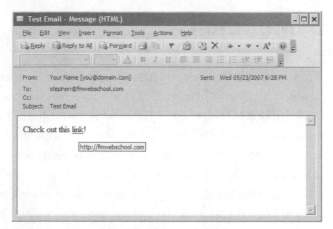

Figure 21-2: HTML email from the example as seen in a mail client

With this knowledge of HTML emails, you can now construct simple links, newsletters, or even complex pages that can be sent out based on your FileMaker data.

Custom Character Encodings

When working with PHP, FileMaker, or just about any other system, non-English characters often cause hours of agony for the developer. Often you will have data that is encoded in UTF-8, UTF-16, or ISO-8859-1. If you will be sending emails that include this data, it is best to set the content-type header with the additional charset parameter. This can be accomplished by selecting the correct content type, usually either text/plain or text/html, and then using the following syntax:

Content-Type: text/plain; charset="utf-8"

For other character sets, replace utf-8 with the appropriate encoding name. It should show up properly in the recipient's inbox without them having to override the encoding type and guess which one was used when the email was sent.

Email Security and Post Data

Have you ever had junk mail in your inbox? What a strange question, you might think — everyone has to deal with an overwhelming volume of junk mail at one point or another. Well, quite often junk mail is sent using innocent sites that do not use caution with forms that send out emails, turning those web sites into junk mail sending automatons. Not only does it waste your bandwidth and slow down the web site for all your users, but your ISP can disconnect your account at any time without prior notice due to junk mail. These days it is a serious federal offense, and junk mail issues have to be taken care of promptly to avoid legal problems. The bright side, however, is that it is extremely easy to protect your site from such takeover attempts with a few minor precautions. We will first explore the techniques that are used to perform this exploit, followed by the introduction of a function that will stop spammers dead in their tracks.

Scripts that send emails can be exploited to send junk mail by injecting invalid data into the header portion of the message. For example, you are collecting an email from the user and then placing that value into the reply-to header to make replying to the user easy. A valid email address in the post data from the user will work perfectly and make it easy to reply to this email. However, consider what happens if the email address contains malicious data such as a reply-to email followed by an end of header symbol and then a body section with an advertisement for the latest pharmaceutical product on the market. With a bit more crafting of the header, an end of body section is also forced into the header, turning the section that was previously the header into a full message, with the body portion that you enter into the mail function being discarded before the message is sent. This scenario is very real. If you have the proper protection in place, you will occasionally get messages from your feedback form that contain strange characters and weird data — evidence that an attempt was made to compromise your form — but with your security in place, all you have to do is smile at the futile attempt.

Now that you know how malicious users will attempt to attack your email forms, you can use simple PHP to defend yourself. Defeating this straightforward attack while allowing post data into your email headers requires removing special characters from the post data before adding them to the header. The special characters in this case are the end line characters "\r" and "\n", which separate headers and allow a header block to end. PHP allows this replacement to be easily performed using the str_replace function, which can take an array of search characters and replace them with an empty string:

```php
<?php
str_replace(array("\r","\n"),"",$_POST['name']);
?>
```

When combined with an actual header, the resultant code would resemble the following:

```php
<?php
$headers.= "\nReply-To:
".str_replace(array("\r","\n"),"",$_POST['name']);
?>
```

Note that the two items in the array have double quotes around them. You can use \n and \r as special characters only with the double quotes; otherwise, the slash becomes a literal slash and the search string will not detect those two special characters.

With this simple str_replace replacement, the post data is now safe to use in the email header variables and would force any malicious code into the single header line that you would be able to easily see if such an email came into your inbox from the form. We strongly suggest taking a few minutes to do this with all user-supplied data within your forms. It will save hours of headaches down the road and allow your business to function smoothly within the turbulent Internet network.

Building a Feedback Form

It is best to start learning about interactive PHP email scripts by creating a simple feedback form. Feedback forms allow you to take data from the user and directly submit it as an email to a hard-coded recipient. These forms provide a good way to interact with the user while keeping the database interaction out of the picture.

1. We will start creating a feedback form by building the actual form itself. Let's name this new PHP page **feedbackForm.php**. This form will submit itself to feedbackFormResponse.php, which will actually use PHP to process the submitted data and generate the email to the hard-coded user. This form is a very simple form in a table format. The HTML code for this form should resemble Figure 21-3 and will produce the HTML output of Figure 21-4.

```
 1   <!DOCTYPE HTML PUBLIC "-//W3C//DTD HTML 4.01 Transitional//EN"
     "http://www.w3.org/TR/html4/loose.dtd">
 2   <html>
 3   <head>
 4   <meta http-equiv="Content-Type" content="text/html; charset=utf-8">
 5   <title>Feedback Form</title>
 6   </head>
 7
 8   <body>
 9   <p>Feedback Form</p>
10   <form action="feedbackFormResponse.php" method="post">
11     <table width="300" border="1">
12       <tr>
13         <th valign="top" scope="row">Name: </th>
14         <td><input name="name" type="text"></td>
15       </tr>
16       <tr>
17         <th valign="top" scope="row">Email:</th>
18         <td><input name="email" type="text"></td>
19       </tr>
20       <tr>
21         <th valign="top" scope="row">Subject: </th>
22         <td><input name="subject" type="text"></td>
23       </tr>
24       <tr>
25         <th valign="top" scope="row">Message</th>
26         <td><textarea name="comments"></textarea></td>
27       </tr>
28       <tr>
29         <th valign="top" scope="row"> </th>
30         <td><input type="submit" name="Submit" value="Submit"></td>
31       </tr>
32     </table>
33   </form>
34   </body>
35   </html>
```

Figure 21-3: HTML code for feedback form

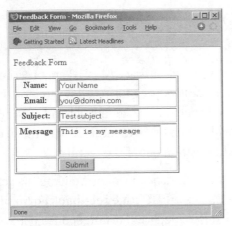

Figure 21-4: Browser output of feedback form

2. Once this form has been built, it is time to construct feedback-
    FormResponse.php, which will contain the code to actually
    construct a well-formatted message for your inbox. We will be
    using the post data security knowledge from the previous section
    in this form to make the headers functional yet secure, so please
    review that section if the str_replace references arc not clear to
    you.

    We will start this page by constructing the body of the message
    first. This will use a quick introductory string and the post data
    from the comments variable. The introductory string will be
    "Feedback form submission:," which will precede the actual sub-
    mitted comment. The post data is then appended to the body
    variable. Please enter the following code into your page at the
    beginning of a blank PHP page:

```php
<?php
  $body = "Feedback form submission:\n";
  $body.= $_POST['comments'];
?>
```

    Notice that we have used "\n" within double quotes on the first
    line. This will place a line break between the introductory sen-
    tence and the comments supplied by the user.

3. With the body variable completed, let's move on to creating the header for this message. This time the header will include the from and the reply-to headers. The following code uses three lines of code to make the reply-to header construction easier to read and edit. The first line sets up the first half of the header with the leading new line, and the second line removes any dangerous characters and constructs a reply address with both a name and an email address in it. The following three lines should be placed right after constructing the body variable, within the <?php and ?> tags:

```
$headers = 'From: "Your Name" <you@domain.com>';
$headers.= "\nReply-To: ";
$headers.=
str_replace(array("\r","\n"),"","".$_POST['name']."'
<'.$_POST['email'].'>');
```

4. With the body and headers completed, only the subject line is left and then we can send it using the mail function. The subject is also taken from the user; therefore, it uses the replacement for special characters as part of the variable assignment. The mail function is used right after the subject, so both of those lines should be placed after the headers variable construction:

```
$subject = 'Feedback Form: '.str_replace(array("\r","\n"), " ",
$_POST['subject']);
$result = mail('you@domain.com', $subject, $body,
$headers);
```

Now that the mail has been sent, you can place a message to the user after the closing PHP tag indicating that it was sent successfully and then suggest the next action on your site, such as a link to your catalog or home page.

```
 1   <?php
 2       $body = "Feedback form submission:\n";
 3       $body.= $_POST['comments'];
 4       $headers = 'From: "Your Name" <you@domain.com>';
 5       $headers.= "\nReply-To: ";
 6       $headers.= str_replace(array("\r","\n"),"",'"'.$_POST['name'].'" <'.$_POST['email'].'>');
 7       $subject = 'Feedback Form: '.str_replace(array("\r","\n"), " ", $_POST['subject']);
 8       $result = mail('you@domain.com', $subject, $body, $headers);
 9   ?>
10   Thank you, your feedback submission has been sent.
```

Figure 21-5: Source code of feedbackFormResponse.php

Adding an "Email a Post" Option to the Blog

Now that you understand how to email safely from PHP, it is time to implement it into something useful within the blog project. The most logical place to use emailing within the blog project is to add an option to email a blog post to a friend, or even to your own email for future reference. The overall process in this case resembles any other page that works on a single record:

■ The record is retrieved from the database.

■ The record fields are used to construct PHP variables for the email subject and body.

■ The email is then sent out.

1. We will start by creating a link to the Email a post page and retrieving the record on that page. First, let's create the link to the record on our viewPost.php page. This will require the addition of the standard <a> tag with a link to emailPost.php. Add the following code before the closing <td> tag within viewPost.php:

```
<a href="emailPost.php?id=<?php echo $post->
getField('postId'); ?>">
    Email Post to a Friend
</a><br>
```

2. Next, we will use the viewPost.php page as the beginning of the email form page, since viewPost.php already has the functionality to retrieve the single post record from the passed-in id get variable. The source code to start emailPost.php can be copied from Figure 21-6.

```
1   <?php require_once('include/db.inc.php');
2   $findPostCmd = $blogDB->newFindCommand('Posts');
3   $findPostCmd->addFindCriterion('postId', '==' . GET('id') );
4   $findPostResult = $findPostCmd->execute();
5
6   if(FileMaker::isError($findPostResult)) {
7       die('Database Error: '.$findPostResult->getMessage());
8   }
9
10  $posts = $findPostResult->getRecords();
11  $post = $posts[0];
12  ?>
13  <?php include('blogHeader.php'); ?>
14          <td valign="top">
15              <h1>Email Post: <?php echo $post->getField('title'); ?></h1>
16          </td>
17  <?php include('blogFooter.php'); ?>
```

Figure 21-6: Initial source code of emailPost.php

3. The form should then be added to this HTML page to allow users to enter their own email address as well as the address of their friend. At this stage, we will also add the conditional message variable printing, which has been used with other forms. We will use this variable to tell the user when the message was sent correctly. The source code for this form is in Figure 21-7, and the output of this page in a browser should resemble Figure 21-8.

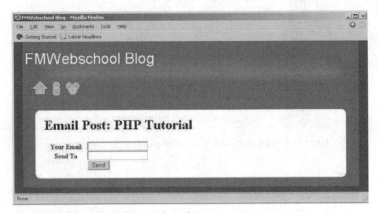

Figure 21-7: Source code of the email post form

Figure 21-8: Browser output of the email post form

4. Next we should define a blank error message, and then add the if statement to detect when the form was submitted. Place your cursor after the line that isolates the post record into the PHP post variable. First, we will initialize the message variable using this very simple PHP line:

$message = "";

Next we add the if statement that checks whether there is a post to variable that contains some text; in that case, the email code will be executed. The code to add is:

if(POST('to') != '') {
}

With that if statement in place, that part of the page should closely resemble Figure 21-9.

```
▼ Code Inspector
     6  if(FileMaker::isError($findPostResult)) {
     7      die('Database Error: '.$findPostResult->getMessage())
        ;
     8  }
     9
    10  $posts = $findPostResult->getRecords();
    11  $post = $posts[0];
    12
    13  $message = "";
    14  if(POST('to') != '') {
    15
    16  }
    17
    18  ?>
    19  <?php include('blogHeader.php'); ?>
```

Figure 21-9: if statement that will send the email

5. The last step in this process is to add the email sending code to the if statement. We will start this code by constructing the body, subject, and header variables. First, we construct the body using the from post variable as well as the body of the FileMaker post record:

$body = POST('from')." has recommended this blog post:\n";
$body.= $post->getField('body');

Next, we create a header that will include the from information for your blog:

$headers = 'From: "Your Name" <you@domain.com>';

The last variable is the subject variable, which integrates the title FileMaker field as part of the email subject:

$subject = 'Blog Post: '.$post->getField('title');

Once that is done, we use the mail function along with the post to variable to send the actual email. The result from the mail function, which is either true or false, is checked and the appropriate message is displayed to the user:

$result = mail(POST('to'), $subject, $body, $headers);
if($result) {
  $message = 'Your message has been sent';
}else{
  $message = 'Failed sending email';
}

The complete source code for the if statement can be seen in Figure 21-10.

Figure 21-10: The email if statement

This completes the lesson of integrating the email function into your application. You should review this section thoroughly if the concept of constructing the email body and subject lines with FileMaker data within them is not clear. This knowledge is vital to both constructing emails and other future data manipulation that mixes text, post variables, and FileMaker records.

Summary

Email can be a very powerful tool when used properly and in moderation within your PHP projects. Please remember to always remove new lines and other dangerous characters from user-submitted data before sending emails, so as to keep the Internet a pleasant and spam-free environment. When you feel that you have reached the limits of your email capabilities or want to try more advanced topics such as using attachments, take a look at Appendix B for the PEAR Mail and MIME classes that will allow you to send complex multipart emails.

Chapter 22

Debugging Connectivity Issues

In the real world, sites go down, databases change locations, and something always seem to go wrong. While we all hope that our projects will be functioning smoothly for years into the future, it never hurts to be prepared for your database going offline. There are many reasons for a database connection to suddenly stop working and constantly return the FileMaker_Error object instead of the FileMaker_ ResultSet; the most common ones are outlined first and should solve 95 percent of your connectivity issues. The bulk of this chapter focuses on debugging the actual FileMaker_Error object and figuring out the issue with it through inspection of internal variables.

Common Connectivity Issues

The following are some common causes for a database connection to fail:

- Incorrect IP address or host name in your PHP connection settings

- Incorrect user name or password set in PHP
    - Try resetting the FileMaker account password and the password within the PHP connection settings file

- The user or their group does not have the fmphp extended privilege enabled
- Database file that is closed on the server
- Firewall blocking outgoing connections to the Web Publishing Engine

Printing Debugging Information

Before debugging can be efficient, you must be able to print the PHP object that is causing issues. The easiest way to do that is by combining a print_r($var) operation with a pair of <pre> tags to output the entire object in your browser. Below is a deliberately invalid FileMaker API request that will output a FileMaker_Error object into the browser.

```php
<?php
require_once('../FMAPI/FileMaker.php');
$fm = new FileMaker('Blog','127.0.0.2','webuser','webpass');
$find = $fm->newFindAnyCommand('Posts');
$result = $find->execute();
echo '<pre>';
print_r($result);
echo '</pre>';
?>
```

The output in your browser should resemble Figure 22-1. We will be using it throughout this chapter to analyze the different sections and isolate your connection problems.

```
FileMaker_Error Object
(
    [_fm] => FileMaker_Implementation Object
        (
            [V73ee434e] => Array
                (
                    [charset] => utf-8
                    [locale] => en
                    [logLevel] => 3
                    [hostspec] => 127.0.0.2
                    [recordClass] => FileMaker_Record
                    [prevalidate] =>
                    [database] => Blog
                    [username] => webuser
                    [password] => webpass
                )

            [Vea4b3413] =>
            [Vff1d7746] =>
            [V9a3dcbce] => -12385362
        )

    [error_message_prefix] =>
    [mode] => 1
    [level] => 1024
    [code] => 802
    [message] =>
    [userinfo] =>
    [backtrace] => Array
        (
            [0] => Array
                (
                    [file] => F:\FM\PHPBook\FMAPI\FileMaker\Error.php
                    [line] => 50
                    [function] => PEAR_Error
                    [class] => PEAR_Error
                    [object] => FileMaker_Error Object
 *RECURSION*
                    [type] => ->
                    [args] => Array
                        (
                            [0] =>
                            [1] => 802
                        )

                )

        )
```

Figure 22-1: Output of a FileMaker_Error object

Next we will deconstruct that bit of output and learn how to gain useful information from it when your application misbehaves.

Checking the Database Authentication Credentials

Within the first few lines of the output you will see the connection settings (Figure 22-2). The host name is listed first followed by a few
options, the database name, the user name, and finally the password.
You should carefully examine this information to see if the expected
values appear in this area since those are the settings that were used
to initiate the connection. If your connection file says otherwise,
recheck your PHP logic to see where this information was reset.

```
FileMaker_Error Object
(
    [_fm] => FileMaker_Implementation Object
        (
            [V73ee434e] => Array
                (
                    [charset] => utf-8
                    [locale] => en
                    [logLevel] => 3
                    [hostspec] => 127.0.0.2
                    [recordClass] => FileMaker_Record
                    [prevalidate] =>
                    [database] => Blog
                    [username] => webuser
                    [password] => webpass
                )

            [Vea4b3413] =>
            [Vff1d7746] =>
            [V9a3dcbce] => -12385362
        )

    [error_message_prefix] =>
    [mode] => 1
    [level] => 1024
    [code] => 802
    [message] =>
    [userinfo] =>
    [backtrace] => Array
        (
            [0] => Array
                (
                    [file] => F:\FM\PHPBook\FMAPI\FileMaker\Error.php
                    [line] => 50
                    [function] => PEAR_Error
                    [class] => PEAR_Error
                    [object] => FileMaker_Error Object
 *RECURSION*
                    [type] => ->
                    [args] => Array
                        (
                            [0] =>
                            [1] => 802
                        )

                )

        )
```

Figure 22-2: Finding database credentials

Investigating Specific Error Codes

Once you have verified that your connection settings are correct, take
a look below to find entries for error codes and messages (Figure
22-3). Generally, this area will display the FileMaker error codes that
this query returned, and for some errors it will even include an actual
error message. When there is an error code but no error message,
take a look at Appendix A for a convenient list of error codes, their
messages, and even troubleshooting suggestions for some specific
codes.

```
FileMaker_Error Object
(
    [_fm] => FileMaker_Implementation Object
        (
            [V73ee434e] => Array
                (
                    [charset] => utf-8
                    [locale] => en
                    [logLevel] => 3
                    [hostspec] => 127.0.0.2
                    [recordClass] => FileMaker_Record
                    [prevalidate] =>
                    [database] => Blog
                    [username] => webuser
                    [password] => webpass
                )

            [Vea4b3413] =>
            [Vff1d7746] =>
            [V9a3dcbce] => -12385362
        )

    [error_message_prefix] =>
    [mode] => 1
    [level] => 1024
    [code] => 802
    [message] =>
    [userinfo] =>
    [backtrace] => Array
        (
            [0] => Array
                (
                    [file] => F:\FM\PHPBook\FMAPI\FileMaker\Error.php
                    [line] => 50
                    [function] => PEAR_Error
                    [class] => PEAR_Error
                    [object] => FileMaker_Error Object
 *RECURSION*
                    [type] => ->
                    [args] => Array
                        (
                            [0] =>
                            [1] => 802
                        )

                )

        )
```

Figure 22-3: Finding error codes

Local Firewalls

Occasionally your connection settings will seem correct and everything else will be set up perfectly, but your connection will still either time-out after some loading time or be immediately dropped. This could be a problem with a local firewall on the PHP web server not allowing the outgoing HTTP request to go out to your FileMaker Server; in that case, try disabling all of your local firewall software or testing the PHP files on a different server.

Routers and ISPs

Occasionally routers can present their own set of connection problems, especially when your HTTP ports are not correctly forwarded. Often you will be testing with a local FileMaker Server and a local PHP server, using your public IP address for the actual connection, and everything seems to work properly. However, let's say you want to move your PHP files to a public web server while keeping the FileMaker Server local, but suddenly the public IP will not work from a remote server. In that case, you should suspect port forwarding problems or even your Internet service provider blocking specific ports, which is a common occurrence on North American cable and DSL small office and home grade connections. Try running your FileMaker Web Publishing Engine and the local web server on a port other than port 80. Ports above 8000 tend to work quite well.

Secure Connections

Attempting to use a secure connection to your FileMaker Server Web Publishing Engine can present many different problems. The PHP cURL module does not generally handle secure connections well from within Windows environments due to difficulties verifying SSL certificates. In addition to these problems, the web server you are using must be configured to accept secure connections with a valid certificate; otherwise, the connection will never even reach the FileMaker Server Web Publishing Engine step and be immediately dropped by the web server.

DNS Issues and Dynamic IPs

Attempting to use a dynamic IP to host a FileMaker Server can be unpredictable and risky. ISPs often change dynamic IPs randomly and without notice, often after downtime or outages, at which point double-checking your IP address is usually at the very bottom of your list of tasks to perform. However, if you must use an IP address, it is always a good idea to double-check with a third-party web site regarding your real IP address at the time; we recommend http://whatIsMyIP.com as a quick way to check your IP address.

When running a web server on a sub-domain that is pointed at your dynamic IP, remember that changing the IP will usually take 2 to 12 hours to propagate throughout the Internet. A common misconception is that if you can use it, then the web server that has a failed connection can also use your new IP address. Most likely, the DNS server of your web server will not be at the same synchronization state as your local information, and to bring connectivity back online you should overwrite the host name in the connection file with the actual IP address. However, do not forget to change it back once the DNS information has propagated through the system.

When in Doubt, Search the Web

If you have a persistent error code that you cannot resolve, just use your favorite search engine to search for the error code and a combination of keywords such as "filemaker," "filemaker web publishing," or "filemaker xml." You will be surprised at the number of errors that have been documented and resolved over the years in FileMaker discussion groups all over the web.

Connectivity issues that are not related to FileMaker directly are also often resolved with a few quick searches in your favorite search engine. Remember a very simple rule: If you have a specific error message or an error code, no matter how ambiguous it seems, just type it into a search engine and add the name of your software, such as the web server name or even "FileMaker." The web has had years to fill up with information, and it is there ready to be found. The old rule also applies here: There are no stupid questions, especially since making a few unlikely or unrelated queries can save you hundreds of dollars in one-on-one consulting time to debug your problem, and don't forget the feeling of accomplishment that follows when you solve a difficult problem using your own resources!

Summary

We hope this chapter showed you that it is possible to dig a bit deeper to resolve errors, and that with a few simple debugging outputs you can discover the cause for most web publishing problems. The most important thing to remember is not to give up on pages that cause issues. Instead, try taking a deep breath and peeking under the hood. The techniques from this chapter will be very valuable in your quest to build web-enabled FileMaker applications, as well as to resolve any unexpected errors you've encountered thus far.

Chapter 23

Wildcards

Wildcards are very useful sequences of characters that can be used to perform partial matching within database searches. FileMaker includes a few very useful wildcards to match characters, numbers, and even date ranges. However, wildcards present a huge security risk when using user-entered data to find a record, and thus this chapter will explain how to protect your scripts from wildcard-based attacks.

What Wildcards Are Available?

Figure 23-1 is a screenshot from the FileMaker Pro find screen showing the wildcards that are available to you through both PHP and FileMaker Pro.

The most dangerous wildcards to security are the "@" and "*" symbols, which allow guessing within search strings to access records that do not belong to the user. The @ symbol can also be problematic for email searches in the database if it is not escaped (used with a backslash), often returning "401 Record Not Found" errors.

Figure 23-1: Wildcards within FileMaker Pro

Entering Literal Wildcard Characters

As you have seen above, there are a number of characters that have to be treated with care when doing searches in order to get the results that you expect. In order to treat the special characters as the actual characters they represent, a method called escaping has been devised. Escaping characters involves placing a backslash before the character itself and a double backslash to enter a literal backslash. For example, "sally@example.com" becomes "sally\@example.com." It is really that simple and will save you much grief trying to figure out why simple searches for email addresses do not work. This process can also be automated using PHP when dealing with user-supplied data. This involves a regular expression based replacement process that adds slashes before dangerous characters. The section below goes into some detail about the function and how it works.

Replacing Wildcards through a Regular Expression

PHP includes many methods to search and replace text, from a simple string replace to more complex pattern matching. The function we discuss here, escapeWildCards, uses regular expression matching, which looks for a pattern and applies a transformation to it accordingly.

Regular expressions are special strings that allow very complex pattern matching within a string. They also allow you to extract the matched pattern and manipulate it. In our case, we are using a regular expression to find all the special wildcard characters and then manipulate those found patterns by adding a backslash before them. The regular expression to match wildcard characters is "/([@*#?!=<>\.\/~"])/." While it certainly looks intimidating, it is nothing more than a match for a group of characters. We don't go into details of this regular expression here, but we do recommend learning about the power of regular expressions and PHP.

The function then combines the preg_replace function with the text passed in as a parameter to perform the search and replace operation.

```php
function escapeWildCards($text, $quoted = false) {
  $escapeChars = '/([@*#?!=<>\.\/~"])/';
  $text = preg_replace($escapeChars,'\\\${1}',$text);
  if($quoted) {
    return "".$text."";
  }else{
    return $text;
  }
}
```

Once that is done, we have a string that is free of wildcards and is safe to use within a FileMaker query. As a small bonus, the function also allows you to optionally add quotes around the result if you are expecting a multiword search within the field. By default, quoting is not performed, but passing true to the second argument of the function will return the string without wildcards and with quotes around it.

Usage Examples

The easiest way to use escapeWildCards is in combination with the addFindCriterion command. The following code demonstrates an easy way to call this function while adding the criterion. It also adds a double equal sign in front of the search to make it even more exact:

```php
<?php
$record_find->addFindCriterion('firstName',
'=='.escapeWildCards(POST('firstName')) );
?>
```

Summary

With this knowledge of wildcards, you can safely create login schemes, user name searches, and other exact record searches such as confirmation numbers. We suggest always escaping wildcards when performing any kind of search in which the keywords are obtained from the user, unless a wildcard option is explicitly desired. You can add the function above to your library of common functions and have it available only a few strokes away.

Going Beyond the Basics

You should congratulate yourself for reaching this point on your journey to learn PHP. We hope that you are now comfortable with web publishing FileMaker data using PHP, as well as have a good idea of how dynamic web sites are constructed. Even if you had trouble with some concepts, with a bit of exploration and rereading some chapters we are confident you will be able to proudly extend your FileMaker applications onto the web.

Only the Beginning

Reaching this point on your journey to learn PHP has not been easy, and you should be proud of all the progress you've made. However, the material learned so far is only the beginning of the possibilities that PHP offers to web developers. PHP is a constantly evolving open-source project, which means new features are added all the time and new technologies are quickly adopted to be accessible by PHP.

There are many very exciting topics that you can explore as you continue learning PHP. For example, adding PHP-based web services to your database application can open up your repository of data to a wide range of devices. As for the next paradigm in web development, AJAX applications will become a central part of the workplace. AJAX offers seamless web interfaces with minimal page refreshes and maximum speed and smoothness of navigation. FileMaker and PHP can easily serve as a back end for such applications and should be a very exciting vector to explore if the correct type of project comes along.

The online world of web publishing is not the only place where PHP can be combined with FileMaker for very powerful results. PHP is currently being developed for easy integration into offline applications, allowing the easy PHP syntax to be combined with the power of multi-window menu-driven desktop applications. While many critics will tell you that PHP is best used on the web and will seem slow on a desktop when compared to traditional environments such as C++ or Java, the development cycle of PHP applications can be extremely rapid with unique advantages for the programmer when trying to write secure code. PHP can already be easily combined with an offline application in the form of command line scripting, allowing your FileMaker applications to use scripts that execute PHP to perform advanced data manipulation on exported records and then importing the results back into the database.

We sincerely hope that the possibilities above will get you excited about continuing to learn PHP and integrating it into the next generation of FileMaker solutions that solve business problems many magnitudes more complex than ever before. Just remember to experiment, be persistent, and communicate your ideas to the world!

Things to Know before Continuing

PHP includes a vast amount of language constructs, functions, and classes for writing efficient applications. However, there are a few core concepts that we believe you should know well and be very comfortable with. Without these basic building blocks it will be hard to read the official PHP documentation or understand PHP code written by other developers.

The first main concept that you should familiarize yourself with is the language operators, including the short notation and logical comparisons. Please review Chapter 8, "PHP Basics," if the following list of operators is not clear to you (where n is a number, and s is a string):

- $x += n : Short form for $x = $x + n

- $x .= s : Short form for $x = $x . s

- $x == $y : Check if two variables are equal

- $x === $y : Check if two variables are equal and have the same type (used often outside of FileMaker in general PHP scripts)

- $x && $y : Check if both $x and $y conditions are true

- $x || $y : Check if $x or $y condition is true

- $x[] = s : Add s to the end of the $x array

The operators in this list are widely used throughout the PHP community and are vital to reading PHP code as well as writing efficient code. Whenever you encounter an operator that you have not seen before and cannot guess what it will do, the best reference for understanding PHP operators is the official manual entry on them: http://php.net/operators.

The second core concept within PHP is the notation used for functions within the official manual. It might seem like strange syntax at first, but it has some resemblance to the syntax used within the FileMaker Calculation dialog when using functions.

array array_merge (array $array1 [, array $array2 [, array $...]])

The line above states that an array is returned from the array_merge function, which has to have the $array1 parameter and an unlimited number of array parameters. The square bracket notation denotes an optional argument to the function and may be used for more advanced results from a function.

The last concept that you should become familiar with is using include files to separate sections from your site into logically distinct chunks. Those chunks can be manipulated by setting variables before including them such as a custom title variable before including the HTML header file, or an array of results before including a file that prints a result table. Extensively using include files will allow you to dramatically reduce the amount of work and typing needed to create and maintain projects, directly translating this skill into greater profits and more development time.

Experiment and Learn

The most important thing to remember when learning a programming language, especially for a unique medium such as the web, is that experimentation is your most important tool. When something does not seem to work, it is easy to make and correct mistakes, so just start debugging and simplifying your problems until the correct solution comes along. Most likely the experience of tracking down strange problems will leave you with a great feeling of accomplishment and confidence. When all else fails and you cannot track things down, remember that you are building something for the World Wide Web, the largest community in recorded history, filled with knowledgeable experts in all fields. Just browse the PHP and FileMaker specific resources listed in Appendix B to find starting points for resolving problems and learning more about web publishing. If all that fails, just use a search engine to find mailing lists and forums that will have help-ful members who are glad to look and troubleshoot small bits of code when asked nicely.

The Sky Is the Limit

As you continue working with and building new PHP systems, you will start seeing new possibilities to extend your FileMaker applications. As the global World Wide Web network evolves in the years to come, the Internet will become the common medium of communication and you will be ready to transform your application to be accessible to future devices with very little effort. Currently we are only seeing the tip of the iceberg when using powerful online applications. More is sure to come. Keep your mind open, and your reference sections handy, then use the knowledge you have to envision and build the global network of innovation!

FileMaker Error Codes

This appendix lists the FileMaker error codes and their cause. Some entries also include ways to resolve the error.

–1 = Unknown error

0 = No error

1 = User canceled action

2 = Memory error

3 = Command is unavailable (for example, wrong operating system, wrong mode, etc.)

4 = Command is unknown

❑ Incorrect encoding settings within your PHP pages that contain forms can cause this error due to special characters breaking the request string.

5 = Command is invalid (for example, a Set Field script step does not have a calculation specified)

6 = File is read only

7 = Running out of memory

8 = Empty result

9 = Insufficient privileges

10 = Requested data is missing

11 = Name is not valid

12 = Name already exists

13 = File or object is in use

14 = Out of range

15 = Can't divide by zero

16 = Operation failed request retry (for example, a user query)

17 = Attempt to convert foreign character set to UTF-16 failed

18 = Client must provide account information to proceed

19 = String contains characters other than A-Z, a-z, 0-9 (ASCII)

100 = File is missing

101 = Record is missing

- ❏ Forgetting to set the record ID when doing an edit or a delete query will cause this error.

- ❏ Setting a field name with a period (.) in its name when performing a request will cause this error. Periods cannot be used for field names with the Web Publishing Engine, but displaying fields with periods will work if they are within a returned result set.

- ❏ Setting a blank record ID will cause this error. Double-check your PHP code to make sure the variable you are using for the record ID has a value.

- ❏ The record ID parameter specified is not a valid record ID for records shown in this layout. Sometimes this is caused by a record ID from one layout being used in another layout with the same data but a different table occurrence.

102 = Field is missing

- ❏ The field is not on the layout.

- ❏ All fields you want to search on, read data from, or input data into must be on the layout used for this specific query. Merge fields on the layout and other non-editable text are not accessible through the Web Publishing Engine.

- ❏ If you are certain the field is on your layout but the query still does not work, then double-check that the layout is the only one with this name. If two layouts have the same name, the one that was arbitrarily selected for the query does not have the field that you need.

103 = Relationship is missing

104 = Script is missing

105 = Layout is missing

    ❏ Other than the obvious check for spelling errors in your layout name, make sure the user account that is used for this query has the permissions to access this layout.

106 = Table is missing

107 = Index is missing

108 = Value list is missing

109 = Privilege set is missing

110 = Related tables are missing

111 = Field repetition is invalid

    ❏ Make sure that on your layout the maximum repetition count includes the repetition that you were trying to set.

112 = Window is missing

113 = Function is missing

114 = File reference is missing

130 = Files are damaged or missing and must be reinstalled

131 = Language pack files are missing (such as template files)

200 = Record access is denied

201 = Field cannot be modified

    ❏ Calculation or summary fields often cause this problem. You can only perform searches on them and not modify them directly.

202 = Field access is denied

203 = No records in file to print or password doesn't allow print access

204 = No access to field(s) in sort order

205 = User does not have access privileges to create new records; import will overwrite existing data

206 = User does not have password change privileges or file is not modifiable

207 = User does not have sufficient privileges to change database schema or file is not modifiable

208 = Password does not contain enough characters

209 = New password must be different from existing one

210 = User account is inactive

211 = Password has expired

212 = Invalid user account and/or password. Please try again.

213 = User account and/or password does not exist

214 = Too many login attempts

215 = Administrator privileges cannot be duplicated

216 = Guest account cannot be duplicated

217 = User does not have sufficient privileges to modify administrator account

300 = The file is locked or in use

301 = Record is in use by another user

302 = FM5 & 6: Script definitions are in use by another user; FM7+: Table is in use by another user

303 = FM5 & 6: Paper size is in use by another user; FM7+: Database schema is in use by another user

304 = FM5 & 6: Password definitions are in use by another user; FM7+: Layout is in use by another user

305 = Relationship or value list definitions are in use by another user

306 = Record modification ID does not match

400 = Find criteria are empty

401 = No records match the request

❑   If using record ID for the search, make sure it is a valid record ID from the same table occurrence and preferably from the same layout.

❑   Special characters and incorrect encoding settings can cause this error.

❑   Special characters such as *, @, and ? have to be escaped if you are trying to search for a literal value. For example, the email address "sally@example.com" must be entered as "sally\@example.com." See Chapter 23 for information on proper character escaping and a convenient function to use whenever you want all characters to be escaped.

402 = Selected field is not a match field for a lookup

403 = Exceeding maximum record limit for trial version of FileMaker Pro

404 = Sort order is invalid

405 = Number of records specified exceeds number of records that can be omitted

406 = Replace/Reserialize criteria is invalid

407 = One or both match fields are missing (invalid relationship)

408 = Specified field has inappropriate data type for this operation

409 = Import order is invalid

410 = Export order is invalid

411 = Cannot perform delete because related records cannot be deleted

412 = Wrong version of FileMaker Pro used to recover file

413 = Specified field has inappropriate field type

414 = Layout cannot display the result

415 = One or more required related records are not available

500 = Date value does not meet validation entry options

501 = Time value does not meet validation entry options

502 = Number value does not meet validation entry options

503 = Value in field is not within the range specified in validation entry options

504 = Value in field is not unique as required in validation entry options

505 = Value in field is not an existing value in the database as required in validation entry options

506 = Value in field is not listed on the value list specified in validation entry option

507 = Value in field failed calculation test of validation entry option

508 = Invalid value entered in Find mode

509 = Field requires a valid value

❑ Field validations can work differently on the web than they do in FileMaker Pro, so try relaxing some validation restrictions if you encounter this problem.

510 = Related value is empty or unavailable

511 = Value in field exceeds maximum number of allowed characters

600 = Print error has occurred

601 = Combined header and footer exceed one page

602 = Body doesn't fit on a page for current column setup

603 = Print connection lost

700 = File is of the wrong file type for import

701 = Data Access Manager can't find database extension file

702 = Data Access Manager was unable to open the session

703 = Data Access Manager was unable to open the session; try later

704 = Data Access Manager failed when sending a query

705 = Data Access Manager failed when executing a query

706 = EPSF file has no preview image

707 = Graphic translator cannot be found

708 = Can't import the file or need color computer to import file

709 = QuickTime movie import failed

710 = Unable to update QuickTime file reference because the database is read only

711 = Import translator cannot be found

712 = XTND version is incompatible

713 = Couldn't initialize the XTND system

714 = Password privileges do not allow the operation

715 = Specified Excel worksheet or named range is missing

716 = A SQL query using DELETE, INSERT, or UPDATE is not allowed for ODBC import

717 = There is not enough XML/XSL information to proceed with the current import or export

718 = Error in parsing XML file (from Xerces)

719 = Error in transforming XML using XSL (from Xalan)

720 = Error when exporting; intended format does not support repeating fields

721 = Unknown error occurred in the parser or the transformer

722 = Cannot import data into a file that has no fields

723 = You do not have permission to add records or to modify records in the target table

724 = You do not have permission to add records to the target table

725 = You do not have permission to modify records in the target table

726 = There are more records in the import file than in the target table. Not all records were imported.

727 = There are more records in the target table than in the import file. Not all records were updated.

729 = Errors occurred during import. Records could not be imported.

730 = Unsupported Excel version. (Convert file to Excel 7.0 (Excel 95) Excel 97, 2000, or XP format and try again)

731 = The file you are importing from contains no data

732 = This file cannot be inserted because it contains other files

733 = A table cannot be imported into itself

734 = This file type cannot be displayed as a picture

735 = This file type cannot be displayed as a picture. It will be inserted and displayed as a file.

800 = Unable to create file on disk

801 = Unable to create temporary file on system disk

802 = Unable to open file

    ❑ This error is often caused by an incorrect user name and password combination.

    ❑ The user name and password used do not have the required fmphp extended privilege that is required for PHP access.

    ❑ The file you are trying to access is closed on the FileMaker Server; make sure you can access it with FileMaker Pro using Open Remote.

    ❑ FileMaker Server has not been properly installed for web publishing with PHP.

803 = File is single user or host cannot be found

804 = File cannot be opened as read only in its current state

805 = File is damaged; use Recover command

806 = File cannot be opened with this version of FileMaker Pro

807 = File is not a FileMaker Pro file or is severely damaged

808 = Cannot open file because access privileges are damaged

809 = Disk/volume is full

810 = Disk/volume is locked

811 = Temporary file cannot be opened as FileMaker Pro file

812 = Cannot open the file because it exceeds host capacity

813 = Record synchronization error on network

814 = File(s) cannot be opened because maximum number is open

815 = Couldn't open lookup file

816 = Unable to convert file

817 = Unable to open file because it does not belong to this solution

818 = FileMaker Pro cannot network for some reason

819 = Cannot save a local copy of a remote file

820 = File is in the process of being closed

821 = Host forced a disconnect

822 = FMI files not found; reinstall missing files

823 = Cannot set file to single user; guests are connected

824 = File is damaged or is not a FileMaker file

900 = General spelling engine error

901 = Main spelling dictionary not installed

902 = Could not launch the Help system

903 = Command cannot be used in a shared file

904 = Command can only be used in a file hosted under FileMaker Server

905 = No active field; selected command can only be used if there is an active field

920 = Can't initialize the spelling engine

921 = User dictionary cannot be loaded for editing

922 = User dictionary cannot be found

923 = User dictionary is read only

950 = Adding repeating related fields is not supported

951 = An unexpected error occurred

952 = Email error message mail format not found

953 = Email error message mail value missing

954 = Unsupported XML grammar

955 = No database name

956 = Maximum number of database sessions exceeded

957 = Conflicting commands

958 = Parameter missing in query

971 = The user name is invalid

972 = The password is invalid

973 = The database is invalid

974 = Permission denied

975 = The field has restricted access

976 = Security is disabled

977 = Invalid client IP address (for the IP restriction feature)

978 = The number of allowed guests has been exceeded (for the
      10-guest limit over a 12-hour period)

1200 = Generic calculation error

1201 = Too few parameters in the function

1202 = Too many parameters in the function

1203 = Unexpected end of calculation

1204 = Number text constant field name or '(' expected

1205 = Comment is not terminated with */

1206 = Text constant must end with a quotation mark

1207 = Unbalanced parenthesis

1208 = Operator missing function not found or '(' not expected

1209 = Name (such as field name or layout name) is missing

1210 = Plug-in function has already been registered

1211 = List usage is not allowed in this function

1212 = An operator (for example, + or *) is expected here

1213 = This variable has already been defined in the Let function

1214 = AVERAGE COUNT EXTEND GETREPETITION MAX MIN NPV STDEV SUM and GETSUMMARY: expression found where a field alone is needed

1215 = This parameter is an invalid Get function parameter

1216 = Only Summary fields allowed as first argument in GETSUMMARY

1217 = Break field is invalid

1218 = Cannot evaluate the number

1219 = A field cannot be used in its own formula

1220 = Field type must be normal or calculated

1221 = Data type must be number, date, time, or timestamp

1222 = Calculation cannot be stored

1223 = The function referred to does not exist

1400 = ODBC driver initialization failed; make sure the ODBC drivers are properly installed.

1401 = Failed to allocate environment (ODBC)

1402 = Failed to free environment (ODBC)

1403 = Failed to disconnect (ODBC)

1404 = Failed to allocate connection (ODBC)

1405 = Failed to free connection (ODBC)

1406 = Failed check for SQL API (ODBC)

1407 = Failed to allocate statement (ODBC)

1408 = Extended error (ODBC)

Additional Resources

The FileMaker community contains a wealth of resources available through many channels. The following list of resources will help further your skills not only as a web developer but also as a FileMaker developer.

FileMaker Forums

FMWebschool web forum: http://www.fmwebschool.com/frm

The FMWebschool Forum is a moderated forum focusing on FileMaker web technology and consulting.

FMForums: http://www.fmforums.com

FM Forums

FMForums is a wonderful FileMaker resource, containing dozens of topics relating to FileMaker.

FileMaker Developer Tools

FMStudio: http://www.fmwebschool.com/fmstudio.php

FMStudio is a Dreamweaver extension that enables you to work with live FileMaker data in Dreamweaver. FMStudio includes a Site Builder that allows you to build multipage PHP web sites by answering questions about your database. FMStudio works with FileMaker 6 through 9 and with Dreamweaver MX, Dreamweaver 8, and Dreamweaver CS3.

JumpStart: http://www.fmwebschool.com/jumpstart.php

JumpStart is a rapid development tool that enables you to quickly build FileMaker web sites. JumpStart automatically builds multipage FileMaker-driven web sites in a matter of seconds.

FMColor Pro: http://www.fmwebschool.com/fmcolorpro.php

FMColor Pro provides a beautiful FileMaker interface that combines hundreds of colors into beautiful matching color schemes. FMColor Pro takes away the guessing game as to what colors match. Simply select any color from the hundreds presented in the palette. Immediately, six matching colors will be displayed. FMColor Pro gives you the RGB and hex value of each color and provides a graphic image of what a database would look like using those same colors. Choose the View in HTML setting, and a web page will launch showing the collection of colors together.

FileMaker buttons and icons: http://www.fmwebschool.com/buttons.html

FMWebschool provides professional buttons and icons for FileMaker databases and web sites. Each set is hand drawn, and they offer a consistent and uniform look that gives an air of professionalism to your user interface.

FileMaker User Groups

FMPug: http://www.fmpug.com

FMPug consists of dozens of user groups throughout the world that meet on a monthly basis. Andy Gaunt, founder of the Pug, has done an amazing job providing technical resources, discounts on third-party products, and listings of FileMaker related activities. FMPug also allows you to set up a web page on the Pug site with a virtual business card and details about your business and services.

Web Editors

Adobe Dreamweaver: http://www.adobe.com/products/dreamweaver

Dreamweaver is considered to be the most popular web editor on the market. Dreamweaver works with both Macintosh and Windows and now integrates with FileMaker Pro through FMStudio.

BBEdit: http://www.bbedit.com

BBEdit is the leading professional HTML and text editor for the Macintosh.

Nvu: http://www.nvu.com

Nvu (which stands for "new view") is a free, open-source web editor. Nvu enables you to easily create web pages and manage a web site with no technical expertise or knowledge of HTML.

Online Resources

Official PHP web site: http://www.php.net

Where do you get PHP? From the PHP web site. The official PHP web site is full of tutorials, the official PHP manual, and helpful links to other resources. The FAQ section is extremely helpful, and there are numerous links to forums, email lists, and other PHP services.

W3 Schools: http://www.w3schools.com

The W3 Schools web site provides hundreds of free tutorials on all aspects of web publishing. Learn by exploring their free sample files and online quizzes. This site is a must for every web developer.

Apache: http://www.apache.org

The Apache site is full of useful information. The Apache server is the most popular server on the Internet, and is available for download from this site.

JavaScript: http://www.javascript.com

A great searchable archive of JavaScript code.

HTML Goodies: http://www.htmlgoodies.com

HTML Goodies is a great site filled with HTML, CSS, and JavaScript tutorials focusing on the beginner to intermediate level.

CSS: http://www.w3.org/Style/CSS

Cascading style sheet home page.

FMWebschool resources: http://www.fmwebschool.com/resources.php

FMWebschool provides numerous resources for the FileMaker developer, including free tutorials, whitepapers, and numerous developer resources to facilitate FileMaker web publishing.

Useful PHP Classes

PHP PEAR Mail Class: http://pear.php.net/package/Mail

The PEAR Mail class allows the sending of emails using a variety of technologies and security settings. Protocols such as SMTP are supported, allowing the usage of email sending functionality using a third-party mail server.

PHP PEAR Mail_Mime Class: http://pear.php.net/package/Mail_Mime

The PEAR Mail_Mime class allows you to construct advanced email messages using the standard MIME architecture. Features of this class include mixing of text and HTML email parts, inline images, and even file attachments.

FileMaker Hosting

Point In Space: http://www.pointinspace.com

Point In Space is a professional FileMaker web publishing hosting company owned and operated by John May.

Long Term Solutions:
http://www.longtermsolutions.com

Long Term Solutions is a hosting and consulting company based in Tennessee and owned and operated by Bob Patin.

Adatasol: http://www.adatasol.com

Adatasol is a FileMaker hosting company owned and operated by Dan Weiss, a FileMaker Partner.

dbdom: http://www.dbdom.com

dbdom.com is a FileMaker hosting company with offices in California, New York, and the United Kingdom.

FileMaker News and Email Lists

FMPro.org: http://www.fmpro.org

FMPro.org is a fantastic source of FileMaker information. Whether you are looking for FileMaker news, plug-ins, publications, or training, you will find it all at FMPro.org.

Database Pros: http://www.databasepros.com

Created by John Mark Osborne, Database Pros continues to be one of the best sites for free FileMaker tips, tricks, and techniques. Database Pros is constantly updated and provides a wealth of information for developers of all levels. John also offers expert FileMaker training services.

FMPexperts: http://www.ironclad.net.au/lists/FMPexperts/index.html

FMPexperts is a mailing list where individuals discuss advanced FileMaker techniques. Beginners and novices are also encouraged to join.

RealTech: http://www.fmpug.com

FMPug.com, the leading FileMaker-centric networking community, launched its newest benefit specifically designed to help its members connect with one another. RealTech enables members to upload screenshots and files, ask questions, share ideas, communicate experiences, post issues, or simply read through contributions from other members. Moreover, because it's a listserv, all the information is delivered directly to the member's inbox, where messages can be read through at leisure. As members of FMPug will firmly attest, RealTech is a fantastic resource for everyone who utilizes the FileMaker application. It's a great avenue for users and developers to troubleshoot day-to-day FileMaker issues and a way to seek out answers to even the most frustrating questions.

FMPug promises RealTech will continue to cover topics, whether large or small, to meet the needs of the growing community. If the steady following is any indication, there is little doubt RealTech will remain a hot commodity in the world of FileMaker.

Comp.Databases.FileMaker:
http://groups.google.com/group/comp.databases.filemaker/topics

Comp.Databases.FileMaker is a Google group for discussing FileMaker that is open to those at all levels of expertise.

FileMaker Newsletters and Blogs

Confessions of a Webaholic: http://www.fmwebschool.com

Confessions of a Webaholic is a free monthly FileMaker newsletter sent to over 5,000 FileMaker enthusiasts. The newsletter contains FileMaker related articles as well as tutorials, book reviews, and free sample files. You can sign up for the newsletter at the FMWebschool home page.

FileMaker Consultant Blog: http://www.fmwebschool.com/filemaker_consultant.htm

The FileMaker Consultant Blog was created to offer FileMaker developers resources to market their products and services. The blog contains articles on marketing, search engine optimization, and customer acquisition. All articles and resources are tailored to the FileMaker developer.

FileMaker Web Training Classes

FMWebschool offers FileMaker web-training classes for PHP and FileMaker. To find out more about training and class schedules, email Stephen Knight at stephen@ fmwebschool.com or check out our training page at http://www.fmwebschool.com/phpclass.php.

FileMaker Web Consulting

FMWebschool offers professional FileMaker web development services. Since 1999, FMWebschool has developed and deployed over 350 FileMaker web sites and has trained hundreds of individuals. If you would like to have FMWebschool help with the development of your site, or you just have some questions about FileMaker web publishing, please fill out our consulting form at http://www.fmwebschool.com/services.php.

Web Publishing Books

Teach Yourself Visually HTML by Sherry Willard Kinkoph (ISBN 978-0764579844)

This is a great book for complete beginners and individuals who like to see how things are done without a lot of heavy code. This book has several great lessons to help you become more familiar with HTML.

PHP Solutions: Dynamic Web Design Made Easy (Solutions) by David Powers (ISBN 1-59059-731-1)

An easy-to-read, easy-to-understand book that covers PHP basics with an introduction on implementing MySQL.

Foundation PHP for Dreamweaver 8 by David Powers (ISBN 1-59059-569-6)

This is a great tool for learning both Dreamweaver and the power of PHP simultaneously. This book goes into detail about working with PHP and CSS within Dreamweaver.

CSS: The Definitive Guide by Eric Meyer (ISBN 978-0596527334)

This book is a great resource and should definitely be added to your web publishing library. Eric Meyer does a tremendous job of showing you how easy it is to integrate CSS into your own solutions with powerful results!

Head First HTML with CSS & XHTML by Eric and Elisabeth Freeman (ISBN 978-0596101978)

This is a great beginners book with detailed examples and explanations. The book is extremely well written and a delight to read.

FileMaker Technical Network

FileMaker Technical Network: http://www.filemaker.com/technet

FileMaker Technical Network is a community of FileMaker enthusiasts that includes users, designers, and developers and provides access to technical info. The program helps members improve their technical expertise in order to build better solutions and solve technical challenges.

FileMaker Business Alliance

FileMaker Business Alliance: http://www.filemaker.com/fba

The FileMaker Business Alliance, for third-party independent developers, provides business opportunities through exclusive sales and marketing support from FileMaker. The FBA provides a host of resources including promotional benefits, sales resources, comarketing opportunities, and product discounts to help you grow your business.

FileMaker TechInfo Database

FileMaker TechInfo database: http://www.filemaker.com/support/techinfo.html

The FileMaker TechInfo database is an online support database with thousands of articles. If you have a problem that you need to troubleshoot, chances are you will find the solution here.

Index

A

About blob, creating for blog application, 231-232
absolute links, 192
account-based authentication, 367, 373-376
accountLogin function, 374, 376-378
accounts, setting up, 78
Active Directory authentication, 378
Add Fields to Portal window, 74, 77
addFindCriterion function, 262
addSortRule function, 252-253
Admin Console,
    creating account, 35
    opening, 45
    using, 46-49
AJAX, 423-424
alignment, 153-155
anchors, 97, 102-104
AND find, 262
Apache, setting up on Macintosh, 15
API, 219-221
    using for a query, 235-237
API for PHP, 221
    using, 222-224
application programming interface, *see* API
arrays,
    adding elements to, 169-170, 173
    creating in PHP, 164-168
    in PHP, 163
    printing elements as text string, 176
    removing elements from, 171-172
    replacing elements in, 168-169
    sorting in, 174-175
    working with in PHP, 168-176

authentication, 365
    account-based, 367, 373-376
    table-based, 366, 368-373
authentication credentials, checking, 414
authentication schemes, 366, 378
    troubleshooting, 379-380

B

background color, setting, 146-147
background images,
    adding, 147-152
    fixed, 148-149
    repeating, 149-152
background position, 152-153
background properties, setting, 155-156
bcc header, 395-396
blog, 51, 225-226
blog application,
    adding email option to, 404-408
    adding PHP includes to, 232-233
    adding record to, 250-252
    adding sort functionality to, 253-254
    adding value lists to, 335-339
    creating About blob for, 231-232
    creating editable form in, 285-289
    creating feedback form for, 401-404
    creating filled-in form for, 344-348
    creating header and footer files for, 227-228
    creating index page for, 234-235
    creating input form for, 245
    creating navigation links in, 268-273
    creating results page for, 266-267
    creating search form for, 263-265
    creating style sheet for, 229-230
    deleting records in, 289-291
    displaying result set in, 238-240
    finding records in, 258-261